FLORIDA STATE
UNIVERSITY LIBRARIES

OCT 23 2000

TALLAHASSEE, FLORIDA

Second Nature

Space, Place, and Society
John Rennie Short, *Series Editor*

OTHER TITLES IN *Space, Place, and Society*

At Home: An Anthropology of Domestic Space
IRENE CIERAAD, ED.

Becoming a Geographer
PETER GOULD

The Global Crisis in Foreign Aid
RICHARD GRANT AND JAN NIJMAN, EDS.

New Worlds, New Geographies
JOHN RENNIE SHORT

Putting Health into Place: Landscape, Identity, and Well-Being
ROBIN A. KEARNS AND WILBERT M. GESLER, EDS.

Second Nature

The History and Implications
of Australia as Aboriginal Landscape

LESLEY HEAD

Syracuse University Press

Copyright © 2000 by Syracuse University Press
Syracuse, New York 13244-5160

All Rights Reserved

First Edition 2000

00 01 02 03 04   6 5 4 3 2 1

The paper used in this publication meets the minimum requirements of American National Standard for Information Sciences—Permanence of Paper for Printed Library Materials, ANSI Z39.48–1984.

Library of Congress Cataloging-in-Publication Data

Head, Lesley.
    Second nature: the history and implications of Australia as Aboriginal landscape / Lesley Head.—1st ed.
       p. cm.—(Space, place, and society)
    Includes bibliographical references.
    ISBN 0-8156-0587-0 (alk. paper)
    1. Human ecology—Australia. 2. Australian aborigines—Land tenure. 3. Landscape assessment—Australia. I. Title. II. Series.
GF801.H36   1999
306'.0899'915—dc21   99-24394

Manufactured in the United States of America

To Richard

Lesley Head is associate professor in the School of Geosciences, University of Wollongong, Australia, where she teaches and researches in physical geography, cultural geography and archaeology. She has published widely in journals such as *Antiquity, Archaeology in Oceania, The Holocene, Transactions of the Institute of British Geographers,* and *World Archaeology.*

Contents

Illustrations   ix

Acknowledgments   xi

Terminology   xiii

Introduction   3

Part One Overview

1. Hunter-Gatherers, Land, and the Past   15

Part Two Embedding

2. Zones and Strata, or How the Aborigines Became Living Fossils   33

   Nomads   55

3. Timeless and Placeless   61

   All the Children She Had   82

Part Three Unsettling

4. Numbering Deep Time   89

viii   Contents

        A History for the People
        Without History   109

5.   Landscape: Pure and Primordial?   110

        No Dams   133

6.   Peopling the Wilderness   138

        New Australia   157

Part Four   Reworking

7.   The New Colonizers   165

        Summerland   190

8.   Aboriginality, Hunter-Gatherers,
        and Tradition   192

        The National Park   213

9.   Beyond the Colonial Heritage
        in Environmental Debate   214

10.   Conclusion   235

        Glossary   241

        Works Cited   243

        Index   267

Illustrations

Figures

1. Lake Argyle   4
2. "You don't look like an Australian"   5
3. "Empty Australia"   47
4. Taylor's zones and strata   49
5. Lava-flow analogy applied to studies of evolution and linguistics   51
6. Gardiners Creek and Yarra River   58
7. "Native women getting Tambourn roots"   59
8. Postcard, Australian Aborigines   66
9. "A Curiosity in her own country"   68
10. Point Macleay Mission   70
11. Aborigines making stone implements   73
12. Buffalo River at Nug Nug Myrtleford   84
13. Toyota LandCruiser advertisement   100
14. Estuarine flats of Cambridge Gulf   115
15. "Aborigines using fire to hunt kangaroos"   119
16. Unburnt country, Ningbingi   120
17. The Franklin blockade   134
18. Yolngu clan structure and land ownership   143
19. Cat Bay jetty, Phillip Island   169
20. Revegetation program, Summerland Peninsula   173
21. Irrigated agriculture on the Ord River   177
22. Biddy Simon and Polly Wandanga hunt for goanna   204
23. Biddy Simon digs for yams   205
24. Biddy Simon waters her garden   206
25. Jodie Hall paints on bark   208

Illustrations

Maps

1. Locations mentioned in text   2
2. Sussex and Kent, England   56
3. Port Phillip district, Victoria   57
4. The Ovens and Buffalo valleys, Victoria   83
5. Archeological and paleoecological sites mentioned in text   94
6. Southwest Tasmania   106
7. Australia and high pressure cells   113
8. Climatic index   114
9. Arnhem Land   141
10. Paraguay and New Australia   159
11. Phillip Island, Victoria   168
12. Ord River area   176
13. Aboriginal land in Australia   219
14. Rainforest in Australia   229

Acknowledgments

This book has been a number of years in the making, and more people have helped me through discussion and argument than I can single out here. I am grateful to them all. Nancy Williams has provided constructive encouragement over many years. Biddy Simon and Polly Wandanga and their families welcomed me and my family into their lives and challenged us in many ways. My field research has been funded at various times by the Australian Research Council, the Australian Institute for Aboriginal and Torres Strait Islander Studies, and the Quaternary Environments Research Centre at the University of Wollongong. For assistance with library research I thank the Inter-Library Loans staff of the University of Wollongong; the staff of the Balfour Library, University of Oxford; and Jennifer Atchison. My parents, Keith and Alison Head, offered their knowledge of family history; in this respect I am also a beneficiary of painstaking research by my aunt Margaret Boston. Chris Gosden, Jane Kaye, Gordon Waitt, and David Bowman provided insights and support at crucial stages of the process.

Robert Wray and Heqing Huang assisted with the production of the manuscript. Sue Pritchard drafted the maps, and Penny Williamson prepared the photographs. I thank the University of Wollongong for the study leave and the Faculty of Science for the teaching relief grant that allowed me to complete the manuscript, which was copyedited by Steve Holmes. Throughout, Richard Fullagar offered practical and intellectual support with his characteristic generosity of spirit.

Terminology

In keeping with common usage in Australia, the term "aboriginal" is used here in reference to indigenous peoples generally. The capitalized terms "Aboriginal people" or, less often, "Aborigines" are used in reference to the indigenous people of Australia. Contemporary usage often differentiates Torres Strait Islanders within this umbrella term (as in "ATSI" peoples); for the flow of the text this is not done here. Many Aboriginal Australians also use more local designations when describing themselves, for example "koori" in southeastern Australia. Terminology for non-Aboriginal Australians is also complex. I commonly use the terms "Euro-Australian" and "white Australian" to refer to non-Aboriginal Australians of predominantly but not exclusively anglo-celtic origin, particularly in historical context. However, non-Aboriginal Australians have always come, and continue to come, from diverse ethnic and cultural backgrounds. As the discussion in the book makes clear (particularly in chapter eight), these terms and their meanings are sites of contestation in relation to identity.

Second Nature

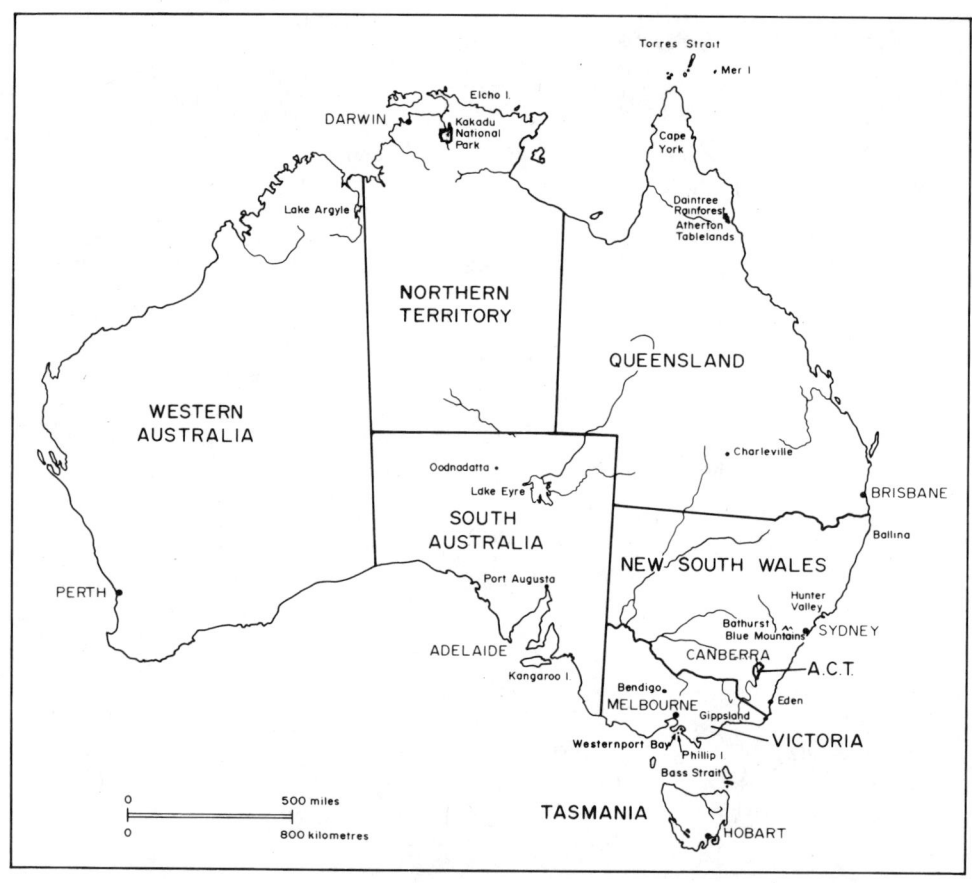

Map 1. Locations mentioned in the text

Introduction

When he opened the Main Dam on the Ord River on 30 June 1972, Australian Prime Minister William McMahon said, "Before us, as you can see, stretch the waters of the greatest man made lake ever made in Australia" (quoted in Graham-Taylor 1978, 360). He was looking at Lake Argyle (see map 1) formed by the dam to facilitate irrigated agriculture in the semiarid tropics of the East Kimberley region. The lake is variously famous for holding nine times as much water as Sydney Harbour and being the only human structure in Australia to be visible from space.

The following year Bulla Bilinggiin, a Miriwoong man, custodian over a cache of sacred artefacts drowned beneath the lake, told anthropologist Bruce Shaw:

> We went out on a boat and I showed a museum feller the place, you know, where it was drowned. That Thing, all that was just like what you call a map for the whole of the earth, see? That's the proper Law . . . The white man couldn't climb over it. You could tell him, "This is my country. See, this my land. This my property." Oh, you can put it in the book now but it's all under water. (Shaw 1986, 171–172)

Increasing numbers of domestic and international tourists are drawn to the Kimberley region which is marketed as Australia's "last frontier." They float on the surface of the lake unaware of the sacred cache and the drowned, named places beneath. Later, in Kununurra's supermarkets, they can buy a book of stunning photographs of *Australia's Kimberley* (Roberts 1995). On the cover is a shot of that same lake, reflecting red rocks and blue sky, as an embodiment of the book's subtitle: "Visions of a lasting wilderness" (fig. 1). The book is a visual plea for the preservation of some of Australia's most beautiful wild places.

4 Second Nature

Fig. 1. Lake Argyle, as depicted on the cover of *Australia's Kimberley* (c. Roberts 1995).

By what conscious or subconscious processes has the largest human structure in Australia become a precious wild place? Is this, in the words of William Cronon, wilderness as "a flight from history" (1996a, 79), both Aboriginal and Euro-Australian? Or, following that strand of academic thought that understands the whole of the continent as an artifact of Aboriginal activity, is such a conceptualization in fact perfectly placed in history?

With his characteristic pithiness cartoonist Ron Tandberg encapsulates a further set of ambiguous images of Australia as Aboriginal landscape (fig. 2). When this cartoon found its way to the breakfast tables of southeastern Australia in December 1996, the reader was assumed to be aware of two things. One was recent publicity over archaeological research in the East Kimberley, in which I was involved, that suggested, among other things, the possibility that Aboriginal people had been in Australia for more than one hundred thousand years; the other was an ongoing racism debate engendered by independent member Pauline Hanson's entry into federal Parliament.

Fig. 2. "You don't look like an Australian." Cartoon by Ron Tandberg, *The Age* (Melbourne), Dec. 1996.

A number of elements are identifiable in the image. Normal Australia, with whom all comparisons are made, is white and male. On the one hand the Aboriginal person (also male) derives enhanced legitimacy in today's Australia from a date provided by an archaeologist; the undertone here is that one hundred thousand years is better than fifty thousand. The older the better. On the other hand the Aboriginal person is implicitly the fossilized representative of an earlier age, simultaneously contemporary and timeless. "Real" Aborigines are associated with landscapes "out there"—at the center, on the frontier. The link is explicitly not with the urban landscapes where the majority of Australians live.

So, we smile wryly over breakfast but also, I think, we feel somewhat uneasy.

These two examples introduce both the tone and the subject matter of this book. We start from the position of discomfort that a number of authors (in Australia and elsewhere) refer to as postcolonial anxiety (Gelder and Jacobs 1995; Griffiths 1996; Jacobs 1996; Willems Braun 1997). Aboriginal people, the land, and the past are inextricably linked in a series of issues critical to contemporary Australia; in most debates, however, very essentialist visions of these three things persist. Culturally and scientifically, we are part-way through a process of profound reorientation in our understanding of the Australian environment and of the human role in its creation; but still there is a persistent reluctance to articulate (as Rose 1996a encourages us to do) the discomforts and ambiguities that process brings to the surface. In preferring the reflective, still surface of Lake Argyle to its messy depths, we continue the "narrative of avoidance" identified by Griffiths (1996, 5) in the late nineteenth and early twentieth centuries.

On paper, recent research in disciplines such as geography, archaeology, and anthropology and a political context in which indigenous voices are heard much more than they were three decades ago have shifted the ground dramatically. Environmentalists have seen themselves as contributing to the rethinking of Euro-Australian attitudes to and use of the environment; some of these creative revisions have been incorporated into the political process. Archaeologists and geographers often encapsulate their contribution as overturning the deception of "an unchanging people in an unchanging land" and as contributing to a more dynamic view of Australia's prehistoric past. In revisiting historical debates and participating in contemporary ones, a central question we must ask is: Given the intellectual strength of the challenge, why has the disruption to understandings developed in the imperial and scientific contexts of the eighteenth and nineteenth centuries been so partial? Why for example has the wilderness ideal been so resistant to the critiques of both deconstructive postmodernism and paleoecology?

I argue that the complexity of the historical situation is commonly understated and the extent of the revolution overstated. The colonial heritage is more deeply embedded in contemporary environmental attitudes and debates than we have acknowledged; many of our own attitudes can be shown to derive from exactly the same dualistic cultural history for which we berate our forefathers. If *terra nullius* (land belonging to no one) was a myth to be discarded in discussions of the ownership of the continent, then it must be similarly discarded when we create and preserve landscapes.

This then is the "second nature" of my title, those habits or characteristics that are "not innate but so long practiced or acquired as to seem so." The term also refers to Glacken's (1967) conception of "second nature," the transformations that humans make of the earth. As he argues it, the question of human transformations is one of the three most persistent questions that "men" have asked about their relationship to the habitable earth since the beginning of Western thought, although the full implications of this third question were not realized until the work of Buffon and Marsh. In what way then have particular understandings of that second nature become second nature to us? In fact, what we have absorbed and assumed is a limited set of understandings of the relations between the people that we now call Aborigines (and who many anthropologists call hunter-gatherers) and the land, including the several dimensions of the way that they transformed the Australian landscape. In seeking to historicize both these transformations and our changing understandings of them, I will examine both physical and conceptual transformations—or socializations—of landscape. Doing so will provide a case-study of how one particular postcolonial country is coming to terms with the prior hunter-gatherer occupation—in the fullest senses of the word—of the land. A range of global connections confirm that the concern is a widespread one; in the old countries too there are challenges afoot to the naturalization of landscapes and peoples.

Although understanding the environment as at least partly an artifact of human activity has a long history in Western thought, it has been problematic even insofar as it applied to agricultural landscapes. Glacken relates the irony that environmental theorizing—emphasizing the role of environment in shaping culture—had its origin in one of the most altered landscapes on earth, the Mediterranean basin:

> It was not like von Humboldt traveling in the tropics, which overwhelmed him with the lushness of their vegetation and in which so little of man was to be seen, nor was it like the young Darwin who saw in the luxuriant forests of Brazil the grand scale of natural wonders compared with the insignificance of man and his doings. One feels that to these writers—Greek and Roman alike—the vineyards, the olive orchards, the irrigation ditches, the grazing goats on the rocky summits, the villages and the villas were inseparable from the landscape of the dry parched hills of the Mediterranean summer, the winds for which there were so many local names, the deep blueness of the sea, and the bright mediterranean skies. It was an altered landscape upon which they gazed and whose beauties they loved. (1967, 119)

Thirty years down the track we can read other things into this example than Glacken presumably intended. It perpetuates the distinction between pristine and altered landscapes, the latter requiring cultivation and villages; we can be blind to other types of transformations and socializations of land because of our cultural imperialism. At the same time, Glacken alerts us to themes that are still relevant: humans have been intimate with transformed landscapes for many thousands of years, and human impacts can be so deeply embedded that they become part of nature.

Glacken also makes the point that when humans were first perceived as environmental agents it was as a positive rather than as a destructive force: "Man was a creator of order, an agent of control, a possessor of the unique skill of the artisan."

> In the literature interpreting the changes that men make in their environment, in the attempts to bestow meaning on these changes, there are, as we shall see, recurrent themes of man as a finisher of the creation, of man bringing order into nature, and after the age of discovery, of European man discovering new lands, which despite the presence of primitive peoples, are considered to be unchanged since the creation and awaiting his transforming hand. (1967, 116, 117)

The first significant recognition of potentially destructive human powers is usually attributed to George Perkins Marsh ([1864] 1965) in the second half of the nineteenth century. Grove argues that the elevation of Marsh and others "to the pantheon of conservationist prophets" (1995, 2) has meant that a much longer history of conservation, particularly in tropical and island colonial environments, has been overlooked. However, even if Marsh has been wrongly mantled as the father of modern environmentalism, his writings do provide some clues to its colonial heritage in the continental colonies of North America and Australia. As he saw it these "new countries," "now first brought under the occupation of man," would provide testing grounds for the questions of distinguishing anthropogenic landforms from geological causes and of the influence of clearing and cultivating upon climate:

> Australia is, perhaps, the country from which we have a right to expect the fullest elucidation of these difficult and disputable problems. Its colonization did not commence until the physical sciences had become matter of almost universal attention, and is, indeed, so recent that the memory of living men embraces the principal epochs of its history; the peculiarities of its fauna, its flora, and its geology are such as to have excited for it the liveliest interest of the votaries of natural science; its mines have given its people the necessary wealth for procuring the means of instrumental observation, and the leisure re-

quired for the pursuit of scientific research; and large tracts of virgin forest and natural meadow are rapidly passing under the control of civilized man. ([1864] 1965, 49)

Of course Marsh was not alone in seeing Australia as a blank slate (many social and environmental experiments were to be carried out here) or of considering its Aboriginal inhabitants, if he thought of them at all, as implicitly part of a curious fauna. Although a few people on the ground in Australia were starting to comment on the ways in which Aborigines manipulated the landscape through their use of fire, it was to be many years before such thoughts were routinely discussed by mainstream environmental critics.

However peculiar Australia is, it is not alone in having to come to terms with a colonial heritage in land management and cultural heritage debates, and in this study I situate these debates in their global context. An important part of this challenge is that answering questions about human interactions with the environment requires spanning the sciences and the humanities. Across the social sciences and humanities, the trend is increasingly to view knowledge and disciplines as socially constructed and historically contingent. Indeed, many of the themes relevant to these issues have already been subject to rigorous historicization; the most valuable of these bring forward the new insights of postmodernism without becoming paralysed by relativism. I draw heavily here on Livingstone's (1992) expression of geography as contested tradition, Stocking's (1987) notion of anthropology as a set of nested contextualities, and on discussions stimulated by Gosden (1994) on time, Evernden (1992) and Cronon (1996b) on nature, and Attwood (1989, 1992) on Aboriginality.

In contrast, much of our understanding of the prehistory of environments and of the human role in them now comes from evidence derived from the natural and physical sciences, where positivistic approaches are still dominant. Such approaches have both myths and narratives of their own, which need to be contextualized by asking questions both about the way that knowledge of the environmental past is produced and about how it is used in public debates over management. Why for example has the rhetoric of environmental change been appropriated almost completely by the development lobby, with conservationists clinging to imagery of the timeless and the pristine?

Although fascinating in scholarly and disciplinary terms, these are not simply intellectual questions; rather they go to the heart of the pressing environmental and social dilemmas of our time. Consistent with the subject matter, my theoretical position is itself ambiguous. I draw on a range of approaches that fall under the very broad postmodern umbrella, finding them extremely useful to analyze questions of difference and otherness, language and representation. At the same time, of course, in Australia the voice of the Other did not wait for postmodernism. Indigenous people's struggle for representation has become an important influence on Australian thinking in recent decades. The distinctive interactions of Aboriginal people with place and the challenge that these provide to unproblematized understandings of landscape—now somewhat commodified as the touchstone example in many a cultural text—were first articulated in Australia by scholars who would blanche at the appellation postmodernist. Indeed, it is in the arena of environmental debate that I find postmodern approaches most deeply problematic (notwithstanding the claims of some that there is a natural affinity between them and solutions to environmental crisis; see e.g. Dear 1994). My reasons are twofold. First, our understanding of environmental problems in the long term and on the broad scale is inescapably dependent on science in all its remotely sensed, computer-modelled glory; however important it is to deconstruct science's narratives and to understand its social context, it remains a tool that we cannot do without. Second, moving forward on these issues requires a certain sort of positionality that is often foreclosed by postmodern assumptions. Quite simply, these are issues that matter.

Revisitation of historical debates and participation in contemporary ones can reveal that the colonial heritage is more deeply embedded in Australian thought and practice—both academic and otherwise—than is generally acknowledged. Fuller articulation of the ambiguities and contradictions in current positions is necessary in order to work toward a reconstituted set of founding myths that will facilitate socially and environmentally sustainable occupation of this continent. In working through those issues, a key starting point is an awareness that there is something distinctive and special about Aboriginal relations to land, independent of the postmodern critique. That something is not part of an essential nature, and it is not static; drawing up on it as a source of inspiration requires us to pay attention to a range of historical and theoretical themes:
- the way that ecological interactions are socially mediated
- human intimacy with the environment

- the interplay of local, national, and global processes
- reworking of traditions to maintain continuity

Aboriginal people themselves have agency in the way that their interactions with the land are depicted in public debates, but they are also constrained by the structures of the colonizing society. Along with the differences between the colonizers and the colonized, there are many points of commonality as well, for example, the notion of *country* is a multilayered motif that resonates both in Aboriginal and in Euro-Australian imaginations.

In keeping with the notion of the multiple temporalities and spatialities of colonialism and of postcolonialism (Thomas 1994; Gelder and Jacobs 1995; Willems-Braun 1997), my explorations range widely across time, space, and academic discipline. Seeming paradoxes abound: specific historical processes—local, national, and global in scope—were required for the construction of the Australian Aborigine (and, correlatively, the Australian environment) as "timeless." Indeed the construction of timelessness was more a spatial than a temporal process; it was closely linked to the physical and conceptual dispossessions that together rendered Aboriginal people "placeless." The colonizers' intellectual tools, for example archaeology and geography, have successfully contributed to the disruption of the colonial narrative. However, nineteenth-century narrative devices such as antiquity and linearity persist. Despite the increasing presence and power of Aboriginal people in expressing their own version of relations to land, the naturalization of Aborigines and of land has only partially been dislodged both in academic and in public debates. Essentialism, of people and of land, can be used both for oppression and for resistance, as we struggle to go beyond a dualistic approach to our place in the environment.

Throughout the book I try to present different authorships in historical context, quoting extensively from scholarly sources where appropriate. The historical context of my own authorship, as a descendant of the colonizers, is illustrated by interweaving aspects of family history that bear on the themes under discussion. As today's generations continue to be implicated in the processes of colonization, this weaving continues to the present.

Part One
Overview

1

Hunter-Gatherers, Land, and the Past

Australia is, perhaps, the country from which we have a right to expect the fullest elucidation of these difficult and disputable problems.

—G. P. Marsh, *Man and Nature*

My claim is not as ambitious as Marsh's, nor am I as confident that the application of a scientific culture to a situation of sudden and massive environmental transformation would in itself provide the tools to counter any ill-effects. However, I do contend that Australian evidence, drawn from a particular set of social and ecological conditions, offers important insights into the questions at hand. As in Marsh's time, we need to ask questions that distinguish anthropogenic from geological causation in environmental change, and to consider why the distinction matters. However, we also need to address the contexts in which the questions are asked, both historical and contemporary. Australians are conscious of multiple Otherings, both oppressive and affectionate. As white Australians locate Aboriginal people metaphorically "out there," so the rest of the world locates us all "down under." In the global economic village such otherness has both advantages and disadvantages. Niche marketing demands difference; the Australian Tourist Commission uses images of the last frontier to attract visitors and their holiday dollars from the other side of the world. My exploration of the interplay of commonalities and differences between the Australian and the international contexts is structured around five overlapping themes: transformed landscapes, landscapes of social negotiation, change among hunter-gatherers, traditionality and primitivism, and the politics of the past. It is in the light of these debates that we must frame and explore the Australian evidence.

Transformed Landscapes

The extent to which hunter-gatherers can and did transform their environment, for example through the use of fire, continues to be controversial. Two dimensions to the debate must be distinguished: first, the extent to which hunter-gatherers were agents of landscape (especially vegetation) change; and second, the political or moral complexions that have been put on this evidence in relation to contemporary management issues.

In the Americas the debate took place with respect to the genesis of grasslands (Stewart 1956; Sauer 1952). Sauer in particular—while often pointing out the lack of research on the topic (1952, 10–13; 1956, 544; 1965a, 224; 1965b)—was vocal on the issue of hunting and collecting peoples having an impact on vegetation over long periods of time. However, Sauer's conclusions were constrained by his times: the tools to pursue the issue further, in the form of pollen and charcoal analysis datable by radiocarbon, were not well developed until the very end of his life; the issue was seen to be confined to temperate latitudes, since "[b]urning is ineffective at the climatic extremes" (Sauer 1952, 13); and in general researchers were still coming to terms with the extent of prehistoric agricultural impacts. Although Sauer was clearly conscious (within the limitations of the then available evidence) of deliberate management and substantial impacts by hunting and collecting peoples, he did not consider this to be "destructive exploitation," a term he reserved for "the rapid and wanton extermination of species under commercial economies" (Speth 1977, 150)—within which he included the impoverishment of aboriginal cultures.

Overviews of human impacts on the environment are now likely to concede that hunter-gatherer impacts were probably greater than has been generally recognized (Simmons 1989), just as earlier views of "natural" landscapes required revision when the profound effects of agricultural activity became apparent (Faegri 1988). In recent decades advances in radiometric dating techniques, microfossil analysis, and sediment analysis have dramatically increased our powers to discern these impacts, although interpretations are still vigorously debated. Australian evidence has been crucial in these debates, because indications of "modified" landscapes are much older here than in glaciated parts of the northern hemisphere (where cultural landscapes do not really become visible until the Holocene, although they are probably much older than that [Birks et al. 1988; Roberts 1989]).

However, the moral dimensions of knowing about the past are found in Old World situations also. For example, there is considerable debate in England about the destruction of historic countryside, and authority for preservation is often sought via an appeal to the antiquity of different vegetation types (Rackham 1995, chap. 3). The debate has been constructed in such a way that if certain communities are shown to be younger or less pristine than had been thought, there is more of a question mark over their value.

Landscapes of Social Negotiation

In a parallel development the so-called new cultural geography has alerted us to other types of landscapes than materially modified ones: landscapes that express aspects of social relations, or symbolic and textual landscapes. In eschewing the notion that culture is the preserve of the "exotic other," cultural geographers have directed energy recently to analysing the contingent nature of culture in mostly urban, mostly capitalist situations (Anderson and Gale 1992). The recognition of landscapes as "transformations of social and political ideologies into physical form" (Duncan and Duncan 1988, 125) is part of the reason for the recent "dismantling of boundaries" between cultural and social geography (Smith 1990; Gregson 1992). At the same time these approaches provide conceptual tools to take another look at the Other and at the historical processes by which specific Others were so defined.

With some exceptions (e.g., Young 1992, Baker 1989), interest in hunter-gatherer understandings of landscape is now just as likely to be found in anthropology (Bender 1993; Hirsch and O'Hanlon 1995) and in archaeology (Head, Gosden et al. 1994) as in geography. Archaeologists such as Gosden, in considering very long-term change, adopt the notion of social landscape "because the use of different parts of the landscape is seen to be structured by the needs of the social system" (1989, 47). Because of their dependence on material evidence to get at the long-term record, archaeologists have had to think in new ways about how social organization is linked to and preserved in the physical landscape; Pardoe's (1994) notion of "bioscape" is a good example of this. Although a few geographers might look askance at the recent discovery by other disciplines of a concept that has been central to geography's identity for hundreds of years—just as historical geographers might be bemused by history's discovery of "the environment"—there is little doubt that the field of geography is richer for the range of disciplinary approaches now utilizing concepts from it.

In all of these disciplines, the relationship between landscape perception and landscape transformation is an issue of ongoing interest. To what extent do people's understandings of their environment affect the ways in which they alter it? How have understandings of the past influenced transformations, both recently and in prehistoric times? How have our explanations been influenced by the nature of the available evidence? Literature from the northern hemisphere often uses an Australian Aboriginal example to illustrate people's transformation of "space" into "place" by drawing the physical landscape into the conceptual order, classifying and domesticating it (e.g. Thomas 1991, 30; Bradley 1993, chap. 1); these authors can then return to monuments and long barrows to discuss the prehistory of such transformations. In Australia, however, researchers return to a less tractable set of archaeological and paleoecological evidence, for which the default mode has been to interpret change in purely ecological terms. The discrepancy, as observed ethnographically, between the social complexity and the material simplicity of Aboriginal societies has been a longstanding issue for Australian archaeology. Recently, it has been argued that the concept of landscape provides one tool for overcoming these problems; for example, Tacon has focused on the relationships between landscape perceptions and archaeologically durable materials such as stone (Tacon 1991, 1994).

Because the increasing academic interest in landscape is often argued to have arisen out of the West's sense of ecological crisis, it is important to consider whether the interest in hunter-gatherer landscapes is just another phase of the colonial enterprise. In fact (as will be explored in later chapters), Aboriginal voices about their relations to land, albeit constrained in certain ways, are transforming academic practice and understanding. Indeed, Morphy argues that this has long been the case and that landscape has been a central if undertheorized concept in Australian anthropology: "The pre-post-modernist in me would argue that it is not a coincidence that many of the issues in the anthropology of landscape are pre-figured in the Australian literature ... Australian Aborigines made landscape a key concept in the study of their society. Indigenous people have played a far more active role in the outsiders' construction of their societies than some theorists have allowed" (1993, 206).

Change among Hunter-Gatherers

The term *hunter-gatherer* is usually applied as an economic definition, based on what people do for a living. Hunter-gatherer understandings of and relations to the land are seen to arise out of this basic ecological relationship. However, things are not that simple: the social constructions of relations to land have a dynamic of their own, particularly in questions of change over time. At more immediate issue is the fact that most hunter-gatherers now also do other things for a living, such as participate to some extent in the cash economy. This raises the question of the relationship between the present and the past or, less analytically, whether such people are still "real" hunter-gatherers. The approach I use here is to problematize the notions of change and continuity and to critically examine which aspects of relations to land are more or less amenable to change, and why.

It is not my intention to review the so-called hunter-gatherer revisionist debate (e.g. Wilmsen and Denbow 1990; Solway and Lee 1990; Lee 1992; Headland and Reid 1989; Headland 1997), most of which has focused on southern Africa, but there are a few points arising out of it that are pertinent to this discussion. Recent Australian research by and large has not become bogged down in the polarized caricatures of hunter-gatherers either as primitive isolates or as constructions of the observer (although "the primitive" persists in various aspects of popular culture). Academically there is a discernible trend towards examining the process of contact and cultural interpenetration, quarrying it for useful information about periods of rapid social and ecological change. Historically Australia has provided an important ethnographic laboratory for hunter-gatherer researchers. It is therefore salient that recent landmark studies into Aboriginal subsistence (Meehan 1982; Altman 1987) are no less significant for having been carried out in situations where hunting, gathering, and participation in the cash economy all interact. Indeed, the considerations of post-European changes are among the most significant of the contributions of these two authors; for example, Meehan's time-budget studies of contemporary women's work allowed her to hypothesize about possible prehistoric scenarios. Both Altman (1981) and Meehan (1991) have discussed the introduction of buffalo into Aboriginal diets and its potential effect on the social organization of production, providing different interpretations for the different communities with whom they worked.

Although there is not necessarily anything static about hunter-gatherer lifeways, there have been important continuities through "what appears to be the greatest stress Aborigines have ever known—the dislocation of their lives and radical depopulation of their land as a direct consequence of European invasion" (Schrire 1984, 77; see also Bird-David 1988; Grinker 1992; Burch and Ellanna 1994, 244). It is the comparison of continuity and change and the exploration of the circumstances under which they are negotiated in current political contexts that provide some of the most interesting research in hunter-gatherer studies today. There is considerable interest in the contact process across a range of disciplines, and the focus of the subject matter is similarly broad, from renegotiation of gender roles (Shoemaker 1995) to trade networks (Clarke and Torrence in press). Although it is of course somewhat artificial to treat aspects of integrated systems separately, the examples I have chosen to focus on here concentrate on the implications of change for relations to land, in particular the interaction between hunter-gatherers and Western-based resource management strategies and debates.

This is not to deny the importance of other dimensions, particularly gender, to these interactions. For example, as will be discussed more fully in chapter three, the refusal or inability of the European colonizers in Australia to recognize the similarities between Aboriginal landscape transformations and horticulture arose at least in part because much of the former was women's work; the digging stick was a woman's tool. Moreover, Western perceptions of Nature are tied closely to perceptions of Woman, as (for example) Sparks has detailed in her study of changes in Anglo images of Navajo women in the nineteenth century. At the beginning of the century the Pocohontas image—young, beautiful and untouched—symbolized a land that "surrendered itself to the redeeming touch of the white male colonizer" (1995, 140). Somewhat later the Pathetic Dusky Heroine, whose men could not adequately protect her from Mexican incursions, was used to justify American intervention. Of course, the realities of Navajo women's lives (such as their ownership of herds of livestock) often collided with these images and forced a limited reassessment of the Land-as-Woman metaphor.

In exploring the complexities of continuity and change in hunter-gatherer societies the experience of the Nunivak Eskimos of southwestern Alaska in dealing with an externally imposed wilderness designation highlights a number of issues that resonate with Australian Aboriginal experiences. The Nunivak are embedded in the

Western cash economy and also undertake traditional subsistence activities throughout the year, particularly fishing and berry-picking. They re-use particular sites to which they have ancestral attachments, and their conceptualization of the landscape is expressed in over nine hundred place names on Nunivak Island (Pratt 1994, 355). In 1980 half of the island was designated as wilderness under a definition that accorded with the 1964 U.S. Wilderness Act as "an area where the earth and its community of life are untrammeled by man, where man himself is a visitor who does not remain" (337). In fact, Pratt argues, there are special provisions in the Alaska National Interest Lands Conservation Act (ANILCA) of 1980 that recognize "the unique relationship of Alaskans to the land" and allow cabin construction and use of motorized transport under certain conditions. However, these have never been well communicated to local people, who expressed opposition to the wilderness proposal the only time they were asked about it. For them, the wilderness designation is another in a long line of external interventions over which they have had no control. Pratt's study also shows that the Nunivak conflicts with the wilderness designation were much greater than they needed to be because of the poor implementation procedures by the U.S. Fish and Wildlife Service. Clearly, the political context of the declaration of the Nunivak Wilderness was not conductive to recognition of patterns of land use and attachment by the Nunivak themselves. Alaska's situation in the American national consciousness as "the last frontier" (simultaneously the last possibility for resource development and the last bastion of wilderness) echoes, for example, the situation of Kakadu National Park in Australia. For conservationists, the wishful image of a blank slate—a terra nullius—where "here, finally, we can do it right" (339) is powerful.

To consider another example, in India hunter-gatherers "are caught between deforestation, on the one hand, and environmental restoration programs, on the other" (Prakash Reddy 1994, 364). Prakash Reddy argues that hunter-gatherer communities have been made scapegoats in battles over the massive destruction of Indian forests currently occurring. On the one hand an industrializing economy and expanding population have increased the demand for forest products, irrigation dams, and hydroelectric projects; on the other hand increased awareness of environmental issues has led to a demand for wildlife sanctuaries and reserves. Under such pressures, "Hundreds of wildlife sanctuaries and a few national parks have been established in various parts of the country over the past decade. Unfortunately, many of them are located in the heart of tribal areas and, in many cases, they were established over the protests of the tribal communities" (364). In practice the management of these sanctuaries and parks leads to choices between tigers and people; for the Chenchu people the conclusion is that "the government prefers tigers to human beings" (365). Prakash Reddy shows that hunter-gatherers in India are still being treated within a government rhetoric of "progress" that assumes the appropriate path for them is to be resettled, often by force, and turned into cultivators; where there is a conflict of interest between their rights and the "national interest," the latter prevails. The differential application of legal principles in this situation has clear parallels with the application of terra nullius in Australia:

> *Lex loci* concerns the law of the place where something is located; by this law, indigenous groups hold rights over the resources and territories in which they live and whose resources they exploit . . . *Res nullius* refers to the right of property accrued to individuals from the property of nobody. By the extension of this concept, the state claims superior rights over the land. Not only the colonial government, but also the present government, thinks that indigenous groups are too barbaric to have *lex loci* rights recognizable by the courts, and so they are deprived of their land and their territories. (375)

A number of factors mean that many resource management debates are now being played out on an international stage, not only because of global economic activity but also because of an awareness of global resources and biodiversity. This has implications for hunter-gatherers both in the colonized west and in newly industrializing countries. People with influence over decision-making processes are often at considerable remove from the situation on the ground; this in itself does not make them any more or less competent, but it does highlight the fact that perceptions beyond the nation state are becoming more important. For example, Australian obligations under international heritage agreements (first used in the 1983 dispute over southwest Tasmania) are commonly invoked in conservation battles and in issues of indigenous rights. The furor over kangaroo harvesting (discussed below in chapter nine) shows that people overseas have often received even more stereotyped and essentialized images of Australian fauna and landscapes than have Australians themselves. The construction of such debates has almost always favored furry animals over indigenous people.

The international debate over sealing and whaling is another case in point. In the Canadian Arctic, according to Wenzel (1994), the European Community sealskin boycott has occasioned greater changes in social and settlement organization among Inuit people than any other manifestations of "modernization" policy. At the time of the EC ban (1983), the ringed seal *(natsiq)* was both a subsistence resource and a source of the cash income essential to support hunting operations through purchasing and servicing snowmobiles and buying gasoline. The loss of this resource was particularly felt among full-time hunters, "mainly men between thirty and fifty years old, who were central figures in the extended family organization of the village" (303). In response, the community returned to a more constricted pattern of summer camps, now coalescing not around older male kin but around wage-earning men who can buy resources. In northern Japan as well, social and economic implications for local communities have resulted from the moratorium on whaling adopted by the International Whaling Commission in 1982. Although distinguished from industrial-scale oil-based whaling by their localized nature and "the sociocultural significance of the consumption, distribution, and production phases," these small-scale minke whaling operations have been nonoperational since 1988 (Iwasaki-Goodman and Freeman 1994, 383). Consequences include a weakening of social ties dependent on gift exchange of whale meat, economic hardship, and threats to a culture historically integrated with whaling.

Conservationists in western countries have turned part of their focus on the newly industrializing nations, where development and population pressures are strong and where the natural environment (particularly tropical forests) is under great pressure. There are a number of interacting factors here, but one that we return to is the extent to which Western conservation movements reproduce a colonial discourse in their characterization of "traditional" modes of resource exploitation.

Traditionality and Primitivism

These two aspects, each of them extremely susceptible to essentializing approaches, are treated together here because of the way that they are stereotyped in contemporary Western society as being ancient, primordial, and unchanging, notwithstanding the fact that many of our own traditions are recent inventions (Hobsbawm and Ranger 1983).

In Brazil, for example, Ramos (1994) identifies a dualistic discourse presenting two apparently conflicting "but in fact complementary, visions of the Indian". An "edenic" discourse presents the Indian as a natural phenomenon, living in innocence and freedom; a "civilizing" discourse emphasises the barbarism of the Indian, the moral superiority of the whites, and the responsibility of the latter to be the rescuer. As Ramos shows, both these visions have a history as old as the colonial process, but of particular interest to this discussion is the way in which the contemporary environmental movement's interest in saving Amazonia is expressed using the same duality. Ramos uses as an example rock singer Sting's 1989 European tour with Chief Raoni.

> The reasoning seems to follow a straightforward exercise in western logic: unspoiled nature is pure; the Indian is part of nature; therefore, the Indian is pure. Such purity then becomes associated with the wisdom that the whiteman once had but has lost on his way to technological progress and with it to the destruction of his environment. Now the whiteman badly needs to recover his lost wisdom in order to preserve, no longer simply a nation, but the planet. The Indian enters this gloomy picture as the unspoiled reservoir of wisdom, ready to be reappropriated by the whiteman. (79)

Having been given this definition—and burden—of purity, an Indian who "sells out" (for example by selling lumber) is then considered to have lost authenticity. The voice of the Indian him or herself is rarely heard in this context, even, Ramos argues, through the filter of the anthropologist.

The notion of tradition can be used in complex ways: for domination or for resistance, externally or internally. Spiegel (1994) focuses on its use in South Africa, arguing that the apartheid government reinvented "traditional/communal" land tenure during the 1950s and 1960s in the form of the Bantustans ("tribal homelands"), in order to control and confine the growing black population and to keep it largely separate from the "white" cities. In another case, although the San of the Natal Drakensberg in the past have been described as everything from "brutal savages" to "harmless people" and "noble savages," contemporary literature often promotes the San as living in harmony with their environment: "It is ironic that, a century after the San fought and lost their struggle for the Natal Drakensberg, they are being used by descendants of their white settler adversaries to promote the conservation of the area" (Mazel 1992, 765). This view of "traditional" Africans as "living in the pristine state of an idealized 'natural' past" is widespread in tourist literature and postcards in South Africa (Spiegel 1994, 192). (In chapter seven I show some parallel examples from Australia.)

The use of traditionality as an expression of resistance is complex. There are anthropological examples where indigenous voices start to cut across the dualisms and in which indigenous people are understood as actors within constraints; the best of these provide useful case studies of how change is negotiated within colonized contexts. Spiegel cites examples of Africanist opponents of apartheid calling for the reinstatement of "traditional" land tenure systems and of the concept of traditionality being used differentially in gender struggles. He argues that where traditionality has been used for purposes of resistance, the deconstructive task is particularly difficult, because the images "are likely to be extremely resilient and their purveyors particularly jealous of their authenticity . . . South African society has for so long been built around images of historical difference that to draw upon them is still a fundamental part of the political process" (1994, 198).

Although the concept clearly needs to be problematized, the understanding of tradition as unchanging is not a stereotype devoid of foundation, particularly in Aboriginal Australia—where Aboriginal Law, as established by ancestral beings during the Dreaming, is in fact represented as unchanging and unchangeable (see more detailed discussion in chapter six). Thus, in the case of Aboriginal women who are custodians of sacred sites, "in order to maintain tradition they must reinterpret that tradition, thus introducing change to maintain continuity" (Mearns 1994, 263). These dilemmas arise in the operation of the Sacred Sites Act, the main mechanism by which the state effects protection of Aboriginal cultural heritage and sites of special significance in the Northern Territory. One of these dilemmas is that because sites can only be discussed by authorized persons and are protected by silence and inaccessibility, people are often reluctant to have sites recorded on the public register until they are actually threatened. Crosscutting this is the gender issue: women's sites are different to men's and may only be discussed by authorized women. Mearns gives examples of areas in which sites were presumed not to exist because male inquirers spoke only to men. In a number of instances sites could only be discussed when female anthropologists and female representatives of mining companies were asking the questions. White men are still dominant in most areas of public life in the Territory—in politics, pastoralism, and mining companies—leading to a situation where Aboriginal men have been assumed to be the spokespersons for their whole community. Mearns sees this practice as having strong historical roots, from the time of the first anthropological researchers; it becomes self-reinforcing because when men are consulted first, their social standing is enhanced, and many of the resources from those interactions (for example consultancy fees) flow mainly to them: "To transmit knowledge from Aboriginal culture within a context structured by the outside world is to transform the conditions under which it may be evaluated and treated" (284). This is a risky business, "for it takes knowledge outside the direct control of those people who have been charged by tradition with its safekeeping" (285). For custodians, the choice imposed by the external society is often between breaching tradition by remaining silent while sites are destroyed or "accepting an interpretation of tradition that is contrary to previous interpretations, and therefore potentially a breach in the continuity of law. To continue tradition thus means to change it" (286).

Analyzing the process of Aboriginal land claims hearings in the Northern Territory, Rose argues that although the Land Rights Act (1976) is an instrument of colonial domination, it nevertheless offers Aboriginal people "zones of empowerment and synergistic accommodation within the structure of restriction and coercion" (1996b, 36). She shows how within these zones Aboriginal people have been active in creating the culture of the land claims process. Paradoxically, however, there is a risk of this particular expression of Aboriginality becoming a "canon of authenticity" that disempowers Aboriginal people in other parts of Australia (cf. Jacobs 1988).

The Politics of the Past

For archaeologists in most parts of the world—but particularly in the postcolonial corners—grappling with social constructions of the past has become part of daily life (McBryde 1992; Bond and Gilliam 1994). At its broadest level, this process is seen in the work of the World Archaeological Congress and in its practical and intellectual attempts to deconstruct the power inherent in controlling knowledge of the past, including ethnic, racial, and gender elements (Ucko 1994). On a more day-to-day level, prehistoric archaeologists in Australia are now required to negotiate permissions to undertake field research with local Aboriginal communities—a politicization and public engagement that is transforming the practice of the discipline (Moser 1995a) but that Smith (1994) argues is undertheorized by postmodern writings in Anglo-American archaeology. Aboriginal demands for control of cultural heritage were crucial in the legislative frameworks developed in Australia in the 1970s and 1980s. They were also, Moser argues, influential in encouraging archaeologists to look more broadly at how Aboriginal people understood the landscape rather than focusing exclusively on "sites" and "relics." Prehistoric archaeologists deal on a daily basis with the challenges of this politicization in a way that historians (for example) do not, because the material remains that constitute evidence for archaeologists are embedded in—or are themselves—a landscape that is also an arena of contested ownership and authorization.

McBryde (1992, 262) identifies four important themes in the relationship between cultural identity and archaeology. The first theme is the process by which archaeologists derive such identity from the material record. The second is the way in which "the past" is constructed and valued differently in different societies; in particular, the construction of "the past" provided by the discipline called archaeology is a product of Western scholarly traditions. The third theme—indigenous peoples' perception of archaeology and archaeologists—follows from the second. A fourth theme links all the others: "the political and social power of the past and its material manifestations," or as Bond and Gilliam put it, "[S]ocial constructions of the past are crucial elements in the process of domination, subjugation, resistance and collusion" (1994, 1).

An important example is provided by the situation of archaeology in South Africa. Focusing on Cape Town, Hall examines how "the early nineteenth-century bourgeois view of the world is used as an artefact of modern domination" (1994, 177) and shows how archaeology challenges the received view of the past. For a bourgeoisie dependent on trade with other parts of the British Empire, "it was essential that Cape Town was seen as a model of prosperity and propriety" (173). This image was expressed in various texts—travelers accounts, newspaper reports, and art—and is still dominant in present-day histories of the period. Hall and colleagues' archaeological work shows that the genteel facade concealed high population densities and considerable poverty among the underclass; in this they found support in reports written by wardmasters in 1840, who had examined conditions of hygiene in response to a smallpox epidemic. Moreover, by showing that the relationship between class and race was complex and that the underclass was very cosmopolitan, Hall uses the past as a weapon to subvert the naturalization of "domination and subservience" (174).

Working in a Thai context, Byrne cautions that "the struggle to achieve management control over the material past is one which takes place not across East-West, national, or cultural lines but across or at the borders of different and often competing discursive formations" (1995, 267). Thus, the problem may not be so much Western imperialism as the hegemonic tendencies of archaeological discourse, which uses the language of "universal" heritage to privilege its own meanings over those of local voices, in this example Thai Buddhism. Byrne outlines the tensions in management of the bell-shaped religious monuments *(stupa)* between attempts to preserve their "original" fabric—often consistent with the nation-building desires of the state—and "the ethic of merit making in Thai Buddhism, [which] puts a premium on the proliferation, reconstruction and rebuilding of *stupas*" (267).

Of course, the politics of the past extend beyond material culture and monuments to broader landscapes, which are also appropriated by different interest groups to enhance their claims to authenticity and to power. This is obviously not a new process. For example, Stonehenge is well known as a site of contestation in recent years, with summer solstice battles between British Prime Minister Thatcher's police state and an amorphous group of New Age travelers; however, as Bender (1993b) shows, contested meanings have attended the site since before the stones. The mythology of landscape extends also to the scale of the nation state: former British colonies Australia and the United States are having to reassess the myths on which they have been built, notably the idea of the pristine, virginal, or empty landscape (Bowden 1992; Butzer 1992; Denevan 1992; Head 1992).

The Contribution of Australian Evidence and Perspectives

The contemporary Australian nation state occupies an entire continent, spanning tropical to cool temperate latitudes and encompassing a great diversity of ecosystems. For most of the continent the great climatic fluctuations of the Quaternary period were expressed not in the advance and retreat of ice sheets but in cycles of greater or lesser aridity. Thus, the landscape—although it certainly changed dramatically—is not one that was scraped clean by ice in the terminal Pleistocene, and so there is at least the possibility (varying with ecological regions) of long paleoecological and archaeological records providing evidence of human interaction with the environment (Dodson 1992). Occupying this land was a diverse and unique biota, adapted in isolation over a timescale of millions of years to stressors such as fire, drought and low soil fertility—a fact that makes it difficult to identify any unique impact of the stress of human arrival.

The land mass of greater Australia was first settled by humans at least fifty thousand years ago, and these inhabitants rapidly occupied the most distant corners of the continent and associated islands. In New Guinea—then part of the continent—agriculture as it is traditionally understood became visible very early, but for the most part the people observed by the first European invaders fitted (in fact provided) the archetype of hunter-gatherers. The interpenetration of Ab original and Euro-Australian societies over the last two hundred years provides a significant written record not only of hunter-gatherer lifestyles at or very close to contact but also of the ways in which those lifestyles changed in the face of a new set of invaders. Increasingly the voices of Aboriginal people express in public forums how they perceive, symbolize, and ascribe meaning to their environments. By drawing on evidence from a range of sources, we can thus begin the task of examining the links between the physical expression of human activity in the landscape and people's perceptions and interpretation of that landscape over these very long periods of time.

By the standards of most of the world the Australian continent is underpopulated, but ecologists and others argue that the current combination of population, technology, and resource exploitation is unsustainable, due primarily to the limits imposed on an industrially-based lifestyle by aridity and low soil fertility. The educated urban middle classes are sensitized both to environmental and to indigenous rights issues and in general have supported moves by the federal government to locate some of the jurisdiction over these issues in international obligations such as World Heritage agreements. Global economic links predate these political ones by two centuries; many large pastoral and mining enterprises have been controlled by offshore owners since the first days of European settlement. Aboriginal Australians are numerically a relatively small ethnic group, but they occupy a unique if ambivalent place in public culture and in the debates by which the rest of the nation seeks to define itself and its place on the continent.

The Continentality Problem

Australian high school students learn that "continentality" is a major factor in Australian aridity, the moisture-bearing winds of the northwest monsoon or the Southern Ocean usually dropping their bundle before they get anywhere near central Australia. Less often is continentality considered as a cultural issue. "Australia" was created when an entire continent was appropriated by a single colonizer (cf. Carter 1987) and later decolonized into a single nation. At the same time, researchers in various fields have alerted us to the regional variability that is hidden by such a conceptualization. Attwood (1989) has argued that any pancontinental Aboriginal identity is a post-European phenomenon; in earlier times, although there were extensive networks of interaction linking Aboriginal groups across the continent, identity was expressed in terms specific to local areas. For White (1996), the nature of colonization and the nineteenth-century classification of Aborigines as a single undifferentiated race have contributed to Australia being treated as a single archaeological region; such an approach contrasts with others applied to areas of comparable size and environmental variability, for example Europe and the United States. White invites us to consider how the archaeological record would be different if, say, Tasmania had been colonized by the French and northwestern Australia by the Dutch. The idea that "the overarching structure of investigation, explanation and story writing has been at the continental level" (White 1996, 1) applies in many areas of Australian life. In exploring the interactions between hunter-gatherers, the landscape, and "the past" in the Australian context, this structure of continentality constitutes a limitation (by making any study of local examples appear indeterminate or partial), but it also provides an illustration of the interplay between local, continental, and broader processes.

Part Two
Embedding

2

Zones and Strata, or How the Aborigines Became Living Fossils

The Zones of to-day are the Strata of to-morrow.

—T. G. Taylor, "Correlations and Culture: A Study in Technique"

A historical overview of the complex processes by which the "unchanging people" stereotype of Aborigines became embedded provides some insights into why that stereotype has been so resistant to the intellectual and social challenges of recent decades. Understanding the stereotype and its associated constructions means understanding its two apparently contradictory dimensions, the notions of "fossil" and of "timeless" people. "Fossil" describes something belonging to the past and out of date; it has been left behind. In nineteenth-century context it also carries the meaning of being incapable of growth or progress. By contrast, what is "timeless" is not subject to time and not affected by the lapse of time. Although there is not a simple chronological progression from one theme to another—indeed, both sides of the coin persist in present attitudes—in broad terms the fossilization metaphor is a feature of nineteenth-century debates on evolution. This chapter focuses on the positioning of Australian Aborigines within those debates. In the first half of the twentieth century, timelessness emerged as a parallel theme. This emergence, and its relationship to Aboriginal displacement in Australia, is discussed in chapter three.

Two very distinct contexts need to be kept in mind. The European exploration and settlement of Australia were happening at some defining moments in intellectual history, of crucial importance is the emergence of evolutionary theory and the nineteenth-century interactions between geology, anthropology, and prehistory. (For more comprehensive accounts of these developments and the ways in which Australian evidence was used in them, see Stocking 1987; Kuper 1988; Mulvaney 1990; Kuklick 1993.) At the same time, the engagement between the "primitive" and the "civilized" was being worked out on the ground, a long way away from these metropolitan debates, and we need to understand the intellectual context simultaneously with what was happening in these concrete local interactions.

I follow Livingstone's (1992) notion of "contested conversations" as a device to emphasise the shifting nature of debates. Although the choice to focus on certain themes necessarily reifies concepts to some extent, I am attempting to historicize our present understandings without being teleological. At the same time, although I focus on themes rather than on disciplinary boundaries, there are important differences in the ways in which different practitioners contributed to the debate. For example, the discussions of antiquity come primarily from people with a geological background, a fact central to the characterization of Aborigines as a fossil people. In the nineteenth century there were strong links between geography and ethnology; Livingstone (1991, 221) notes that "there was a considerable membership overlap between the ethnological and geographical societies in the early Victorian period."

Classification and Civilization

The so-called Age of Discovery symbolized by the Pacific voyages of Captain Cook greatly increased the knowledge available in the Old World about both the natural world and the variety of human cultures. Not surprisingly this information was classified in a way that showed its relationship to the known and accepted order of things. In this respect it is interesting to note some parallels between botanical classifications and human ones, including the assumption of an underlying structure that would pop into focus when the appropriate framework was laid over the data.

> The pleasure of the plant collector, then, was a pleasure in naming uniquely and systematically. It was the pleasure of arrangement within a universal taxonomy, a taxonomy characterized by tree-like ramifications—in short, a pleasure analogous to that felt by the imperial historian, who assimilates occasions and anomalies to the logic of universal reason. Equipped with the artificial system of Linnaeus, novelty ceased to present a problem. Utterly strange forms became type specimens. Less curious plants might be assigned to existing genera. (Carter 1987, 19–20)

Carter was contrasting the approaches of Banks and Cook, arguing that the latter was more interested in specifics and differences, having an explorer's interest in a more dynamic "mode of knowing" (18). However, for our purposes, the parallels between the lens of the naturalist Banks and those of ethnographers more than a hundred years later are striking: "To the ethnographer, the bow and arrow is a species, the habit of flattening children's skulls is a species, the practice of reckoning numbers by tens is a species. The geographical distribution of these things, and their transmission from region to region, have to be studied as the naturalist studies the geography of his botanical and zoological species" (Tylor 1891, 8).

Although by the late nineteenth century the unity of the human race was widely accepted, the continued debate centering on independent invention versus diffusion of traits (editor's introduction to Lubbock [1870] 1978, xxxvii), it is important to remember that in the early part of the nineteenth century, there was still debate about whether the various types of human were all one species. Later discussions about what separated primitive from civilized people followed pre-Darwinian ones about what distinguished humans from the rest of creation. In a summary of his 1826 work, Prichard recapitulates his original aim

> to examine whether in both animal and vegetable worlds, there was only one stock or several . . . The information deduced . . . is sufficient to confirm . . . that the human kind contains but one species, and therefore, by a second inference, but one race. It will, I apprehend, be allowed, by those who have attentively followed this investigation of particulars, that the diversities in physical character belonging to different races, present no material obstacle to the opinion, that all nations sprang from one original, a result which plainly follows from the foregoing considerations. (1826, 589–90)

Even in a later edition, Prichard had to acknowledge the debate—without agreeing with it—that "Negroes, Hottentots, Esquimaux, and Australians, are not, in fact, men in the full sense of that term" (1855, 5).

Whether species difference or levels of civilization were at issue, the pecking order and the criteria used were the same. Central to both debates were the human relationship to nature, in particular the extent of control over nature (including the idea of property) and the complexity of a society's material culture. The four stage theory of human progression was already widely discussed among Scottish philosophers including Adam Smith in the middle of the eighteenth century, and Williams shows the close relationships between these discussions and the development of English property law; hunting savages, representing the lowest stage, were considered to live "in a state of nature in which concepts of property had not yet come into being" (1986, 129). Similarly, Prichard described "that impulse peculiar to man, which urges him to attempt and to persevere through long successive ages in the effort to obtain a conquest over the physical agencies of the elements, and to render subservient to his uses and wants the properties of surrounding bodies" (1855, 3). Morgan ([1877] 1907, vi–vii) argued that the progress from savagery through barbarism to civilization can be traced through four phenomena; inventions and discoveries, social institutions, the family, and the idea of property. Each of those three levels had a lower, middle, and upper status; for example, the lower status of savagery "commenced with the infancy of the human race, and may be said to have ended with the acquisition of a fish subsistence and of a knowledge of the use of fire" (10). There were no living examples of this stage. The middle status of savagery "commenced with the acquisition of a fish subsistence and a knowledge of the use of fire, and ended with the invention of the bow and arrow"; the Australians constituted an example. The criteria for this classification thus included subsistence, and there is a hierarchy of this. Tylor used slightly different criteria: "For the present purpose it appears both possible and desirable to eliminate considerations of hereditary varieties or races of man, and to treat mankind as homogeneous in nature, though placed in different grades of civilization . . . A first step in the study of civilization is to dissect it into details, and to classify these in their proper groups" (1891, 7). The details to be classified include weapons, textile arts, myths, rites, and ceremonies.

Even as a critic of the evolutionary approach, Ratzel would not have disagreed with the criteria of classification: "We speak of natural races, not because they stand in the most intimate relations with Nature, but because they are in bondage to Nature" (1896, 14).

> We may declare in the most decided manner that the conception of "natural" races involves nothing anthropological or physiological, but is purely one of ethnography and civilization. Natural races are nations poor in culture . . .
>
> We call them races deficient in civilization, because internal and external conditions have hindered them from attaining to such per-

manent developments in the domain of culture as form the mark of the true civilized races and the guarantees of progress. Yet we should not venture to call any of them cultureless, so long as none of them is devoid of the primitive means by which the ascent to higher stages can be made—language, religion, fire, weapons, implements; while the very possession of these means, and many others such as domestic animals and cultivated plants, testifies to varied and numerous dealings with those races which are completely civilized. (18–19, 22–23)

Human control over nature was still mainly couched in terms of being able to improve on nature (Glacken 1967), through for example the New World perspective of draining swamps, clearing woodland, and thus improving climate. The concerns raised by George Perkins Marsh in 1864 about the destructive aspects of human impacts in the New World were not yet absorbed into this debate. Grove, however, has argued that "early scientific critiques of 'development' or 'improvement' were, in fact, well established by the early nineteenth century" (1995, 2). Such a critique emerged from colonial expansion in the previous few centuries into tropical environments including India, southern Africa, and particularly tropical islands such as the Canaries, Madeira, St. Helena, and Mauritius. To be sure, the idea of the Australian continent being threatened by land degradation and having environmental limits was considered heretical in Griffith Taylor's time (and still encounters resistance today), but we have become somewhat more willing to accord indigenous people at least the human trait of destroying nature (see also chapter five below).

Classification in Time

With the acceptance of deep time in geology and the Darwinian revolution in biology, it was a short step for classification across space to become one across time, for the most primitive peoples to be associated with the earliest parts of the fossil record: "It being shown that the details of Culture are capable of being classified in a great number of ethnographic groups of arts, beliefs, customs, and the rest, the consideration comes next how far the facts arranged in these groups are produced by evolution from one another" (Tylor 1891, 14). The Other having been found in the most remote places, they were also banished to the most remote times. Whether they had descended to the bottom rung of the ladder from a higher state or had never been able to climb upwards in the progress of civilization, primitive peoples were by definition assigned to an original and lower state. In Australia the apparent inevitability of Aboriginal extinction towards the end of the nineteenth century was accepted by all the players and simply bolstered the arguments for their relict status. Peschel, for example, argued that "it was inevitable that the late surviving and superseded forms of past ages should succumb, that the Australian fauna should find a place in palaeontological books, and the kangaroo hunter disappear with the kangaroo" (1876, 329). More than a century later, neither the kangaroo nor its hunter has disappeared, and some native animals occur in much higher numbers now than in precontact times. Nevertheless, the decreasing Aboriginal population and the widespread belief in the inevitability of extinction played a demonstrable role in influencing people's attitudes. (This point is explored in greater detail in chapter three below.)

This concern for classification in time was expressed most clearly in the emerging discipline of prehistoric archaeology. Although it is not my task here to review these developments comprehensively, two points are important: first, the way in which the Australian evidence was incorporated into general theories; and second, the explicit incorporation of ethnographic material into theories about change over time.

Although there was some hesitation expressed by people such as Ratzel as to the way primitives were co-opted into bolstering the edifice of evolution, and there was debate over which characteristics were most diagnostic of change, the trends in the way in which early overviews by prehistorians treated primitive races were relatively uniform.

> Then came into the world the idea of evolution, dividing races into strata; whereby, as must be clearly pointed out, uncivilized races were, on the basis less of considered facts than of general sentiment, lumped together as a kind of heterogeneous foundation. One can understand the almost passionate need which was felt of providing supports in the world of actual fact for the bold edifice of the theory of evolution, and if we cannot ally ourselves at all points with this feeling, it would be unjust not to recognise that it has called forth, no less in the study of the life of races than in that of all life, a movement which is bringing fruitful truths to light. (Ratzel 1876, 15)

The two most widely quoted and influential practitioners were Lubbock, neighbor and protege of Darwin, and Sollas. The three reasons that Lubbock advances for the study of savage races form a coherent pattern when seen as an aspect of his evolutionist standpoint. First, the ethnographic material can be used in conjunction with archaeological evidence to demonstrate that evolution has occurred; second, as man becomes increasingly master of his own fate, such study can be used to identify "survivals"—which science can then eliminate; and third, the natural progression revealed by the ethnographic record divines man's glorious future, in which the ignorance of the lower races will have been abolished (editor's introduction to Lubbock [1870] 1978, xli–xlii). Lubbock divided prehistoric archaeology into four great epochs; the paleolithic ("when man shared the possession of Europe with the Mammoth, the Cave bear, the Woolly-haired rhinoceros, and other extinct animals"), neolithic, Bronze Age, and Iron Age (2–3). He justified his use of "modern savages" as an analogy for prehistoric times because there is no writing for the periods under study, and because (oral) tradition is shortlived and untrustworthy.

> Deprived, therefore, as regards this period, of any assistance from history, but relieved at the same time from the embarrassing interference of tradition, the archaeologist is free to follow the methods which have been so successfully pursued in geology—the rude bone and stone implements of bygone ages being to the one what the remains of extinct animals are to the other. The analogy may be pursued even farther than this . . . the Van Diemaner and South American are to the antiquary what the opossum and the sloth are to the geologist. (440)

The process of embedding living societies into the fossil record is nowhere more explicit than in the chapter structure of Sollas's *Ancient Hunters and Their Modern Representatives* (1915), in which various "modern representatives" are interspersed with archaeological stages. The Tasmanians (chapter 4) come after the Eoliths and before "The Most Ancient Hunters"; the Australian Aborigines (chapter 7) come between the Lower Palaeolithic and the Aurignacian Age. (The particular position of the Tasmanians in schema such as these has been discussed in greater detail by Murray 1992a and Jones 1992.) For Tylor, "the master-key to the investigation of man's primaeval condition is held by Prehistoric Archaeology. This key is the evidence of the Stone Age, proving that men of remotely ancient ages were in the savage state" (1891, 58).

It is important to remember that this idea of a very long timespan is quite distinct from the ahistoric concept of timelessness. A number of researchers had clear conceptions of long passages of time, although

40 Embedding

they were not usually in a position to put numbers on them. Even Rousseau, a hundred years earlier, explicated this in his discussion of the transition from "natural man" to civil society through the process of enclosing land as property: "Hurried on by the rapidity of time, by the abundance of things I have to say, and by the almost insensible progress of things in their beginnings, I pass over in an instant a multitude of ages; for the slower the events were in their succession, the more rapidly they may be described" ([1755] 1973, 87).

Australian Challenges to the Categories

In the nineteenth century, there already were a number of ways that Australian evidence could have been taken to be subversive of the various categories that scholars had constructed as relevant. The reasons for the persistence of the classifications are complex, but salutary for the discussion in later chapters of the ways they persist through to today. (Interesting comparisons may be made here with Murray's discussion [1992] of the normalization of the high antiquity of man into existing paradigms.) Another important point to make here is that all northern hemisphere commentators were drawing on the same relatively small body of literature describing Australian Aborigines (documented in detail in Mulvaney 1990), including accounts by explorers such as Edward John Eyre, George Grey, and Thomas Mitchell. Specifically anthropological fieldwork by the teams of Howitt and Fison and Spencer and Gillen towards the end of the century was both encouraged and utilized by Tylor, Morgan, and Lubbock. Mulvaney cautions that "the interaction of question and answer, of Old World theory and Australian practice, resulted in circular and misleading argument more often than has been recognised" (1990, 34).

In particular, early scholars were aware that Aboriginal people had a clearly expressed system of land ownership (Strzelecki 1845, 340; Prichard 1851, 269; Haddon 1924, 23; Lubbock [1870] 1978, 312). Lowie noted that "a local group . . . occupied a certain tract and was indissolubly connected to it" (1920, 213). Lubbock, quoting Eyre and Grey, commented that North American Indians seem to have no individual property in land: "It appears, therefore, at first sight remarkable, that among the Australians, who are in most respects so much lower in the scale, 'every male has some portion of land, of which he can always point out the exact boundaries' " ([1870] 1978, 309). It was also notable that "when the Australian ventured to resent, by force of arms, infringement of their valued rights of property, they were abused for being quarrelsome" (Ratzel 1896, 348; see also 376).

Reynolds (1997a) argues that Aboriginal property in land was widely recognized in the colonies in the 1830s and 1840s, both legally and in terms of colonial policy. This was an important basis by which the High Court of Australia in 1992 found that native title had in certain circumstances survived the colonial process and was recognized by English common law. Reynolds charts the process by which those rights became less visible in the second half of the nineteenth century (see also chapter three below).

Moreover, some Aboriginal peoples engaged in agricultural practices. Haddon put forward the curious proposition that they cultivated plants but not the soil: "The Australians can rarely depend on regular supplies of food ... Cultivation of the soil is unknown, except that on the west coast the natives invariably re-insert the head of the wild yams they have dug up so as to be sure of a future crop. The cultivation of purslane *[Portulaca oleracea]* seems to be a well-established fact" (1924, 22). Similarly, Ratzel states:

> One can hardly speak of agriculture among the Australians, only traces of it have been observed. Yams were found in cultivation on the Prince of Wales Island, in the north-west, and in the interior. Grey, in his journey from Gantheaume Bay to the Hutt river, came across a stretch of fertile ground more than 3 miles in breadth, representing a single plantation of warran *(dioscorea)*, literally honey-combed with holes for planting. The prohibition to dig up seed-bearing food-plants after the flowering is merely the necessary result of ever-imminent famine. It is a long step from this to their preservation and increase by cultivation. (1896, 363)

Finally, Aboriginal people were subject to the rule of law: "Law and order are secured by custom and enforced as strictly as in some civilised lands" (Sollas 1915, 229). In various places this is explained away as a conservatism likely to stifle innovation and to maintain cultural stasis. A further anomaly (discussed in the section on Griffith Taylor below) is that many of the Australian primitives inhabited the temperate zone, the heartland of civilization.

The Culture-Stunting Gift

It is important to consider the perceptions of the Australian landscape that attended these discussions. Two persistent themes are the deficiencies of the environment and its influence on people. Once again there are contradictory and contested ideas here; it should not surprise us that much of the early literature on the Australian environment is equivocal. On the one hand the deficiencies (particularly of the tropical and arid parts) are emphasized, whether for specific land uses such as agriculture or as a home for an outpost of civilized people. On the other hand, having settled it, there is a need—both for imperial purposes and for peace of mind—to show off the advantages, partly by stifling criticism. Thus the official rhetoric is much more that of an empty land waiting to be filled than of a wilderness waiting to be tamed.

Crawfurd, discussing the relationship between physical geography and ethnology, described Australia thus:

> The great mass of this continent lies in a temperate region, with well-marked seasons; the rest in a tropical one. The climate of that portion of it which has been tested is one of the finest in the world, and the land is not encumbered with forest, always so formidable an obstacle to the early advancement of civilization. With these exceptions, it possesses no peculiar advantages: it has no great range of high mountains, and hence no great navigable rivers, while, from the same cause, a vast extent of its surface is an arid desert of sand. Compared to its area, it has but a small extent of coast-line, because little indented by gulfs, bays or inlets; hence it is wanting in facility of intercommunication. It contained no native plant available to cultivation for human food and no native animal amenable to domestication, the dog excepted,—of small value in such a climate. Under such discouragements, and without communication with strangers, any advancement in civilization would have been impossible, even had its native inhabitants been of the most highly-gifted races of man. (1863, 4–5)

Similarly, Peschel states:

> So far as we are as yet acquainted with Australia, its most striking feature is the absence of lofty mountain chains, and consequently of great rivers. Thus its remote position on the globe, and its deficiency of projections and indentations of outline, are combined with a want of variety in its elevation. Unfortunately, also, its greatest elevations, the so-called Alps, which reach an altitude of 7000 feet, are situated in the most remote corner of the continent, while the only great river system, of which some thousand miles have proved navigable for steamers, lies on the side most distant from the civilized regions of the Old World. The highest mountains of Australia . . . are moreover

directly hurtful to the continent, for the lofty coasts of the east intercept the damp monsoon, forcing it to deposit its rain on their slopes, so that it reaches the plateaux considerably exhausted and able to bring them only a very small amount of moisture. (1876, 326)

Peschel actually had a quite sophisticated understanding of environmental variables; "the old delusion has been exploded that the interior is entirely occupied by a desert void of vegetation" (327). Rather, the irregular rainfall leads to grassland, parklike woods, and great tracts of brushwood, which "would not in itself have been prejudicial to the development of human society had it not been combined with the unpropitious geological structure of Australia" (327). In this geology, the continent has not been submerged or regenerated and has been heavily eroded. Added to this, the continant's isolation prevented colonization by ungulates: "It may, therefore, be truly said of Australia that it is an island without the advantages of an island climate, a country of productive steppes without the ungulates of the steppes, a land of insular tranquillity or, in other words, of a languid struggle for existence, and an asylum for animal and vegetable forms of past ages' (329).

To be sure, Sollas refers to glaciation in Australia, even if it was only "a few hundred feet in thickness and three miles in length" (1915, 13). This is just one example of the awareness that the environment could change; Horton (1979) has shown that consideration of climate change as a cause of megafaunal extinctions was explicit in the latter decades of the nineteenth century. Like the notion of the timeless people, that of a timeless land is multidimensional and does not have to refer just to a situation where nothing changes.

The influence of the environment on people was debated in terms both of civilized and of savage races. This discussion was bound up in what Livingstone (1991; 1992) calls the "moral economy of climate" and was part of a bigger debate on whether it was possible for the white races to prosper in the tropics. This question was of course central to the colonial enterprise on a global scale.

It was self-evident to many of these writers that Australia was hardly a surprising place to find the archetypal primitive: "Australia, the most insular of all the quarters of the globe, has received a larger share than all the others of that culture-stunting gift—vacant coasts" (Ratzel 1896, 333); "All their accounts agree on the principal points. The only material difference noted is in the bulk and stature, which in the northern parts, and where the people have a better supply of food, are much greater than in barren deserts where the race appears to have dwindled under a process of almost starvation, to which they have been subjected for successive generations" (Prichard 1851, 263). Peschel concluded that "nowhere can the retarded development of mankind be more readily accounted for by the unfavourable configuration of the country than in Australia . . . The social development visibly deteriorates both from north to south and from east to west; that is to say, in proportion to the distance from Cape York, the chief point of which has served to connect Australia with the Old World, the customary mode of life of the natives becomes more and more degraded" (1876, 324, 330).

By contrast, Grove (1995, 481) notes that in various colonial situations the people identifying incipient environmental degradation were those most likely to be sympathetic toward indigenous peoples. In the Australian context he cites the "nascent environmentalism" of Strzelecki, who cautioned against the deterioration of Australian soils under tillage or pasturage (Strzelecki 1845, 361). Such sympathy does not pervade the works discussed in this section, notwithstanding their clear identification of the considerable difficulties facing the agricultural enterprise in Australia. Some very astute writing about the Australian environment came from these authors, who drew on themes of environmental deficiency primarily to explain perceived Aboriginal cultural deficiency.

If the land was constructed in a particular way by anthropological and geographical writers to support their theories on the development of civilization, it had to be reconstructed quite differently by governments anxious to encourage white immigration. The dominant theme is one of transplanting a superior culture rather than adapting to local conditions; thus the "electrifying touch" of colonization would be brought to the soil (Collier 1911, quoted in Schaffer 1988, 95). Contemporary Australians can only ponder how different our present situation would be if more notice had been taken of views such as Peschel's on the "unpropitious geological structure of Australia," and less of those on the "retarded development" of its inhabitants.

Griffith Taylor: "The Weakest Goes to the Wall"

Griffith Taylor (1880–1963) makes an interesting case study at this stage of the story for several reasons. He is known as one of the founding fathers of geography as an academic discipline in Australia and was an extremely controversial figure because of his participation in public debates raging in the first few decades of this century (Powell 1980, 1993). Long vilified as an environmental determinist—partly because his particular brand of determinism did not suit the political purposes of the time—he has become something of a latter-day hero among those advocating the idea of limits to settlement (or at least limits to population) in Australia. Most important for our purposes, his writings provide insights into the ways in which both environment and Aborigines were perceived and discussed in the Australia of the early twentieth century.

Trained in geology under Edgeworth David, Taylor traveled to Antarctica with Scott's expedition. He published on a wide range of topics including geology, climatology, the limits to settlement in Australia, ethnology, and general geography (Sanderson 1988, app. 2); I concentrate here on the Australian context of his works on race and climate. In a series of articles and books, Taylor developed and reiterated an argument challenging the assumption that Australia would support a large white population; at the heart of his arguments are his understandings of the patterns of climate in the arid and tropical parts of the continent and of the ability of the white race to cope with them. In a parallel set of writings he developed a global theory of "climatic cycles and evolution" to explain the racial history of the world and the way that human migrations have been affected by climatic change. I will review these two sets of writings separately before examining their common message.

Whites in the Tropics

The general argument is stated most fully in Taylor 1919b and Taylor 1940 and is repeated in a number of other references. Australia "offers sufficient variety for the exercise of the powers of a geographer in explaining the relation of man to his environment, even though Man is 97 per cent 'British' and the Environment perhaps 87 per cent 'warm and dry.' This, then, is the outstanding problem of Australia" (1940, 3).

Taylor chastised geographers and others for promoting "geographic shibboleths" such as the notions that the southern hemisphere tropics are colder than northern tropical latitudes and that the northern quarter of Australia was covered with tropical jungle. He argued in a much more systematic way than anyone else had done that the rainfall of northern Australia is insufficient in amount and reliability and inappropriate in season to support agriculture and that the climate is simply too hot to be comfortable for white settlers. The one exception is the Atherton Tablelands region of north Queensland, where altitude ameliorates the temperature and rain falls throughout the year: "It is a thousand pities that there are not more of these tropical plateaus in Australia. Many valuable crops would grow excellently there" (1919b, 101). He contrasted "economic Australia" with "empty Australia" (Taylor 1940) (fig. 3).

Very aware (as were the politicians who opposed him) of dense human populations to the north of the continent, in Asia, Taylor argued that the best buffer was not to fill up the empty spaces of the continent but to more fully develop the temperate southeastern crescent, for example between Eden and Ballina in New South Wales. He also drew attention to the importance of the extensive coal resources of the Hunter Valley, New South Wales, as the resource base for a settlement heartland. The yellow hordes would not find most of northern Australia suitable anyway, for "the yellow race is nowhere indigenous in regions with a hot, dry climate, such as the Australian hinterland or Rajputana" (Taylor 1919, 107). In the longer term, "slow migration from cooler to warmer regions accompanied by generations of gradual acclimatization" (1919b, 108) might enable whites to colonize the tropics.

Writing in 1940, more than twenty years after his original article, Taylor considered his arguments to have been vindicated: "It will be seen ... that population is spreading very much as I forecasted ... if the population on the *coast* of east Queensland were removed there would be very little left in tropical Australia, in spite of the attempts for more than a century to colonize the tropics" (1940, 409). (NB: All Taylor's population figures exclude Aborigines.)

Race, Climate, and Evolution

If he was considered a renegade for his opposition to the White Australia[1] policy, Taylor's view of racial difference was in other ways quite

---

1. Some of the first legislation passed following Australian Federation in 1901, and not fully dismantled until the 1960s, was designed to entrench the goal of a "white Australia." This included legislation to remove "kanakas" (Melanesian laborers brought to Australia to work in tropical agriculture) and to exclude non-European immigrants. The decline and extinction of the Aborigines was assumed as part of the idea of a "white Australia" (Aplin et al. 1987, 436–37).

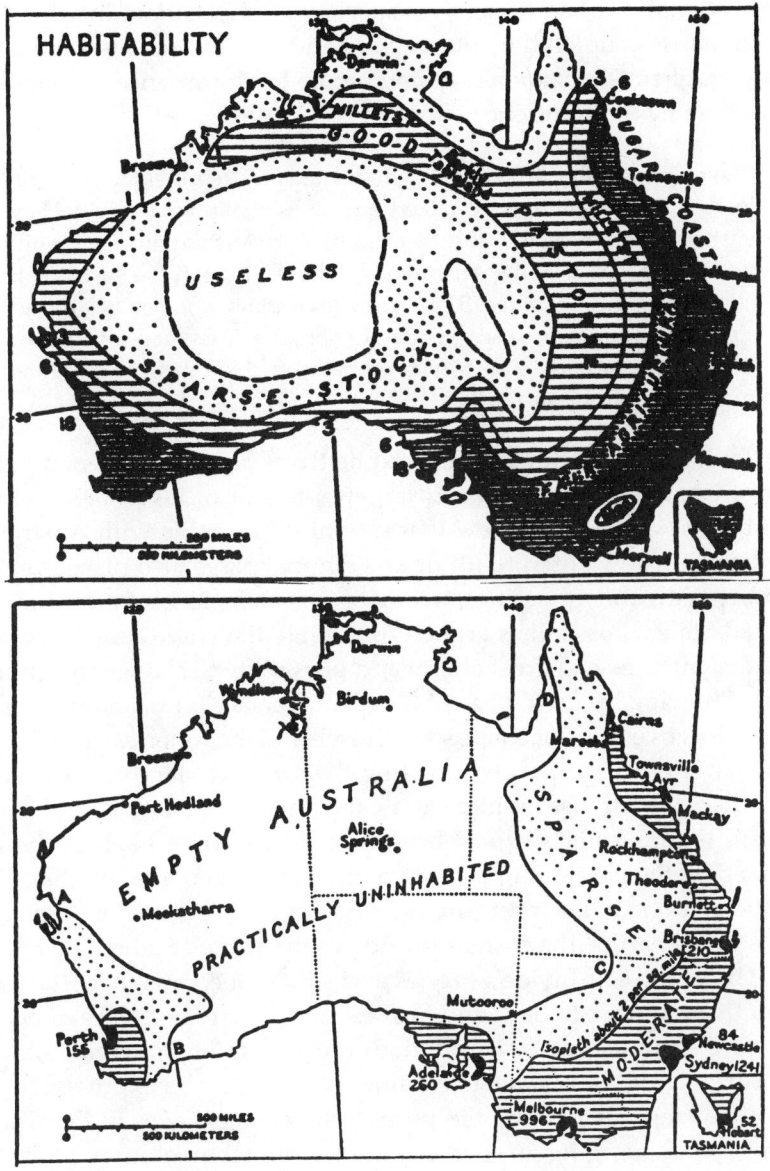

Fig. 3. Griffith Taylor's depictions of "Empty Australia" (based on estimated population density) and of much of the arid zone as "useless" for habitation (Taylor 1946, 390, 391).

conventional. He had a hierarchical view of civilization, in which the Tasmanians occupied the bottom rung and the Australians were a peg or two higher. Civilization is defined more by the absence of characteristics than by their presence.

> The culture of the Tasmanians may be taken as representative of the lowest. They usually went naked but occasionally wore skins. They gashed themselves as a sort of primitive ornamentation. They built nothing so useful as the Australian "wurley," though the Tasmanian climate was much colder (55°F). They used plain wooden spears and clubs and rough stone scrapers and choppers. They had a rude raft like the Californian balsa, which probably enabled them to cross the narrow seas from Asia to Australia. (1921, 73)

Taylor situated himself very explicitly as an environmental determinist, arguing that "culture is largely a result of favorable environment" (1919a, 311). The view that saw him in trouble with Australian politicians who wanted to fill up the empty spaces also placed him in conflict with the emerging stream of possibilistic geography in the United States. Possibilists argued that while the environment set constraints, humans had great ability and possibility to change the ground rules. Showing his own sense of the contingencies influencing theoretical perspectives, Taylor contrasted himself and the Americans: "If he has spent twenty-five years investigating the semi-arid lands of Australia, and thereafter transfers himself to the semi-arctic lands of Canada (which is the writer's experience), he is much more likely to be impressed by the paramount powers of the harsh environment, than if he has been trained (like most American geographers) in one of the richest areas of the earth—the eastern portion of the United States" (1946b, 3).

The essence of Taylor's "zones and strata" theory is that "the most primitive races are to be found farthest away from the centre of evolution of the human races. Throughout the ages the fundamental law of the survival of the fittest has obtained, but it may be expressed more exactly as regards man by the phrase 'the weakest goes to the wall' " (1946a, 6). Envisaging an Asian center for human evolution, he developed a series of maps to show successive migrations out from the heartland (fig. 4). Taylor's classification of races differed from models then current, partly due to his emphasis on the cephalic index (breadth of skull expressed as a percentage of length) as the most diagnostic character of race (profitably studied together with hair cross-section) and the then-popular skin color as the least diagnostic. (The stimulus to increased cephalic index, he argued, was often a struggle against cli-

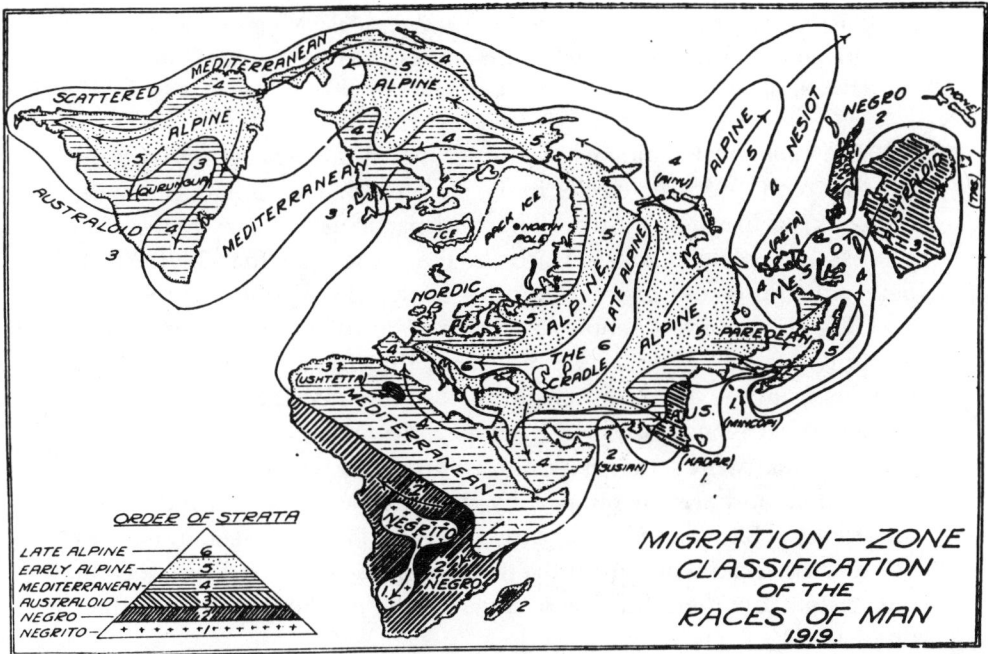

Fig. 4. An illustration of the relationship between Taylor's zones and strata, showing also the position of the Australians and the Tasmanian negritos (Taylor 1946a, frontispiece).

mate [1921, 64].) Interestingly, Taylor's general theory implied a new view of the processes of migration; here, however, I am interested in the way in which "the Zones of to-day are the Strata of to-morrow" (1938, 128) and the implications of this idea for Australia.

Livingstone has identified three metaphors that Taylor used "that betray much about the ideological orientation of moral climatology" (1992, 228): an analogy between racial inferiority and infancy ("the childlike behaviour of the negro"); one between race migration and class-correlated crowd behavior at a football match; and the geological analogy. Before looking in detail at the latter, it is worthwhile to quote the football match "migration"—which applies not only to Taylor's view of evolutionary migrations but also to his understanding of the white settlement of Australia.

> First come the lowest classes and pariahs, who wander freely over the ground long before the general public arrives. They have arrived there by the usual roads and tracks but ultimately are found perched in tree tops and in the least attractive positions of the ground. Then

the proletariat advances along the same roads and corridors. They are driven out of the best seats, which are reserved for the last comers (1919a, 300–301).

The geological analogies are numerous. In this respect Taylor typifies the trend discussed earlier in the chapter (that started at least with Lubbock) of fossilizing Australians and particularly Tasmanians. The process is explained most clearly in the same way that Taylor did, using diagrams and charts. Figure 5 shows the analogy of the lava flow. He also depicted peoples as "inliers," "outliers," and "strata"; for example, Negrito peoples "are scattered through a belt of 'marginal' habitats from the Andaman Island to Tasmania. With the exception of these two extreme regions, all their localities may be described as 'inliers.' In other words, they have almost been overwhelmed by succeeding 'strata,' and are surrounded by the latter, who have driven them into forested highlands in every case" (1946a, 87). As is seen in Figures 4 and 5, the Australians are at the margins of the heartland and deep in the strata. How then did Taylor envisage the mechanics of Australian prehistory?

> It is important to note that the Tasmanian aboriginal presumably crossed [the water barrier surrounding the Asian mainland] before the Australian, and he also must have had some sort of raft for the same reasons. One can picture these primitive folk wandering from Asia into Sunda Land and then retreating slowly before the influx of more advanced tribes. Finally, when their hunting grounds are completely overrun, they despairingly put to sea in their rough rafts made of bark or bundles of rushes. Many are lost but some few reach the islands to the east, whence they ultimately enter Australia. (1946a, 73)

Once there, two factors protect them against further incursions: the drowning of Sunda and Sahul lands and the fact that no one in their right mind would choose to live in northern Australia, where the climate attracted no one who was not forced there (1946a, 73).

Taylor was happy to accept a considerable antiquity for people in Australia, and he also discussed in some detail the environmental changes that must have occurred during human occupation of the continent (1919a). Although we would now understand the specifics of climatic change rather differently, a comparison of his paleoecological scenario and that suggested by modern research is not the point here; rather, it is important to emphasise that like his geological colleagues,

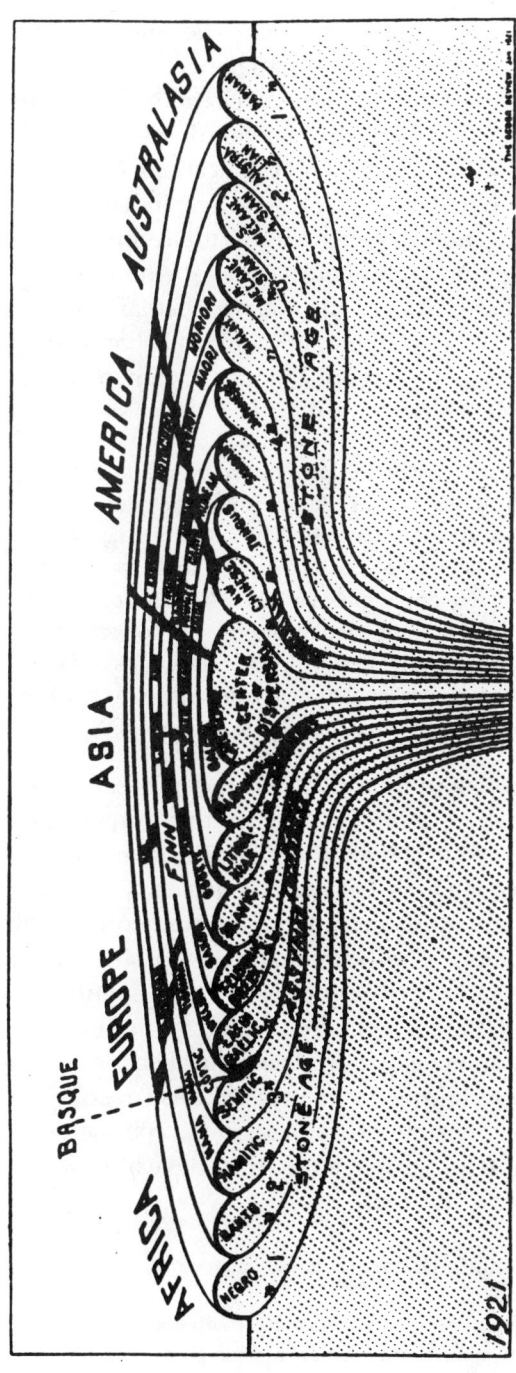

Fig. 5. The lava-flow analogy applied to studies of evolution and of linguistics: "Fossil languages, buried under existing tongues, are seen in section" (Taylor 1938, 121).

Taylor had no conception of "an unchanging land." The landscape that he knew contained abundant evidence of past change, such as that seen in dry lake beds, glacial deposits, and bones of extinct marsupials: "There is overwhelming evidence of the happier conditions which obtained in Pleistocene times" (1919a, 293). The implications of this for people are not developed in detail in Taylor's writings; indeed, in the absence of absolute dating techniques this was virtually impossible. However, in contrast to earlier ethnographers—some of whom saw the different races as having been "placed" in their particular environments—Taylor argued rather that "the chief ethnological characters of man developed largely as a result of marked changes in climate during the Pleistocene age" (1921, 54).

> The continent was now closed to further migration from Asia, and the tribes reached a state of equilibrium. But the environment gradually changed for the worse in southern Australia. The attractive central portion, the ancient corridor, became almost desert, the thick forest of inland New South Wales became open, grassy plains. But it is possible that the tribes were "anchored" to their tribal grounds, and so we find the anomaly of later and probably higher patrilineal migrations occupying poor ground, while the earlier[2] matrilineal tribes have (or had) some of what is now the best country in Australia. (1946a, 99–100)

The link between this developing aridity and the impossibility of agriculture forced the Australian to remain "a primitive hunter living from hand to mouth" (1946a, 99). The anomaly of primitives occupying fertile temperate country such as Tasmania was clearly problematic: "The Australians have always been much more numerous in the tropical portions of the continent.[3] The Tasmanians have probably been in Tasmania for a few thousand years only, whereas they spent half a million years in the tropics" (1921, 57). Finally, of course, "nothing is so dangerous to a people as complete isolation. The natural barrier which preserved the Australian aboriginals from invasion also resulted in their remaining in the same low state of civilization for 100,000 years. At the first approach of a more progressive race they have almost vanished from the face of the earth" (1921, 76).

2. Matrilineal tribes were assumed to be more primitive than patrilineal, as the latter required the ability to identify the father.
3. It is not made clear on what evidence this statement is based. Recent ethnographic research shows very high population densities in some parts of southeastern Australia.

Black and White

There are many obvious parallels between Taylor's racial models and his climatic theories with respect to the presence of whites in Australia. Of particular relevance to this discussion is how he dealt with the Aboriginal people who had survived the colonization process: Because they render the model slightly messy, they are erased in several ways. It is not really clear how conscious Taylor was of doing this. In places he was quite explicit, but he seems to have only felt the need to bring surviving Aborigines into the picture when they fitted a particular theory.

> The fittest tribes evolve and survive in the most stimulating regions ... The least fit are ultimately crowded out into the deserts, the tropical jungles, or the rugged mountains.
>
> Since, however, this "crowding-out" is still occurring, we should expect to find (and *do* find) that there are a few primitive peoples still living in attractive lands, provided they be so far distant from the cradle-lands or centre of evolution that the fitter races have hardly reached them. These primitive people are doomed to extinction, however, as we have seen in the case of the Tasmanians, the last of whom died in 1876. To quote another example, the aborigines in Victoria and New South Wales are reduced to 120 and 1,200 respectively; and a chart of their death-rate shows that these tribes are unlikely to last fifty years. (1946a, 67)

The demise of the Aboriginal population, thus depicted, is the result not of the colonial engagement but the inevitable outcome of a progressivist evolutionary process and of Australia's progress towards a higher type of civilization. In other parts of Taylor's writing, however, Aborigines are simply invisible in the landscape. For example, contrasting the homogeneity of Australia with the complexity of Britain, he wrote:

> There has never been a racial problem; for the few aborigines have almost been ignored in the march of settlement ... If we turn to Africa we find a continent with many more similarities to Australia ... Schwarz has declared that one dominant motif runs throughout, summarized by the phrase "the black man and the thorn tree." In some such fashion we may perhaps venture to assert that the *"mulga-dotted peneplain"* epitomizes the major portion of Australia. We cannot introduce the human factor into our summary, for the Australian is a town-dweller. (1940, 4)

Central to the ambivalent and sometimes contradictory ways in which Taylor deals with postcontact Aboriginal people is the construction of the authentic primitive: "It is very difficult to find aborigines who still retain quite unaltered their primitive culture. But there are a few tribes in this condition, especially in the rarely visited islands off the north coast. The writer has travelled very widely in Australia, and has never seen absolutely primitive aborigines" (1940, 426). His use of biological criteria for characterizing race and primitivism meant that the questions of authenticity could hardly be framed otherwise. In one illuminating paper Taylor and Jardine address the question of culture contact—or, as they put it, the "transition"—by arguing that there are two ways in which research can still be illuminating "among the relics of our eastern aborigines": by comparative anthropometric survey between surviving full-bloods and the full range of hybrids, and by examining "the effect of their changing environment upon these primitive peoples" (1924, 269). The urgency of such research is emphasized by the inevitability of absorption into the general population. The main part of the paper is an attempt to compare a range of anthropometric indicators among full-bloods, half-castes, and quarter-castes and less, with a view to discerning trends. The meaning of any changes (the results are not very conclusive) is not really addressed.

The point of this discussion is not to pillory Taylor but rather to show how an influential Australian who spoke out against several racisms—against the White Australia policy and against Nazism (Taylor 1946b)—could nevertheless not envisage an Australia in which Aboriginal people had a future.

As much as an identity of racial purity was central to the process of national creation at the end of the nineteenth century and within the early decades of the twentieth (White 1981), Australia was much more worried about being yellow than black. This is important to understanding the context of Griffith Taylor's public battles, and emphasizes the limited sense in which Aboriginal issues were to the fore at the time. The imprisonment of Aborigines deep in the geological column and at the bottom of the evolutionary staircase represents an academic counterpart to the far more violent dispossessions that were taking place on the land itself.

Nomads

In 1838 Charles Darwin was pondering the lessons on the struggle for life that were provided by the natural world of the wealthy English landowner—pigeons, dahlias, and greyhounds—penning dissident thoughts in his notebooks, and arguing with himself over whether or not to marry. As he read the sixth edition of Malthus's *Essay on the Principle of Population*, he was struck by the parallels between a society characterized by economic depression, increasing unemployment, and surging emigration and wild populations who "bred beyond their means," only the strongest to survive. In a Whig worldview in which social and biological evolution were conflated, emigration provided a safety valve in the struggle for existence, one that could reduce poverty at home and create new markets abroad. For Darwin the destruction associated with imperial expansion also had a creative edge: "When two races of men meet, they act precisely like two species of animals—they fight, eat each other, bring diseases to each other &c, but then comes the more deadly struggle, namely which have the best fitted organisation, or instincts (ie intellect in man) to gain the day" (Desmond and Moore 1991, 265, 267).

Three weeks after their April 1838 marriage, my great-great-great-grandmother Sarah, an agricultural laborer from Etchingham, Sussex, and her husband William Head, an agricultural laborer from Goudhurst, Kent (map 2), left Plymouth for Australia on one of the first five ships carrying assisted emigrants direct from Britain, arriving in Sydney in August 1838. He was twenty-one and she was nineteen. Sarah, then Ellis, signed her marriage certificate with an X; by the time she arrived in Australia she could read and write and was pregnant with the first of her fourteen children. All things considered, it is hardly surprising that we have so few records of her life. She must have had precious little time for anything other than the demands of the day, at least until

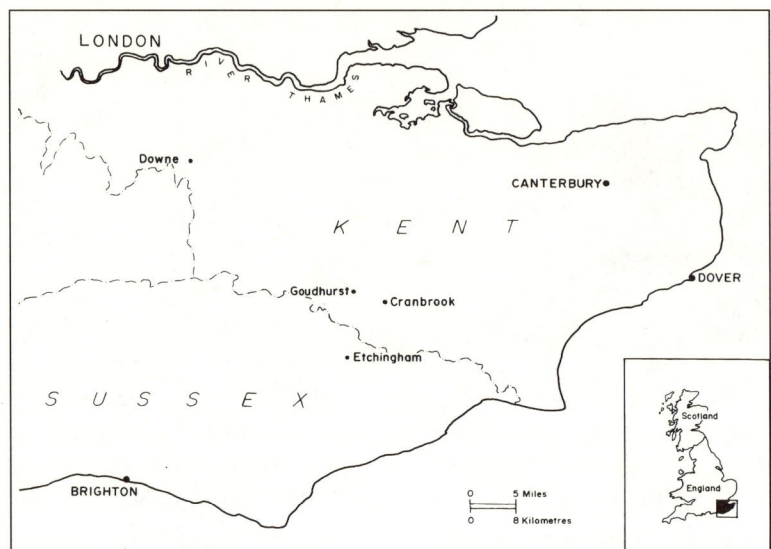

Map 2. Sussex and Kent, England

she was an old woman, from which time there exist some recollections of her reminiscences.

William and Sarah are remembered in our family not as English flotsam who lost the struggle for existence at home, nor as "harbingers of extermination to native tribes" (Desmond and Moore 1991, 266), but as a brave young couple who left everything behind in the hope of a better life. In the way that family histories have of needing superlatives, a number of firsts have been noted; indeed it may be precisely because of these firsts that we commemorate William and Sarah while letting go of other people and other histories. William and Sarah quickly gained employment with John Gardiner, who ran the first cattle station in the Port Phillip area, and left Sydney on the barque *Hope* the first vessel to bring immigrants to Port Phillip. Also on board were four Protectors to the Aborigines. In Gardiner's employ, the couple settled at the junction of the Yarra River and Gardiners Creek (see map 3 and fig. 6), where she worked as housekeeper and supervisor of men's meals and he was the hutkeeper and gardener. According to family legend, William planted the first crop and Sarah gave birth to the first white child in the Hawthorn-Gardiners Creek district (Head 1970). During 1839 William planted ten acres of an unnamed crop, probably wheat or oats. In 1844 their third child was the first person buried at St. Andrew's graveyard, Brighton.

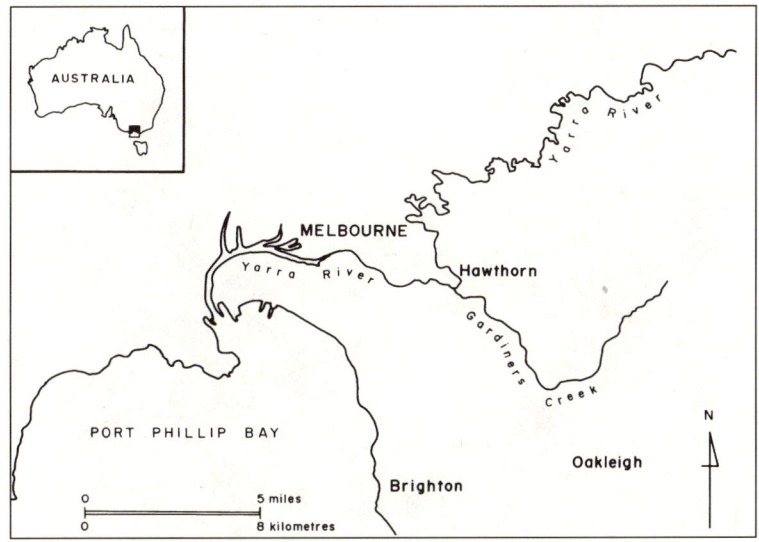

Map 3. Port Phillip district, Victoria

They were not, of course, first at all. History does not record how many patches of Yam-daisy William ploughed under on the river flats, but the owner of the Yam-daisies may have thought justice was done when that first European crop, mown and stooked ready for carting, was washed into the tree tops by a torrential flood.

The Yam-daisy, with its crisp, sweet, radishlike tubers, was widespread across a range of soil conditions in southeastern and southwestern Australia. In places it was so abundant that one early European settler wrote that "the wheels of our dray used to turn them up by the bushel"; Major Mitchell said of Aboriginal children in 1839 that "as soon almost as they can walk, a little wooden shovel is put into their hands, and they learn thus early to pick about the ground for those roots and a few others" (Gott 1983, 9). The continual digging maintained a loose, well-aerated soil, while burning of the grass to better see the aboveground rosettes fertilized the soil and stimulated rapid regeneration (fig. 7). In 1841 George Augustus Robinson, Protector of the Aborigines, described women "spread over the plain as far as I could see them ... each had a load as much as she could carry" (Gott 1983, 9). Not the Gardiners Creek plain, but it could well have been.

Women, children, digging, burning, harvesting, gathering. These are the sort of activities described by male European observers as "ac-

Fig. 6. Junction of Gardiners Creek and the Yarra River, ca. 1873–82. Courtesy La Trobe Picture Collection, State Library of Victoria.

cidental gardening." By 1841 there were seven hundred thousand sheep in Victoria, and by 1843 twice that many (Gott 1983, 12). They grazed the Yam-daisy plains, rooting out the yams with their noses and hardening the soil with continuous trampling.

The bits of Sarah's memories that have survived for us focus on the Aborigines: "At that time the aborigines were very numerous and troublesome. They used to beg flour and tobacco and they terrified Mrs. Head. In later years she used to relate that there was only one door to the house in which they lived, as it would have been too dangerous to have a back as well as a front entrance" (Head 1970, 8). They also apparently begged for her to give them her first piccaninny[1], William.

A March 1839 census of Aborigines in the vicinity of Melbourne

---

1. The term "piccaninny" was commonly used in nineteenth- and twentieth-century Australia to refer to an Aboriginal child. It may have been part of the kriol in which William and Sarah Head presumably communicated with local Aboriginal people. In contrast to American use of the term, there is no necessary association with slavery.

Fig. 7. John Helder Wedge Sketchbook: "Native women getting Tambourn roots, 27 Aug. 1835." Courtesy La Trobe Australian Manuscripts Collection, State Library of Victoria.

recorded one hundred twenty-four members of the Yarra tribe (Wurundjeri) and eighty-three members of the Western Port tribe (Bunurong) (Presland 1983, 28).

William Thomas, Assistant Protector of Aborigines for the Western Port District during 1839–49, described the ecological impacts of the invasion: "In the unlocated parts of the country and other such places as have not been visited by the flocks and herds of the Settler these roots [Yam-daisy] are obtained in great abundance but like the other natural supplies of the Aborigines they diminish and soon disappear when sheep and cattle are depastured" (Gaughwin 1983, 49). A number of references attest to the Aborigines being well aware of the connection; for example, Gott quotes a 1839 reference to a man called Moonin-Moonin: "There were no 'param' or 'tarook' at Port Phillip . . . too many 'jumbuck' (sheep) and 'bulgana' (bullocks, cattle) plenty eat it myrnyong [Yam-daisy]—all gone myrnyong" (1983, 12).

The Head family moved to Brighton some years later, where William junior and his brother Edward made a living felling wood and carting it to Melbourne for sale. They made far more money than did William senior and another brother who headed for Bendigo during the gold rush, particularly when the price of a load of wood jumped from four shillings and sixpence to three pounds. As much as the life of this family is better recorded than that of the daisy-yammers, the scale (let alone the gender) of the individual has always been problematic for traditional Australian history in which political structures have usually been the focus of interest.

> The problem of how to deal adequately with individuals in a work of this kind is always present and always oppressive. They are singularly important, they are the real stuff of such a history, yet only a select number can be described even in the limited manner which the lack of diaries and personal matter makes inevitable. It has been thought best here to use individuals to illuminate their occupations ... A most important group of self-sufficient labourers might be represented by William Head ... so clearly representative of the group of farmers in the area who were hiring themselves out where they could and falling back for subsistence on the home plot, where the tasks were shared by wives and children. (Bate 1962, 119–121)

What did the Wurundjeri make of these nomads, who had forsaken the land of their mothers and fathers for a risky life in someone else's country? They managed a living from the land, then elsewhere exchanged their labor for money—not that the idea of trade was strange to the Wurundjeri. But then the immigrants were gone, only to be replaced by the next wave. From Kent, to Sydney, to Hawthorn, to Brighton, to Oakleigh within a single generation, each move heralding the demise of yet more Yam-daisies. Even as immigrants, we think of ourselves as settled, permanent, owner-occupiers.

Between 1839 and 1863 Sarah and William Head had fourteen children, nine of whom survived to adulthood. Six were born within the first ten years. In the Yarra and Western Port tribes there were five births in the ten years from 1838 (Presland 1983, 30); between 1850 and 1853 two births were recorded (Bride, [1898] 1969, 415).

In 1842 Charles and Emma Darwin moved from London to Downe, Kent, a few miles from the area William and Sarah Head had left. Here Charles, gentleman scholar, paced the sandwalk daily for another seventeen years before his *Origin of Species* was published, and Emma continued to have babies and to run the household. Although their struggle for existence did not compare materially with that of the agricultural laboring families of their village, women of all classes shared the hazardous processes of pregnancy, birth, and bringing children to adulthood. Charles and Emma were particularly devastated by the death of their oldest daughter, Annie, at the age of ten. It was this event that finally "destroyed Charles's tatters of belief in a moral, just universe" (Desmond and Moore 1991, 387).

3

Timeless and Placeless

It is due to no accident that the word "culture" also denotes the tillage of the ground. Here is its etymological root; here, too, the root of all that we understand by it in its widest sense. The storage by means of labour of a sum of force in a clod of earth is the best and most promising beginning of that non-dependence upon Nature which finds its mark in the domination of her by the intellect.

—F. Ratzel, *The History of Mankind*

If the "fossilization" process previously discussed was a translation of spatial into temporal variation, the process by which the Aborigines became "timeless people" in the first half of the twentieth century is also inextricably linked with spatiality. Physical and conceptual dispossessions rendered them "placeless" in Australian society; as links to land were ruptured so were links to history. Aboriginal people were thus characterized as outside time and absent from place.

This is a somewhat stylized summary of a complex set of historical circumstances, five threads of which are traced in this chapter:

1. The conceptual justifications for dispossession of hunter-gatherers on the basis of their perceived lack of purchase on the landscape;

2. As a consequence of continued dispossession and colonization, the numerical decline of the Aboriginal population;

3. Their consequent decreasing visibility in public culture;

4. The rise of ahistorical, functionalist approaches in anthropology;

5. The new Australian nationalism in literature and art, which drew inspiration from essentialized visions of the Australian landscape, summarized in the partner notion of "timeless land."

Common to all these processes was the assumption that the extinction of Aboriginal people, however unfortunate, was inevitable. If one meaning of timeless was "eternal," then it was not assumed to be in this world.

The agricultural metaphor was central to the colonizing culture's vision of itself and its civilizing presence. The apparent absence among the colonized of "tillage" and hence "culture" only served to legitimate both conceptual and physical dispossessions. The interconnections between agriculture, civilization, and property are explored at some length here because they underpin not only the land rights battles of the late nineteenth and early twentieth centuries, but those that continue today.

Conceptual Dispossession

Examining the uses of the agricultural metaphor helps us understand two different land rights struggles. One is the class-based battles between Europeans over land tenure that have long been central to most views of early Australian history; the other is the ways in which Europeans legitimized their dispossession of Aborigines. It also helps us understand a third, the Aboriginal land rights movement of the last thirty years. These most recent legal struggles have had to revisit the seventeenth-century Lockean view of property, underpinned by a particular view of the appropriate use of nature: "As much Land as a Man Tills, Plants, Improves, Cultivates, and can use the Product of, so much is his property. He by his Labour does, as it were, inclose it from the common" (Williams 1986, 121).

It is important to tease out contradictions between theory and practice. The most powerful landholders in early Australia, the wealthy squatters, neither tilled, planted, nor cultivated; they were pastoralists rather than horticulturalists. How is it then that imagery so important in rationalizing the dispossession not only glossed over clear evidence of some agricultural practices among Aboriginal people but was also partial in its application to the colonizers' way of living?

Although narratives of today often emphasise the hostile relationship between the newcomers and the land, Powell offers a different perspective by examining the land relationship from which the immigrants to both Australia and North America came.

> Land remained the prime source of wealth in every European country throughout the eighteenth century and, despite increasing urbanization and industrialization, most Europeans continued to gain their livelihood from agricultural employment. Their images of the New World were in part determined by the kinds of lives they saw and ex-

perienced in Europe. Their reflections on individual perfectibility, on personal dignity and independence, were inevitably based in important measure upon their perception of the intimate and deeply rooted relationship between land and life. (1977, 34)

The New World offered a clean slate, particularly when evoked in Arcadian terms, as it was in attempts to lure free settlers (Lansbury 1970). Hills discusses the pastoral vision as a force for political conservatism: "[P]astoral landscapes . . . represent a model society based on harmony, in which all tensions between the conflicting interests in society are transposed into an equanimity which permits the status quo to prevail" (1991, 15). Here I am more concerned to focus on the way such an ideal served to dispossess societies with different economic bases.

The centrality of property in land to the definition of civilization is one constant running through late-eighteenth- and nineteenth-century thought and politics. For Rousseau it was the thing that distinguished natural man from civil society: "The first man who, having enclosed a piece of ground bethought himself of saying 'This is mine,' and found people simple enough to believe him, was the real founder of civil society" (Rousseau [1755] 1973, 84). For Rousseau many of the consequences of this transition were negative, but a more widespread view was that both people and the land were improved by the process of bringing into cultivation. Hunter-gatherers, however, were not considered sufficiently productive in transforming mere landscapes into things of value, nor were they differentiated sufficiently as subjects in relation to natural objects to meet the criteria for civilized peoples (Povinelli 1993, 8).

Such perceptions also tie into what Grove (1995) has termed an "Edenic discourse" by which European colonizers from the fifteenth through the nineteenth centuries attempted to make sense of the new natures that they were encountering. He argues that the (physical and textual) garden was one of two central metaphors through which perceptions of nature were organized; the other was the island. Australia is peripheral to Grove's discussion, which focuses on tropical island environments and earlier colonizations; nevertheless, his historical perspective on the imagery of the garden provides useful insights into the background to its transfer—perhaps its problematic and ambiguous application—to the Australian context. For, in contrast to the clearly bounded, humid, tropical islands with rich volcanic soils, Australia was continental in scale, mostly arid, and possessed mostly impoverished soils.

Roth, in 1877, discussed the relationship between the development of property and the origins of agriculture, drawing on Australian examples among others. He quotes explorer A. C. Gregory: "A native discovering a Zamia fruit unripe will put his mark upon it, and no other native will touch this; the original finder of the fruit may rest perfectly certain that when it becomes ripe he has only to go and fetch it for himself" (Roth 1887, 109). The fact that, by and large, Aboriginal agricultural practices did not lodge in the imagination of the colonizers was not confined to Australia: "Despite all the evidence to the contrary in the eastern woodlands, the dominating concept of contemporary Indian life in the minds of America's policy-makers became based on the idea of a complex of primitive hunting cultures" (Powell 1977, 85). Powell quotes Wessel's description of the agricultural symbolism of the Ritual on Admission of Indians to Full American Citizenship, used until 1924: "The Indian subject first shot an arrow into the air, intoning an oath to end his wandering days. Then placing his hand upon a plow he swore to abandon the hunt, take up agriculture and live the life of a white man" (Wessel 1976, 19–20).

What neither Powell nor Wessel comment on is the gender dimension of these perceptions. Digging and collection of yams and tubers in Australia is overwhelmingly described ethnographically as the work of women and children (e.g. Gott 1982, 1983) (see also fig. 7 above). Perdue describes the response of the Cherokees to a federal program to civilize them through providing "implements of husbandry": "The Cherokees, devastated by invasion and impoverished by the decline of the deerskin trade, welcomed assistance. Yet they must have been somewhat bemused by the preferred lessons in agriculture. Not only had Cherokee women been farming for centuries, many of the crops and techniques used by Euro-Americans came from Native peoples. Most Europeans, however, assumed that the Native economy rested on hunting" (Perdue 1995, 92). Perdue argues that the Cherokees adapted this "civilization" in terms of their own expectations of men and women.

Roth's paper, drawing on material from all over the world, illustrates some of the contradictions embedded in early analyses of the ethnographic evidence. On the one hand women are even lower on the scale of civilization than savage men, partly at the hands of their menfolk: "Amongst the rudest tribes we find a well defined division of labour between the sexes. The men do the hunting and fishing, and the women the cooking and the general work which goes under the name of drudgery. The women, being the weaker sex, are also terribly knocked about" (Roth 1887, 118). On the other hand he recognised the likelihood that the women made the first steps towards agriculture, thus dragging their society "up the ladder": "As the women appear everywhere with the savage in his lowest known stage to be told off for all work in connection with the collection of vegetable food, it is more than probable that they rather than the men were the first to make tentatives [sic] towards acts which may be regarded as originating agriculture" (120). Roth provides a further clue to the sources of ambivalence to agricultural practices when he reminds us of its eighteenth- and nineteenth-century class-based dimensions—namely, the fact that agriculture was associated with peasantry. In reflecting on the classifications imposed on the Other, we should not forget that the same categories were not necessarily applied to Self: "One reason for the neglect of this study [the origin of agriculture] may lie in the general indifference, if not contempt, with which tillers of the soil are usually regarded. Indeed, history is full of the scorn with which manly or war-like races look down on husbandry" (103).

The "gathering" part of today's concept of the hunter-gatherer, although it was certainly included in the anthropological descriptions of primitive lives, was not used in any of the nineteenth- and early-twentieth-century designations of the scales of civilization (including those referred to in the previous chapter). It arguably did not come into general use until the late 1960s, with the first Man the Hunter conference. Rather, the traditional images of primitivism and savagery have been strongly associated with men and spears rather than women and digging sticks (e.g. fig. 8). This is not to suggest that Aboriginal property rights would have been respected any more had men been turning over the soil; nevertheless, the nexus between women's work and purchase on the earth undoubtedly contributed to its invisibility to the colonizers.

Physical Dispossession

Consideration of such abstract cultural factors should not be taken to suggest that the "frontier" was a zone of purely intellectual rather than physical engagement, for there is extensive documentation now of bloody conflict in most areas of Australia (Atkinson and Aveling 1987,

Fig. 8. Postcard, Australian Aborigines. Courtesy The Image Library, State Library of New South Wales.

chap. 2; Reynolds 1987a). Williams argues that although the English understood Aboriginal rights of possession and ownership quite early, they were quick to create justifications for their own appropriation of land; "The conflict between acting on understanding and justifying expediency" (Williams 1986, 152) is shown in Forster's documentation of the various drafts of a 1838–39 proclamation on Aboriginal rights in New South Wales. In this case, any humanitarian intentions in Britain and on the part of New South Wales Governor Sir George Gipps collided with pressure from wealthy pastoralists:

> The process of drafting and redrafting the proclamation reveals Gipps and his officials in some confusion, for they had to put together a policy which provided some degree of protection for Aborigines and accorded with humanitarian principles expounded in Britain, while at the same time confronting the realities of frontier violence. This task, difficult enough in itself, was made much more complex by inadequacies in the law and ambiguities in the status of Aborigines as subjects of the queen. (Forster 1981, 84–85)

The concept of native title at common law, as decided first in the 1823 Marshall decision in the United States Supreme Court and recognized in the 1992 Mabo decision of the Australian High Court, arose out of exactly this sort of pragmatic quandary: "The European nations wanted the land and they took it. The common law responded by devising a concept that sustained the property rights sanctioned by the government and yet in part maintained the rights of the aboriginal people" (Bartlett 1993, 62).

Ritter helps us to understand more of the relationships between the conceptual and the physical dispossessions with a critique of terra nullius, the concept of empty land belonging to no one—which was widely thought to have been rejected in the Mabo decision. Ritter argues that what was rejected was not terra nullius as a legal doctrine—there is no such thing—but terra nullius as "a discourse of power." The discourse of power that denied Aboriginal land rights in the nineteenth century privileged the ruling interests and emphasized the nomadic, uncertain, and lawless characterizations of Aboriginal life: "The absence of Aboriginal land rights was not a matter for judicial decisions, it was a truth that was self-evident, and the development of the law was predicated upon that truth" (1994, 36). Thus, "Aboriginal people were not denied common law rights to land because of the operation of any single legal doctrine, but rather because of the operation of various socio-historical discourses of power that justified the dispossession of the Aboriginal tribes" (7). By the 1980s, according to Ritter's argument, the rethinking of these self-evident truths within the wider society had created a "discursive crisis," a disjunction between truth and power that the High Court resolved by rejecting terra nullius. (The process of this rethinking is discussed further in later chapters.)

In a number of ways the early decades of the twentieth century marked the nadir of Aboriginal representation both in the symbolic and in the political life of Australia. This is at least partly because all commentators assumed that the Aboriginal race was on the brink of extinction and that it was only a matter of time before half- and quarter-caste people would be completely absorbed into the wider population (fig. 9). In fact, the Aboriginal population declined steadily after European settlement until this period. Although estimates of the lowest Aboriginal population vary slightly in amount and timing and should be considered minimum estimates, there is concurrence that the lowest levels were experienced between the 1920s and the 1930s (Jones 1970; Commonwealth of Australia 1984). The most recent figures suggest a low of 73,828 people of Aboriginal descent in 1933 (Price 1987). Accuracy of Aboriginal population statistics has been hampered

Fig. 9. "A Curiosity in her own country." Cartoon by Phil May, the *Bulletin* (Sydney), 3 Mar. 1888. Courtesy The Image Library, State Library of New South Wales.

by factors including problems of definition; particularly important was Section 127 of the Australian Constitution, which (from 1901 until repealed by referendum in 1967) stated that "in reckoning the numbers of the people of the Commonwealth, or of a State of the Commonwealth, aboriginal natives shall not be counted" (Jones 1970, 5).

Reflecting the fact that the "frontier" was spatially and temporally variable, the lowest numbers were reached at different times across the continent. In Tasmania, the population declined to an estimated eighteen in 1861, and in the population centers of New South Wales and Victoria, lowest levels are noted in 1901. In Western Australia and the Northern Territory, encompassing areas that were not settled by whites until almost the turn of the century, lowest levels were recorded in 1933 (Price 1987, 4).

Notwithstanding the problems of measurement, there is general agreement that following a low point sometime between the 1920s and the 1940s, the Aboriginal population has been growing since, and it maintains a higher rate of growth than the national average. Government policies of the time reflected the assumption that full-bloods would eventually die out and that half-castes and others would be absorbed into the mainstream population.

Invisibilities and Silences

We have come to understand more of the silences in Australian history—and the gaps in individual lives—with the recent publication of the report of the National Inquiry into the Separation of Aboriginal and Torres Strait Islander Children from their Families (also known as the "Stolen Generations" report) (Commonwealth of Australia 1997). The report traces the laws and policies by which thousands of indigenous children—defined by pale skin color rather than by cultural identity—were removed into foster and institutional care right up until the 1970s (fig. 10). Part of the reason that the powerful stories of grief and loss detailed in the report are so disturbing for the contemporary Australian community is that many of them are so recent. These are the stories of living, not always old, people; no longer can we claim that these are the actions of distant generations, that colonialism was something that only happened two hundred years ago.

> When I was 14 years old and going to these foster people, I remember the welfare officer sitting down and they were having a cup of tea and talking about how they was hoping our race would die out. And that I was fair enough, I was a half-caste and I would automatically live with a white person and get married. Because the system would make sure that no-one would marry an Aborigine person anyhow. And then my children would automatically be fairer, quarter-caste, and then the next generation would be white and we would be bred out. I remember when she was discussing this with my foster people, I remember thinking—because I had no concept of what it all meant—remember thinking, "That's a good idea, because all the Aborigines are poor." (Commonwealth of Australia 1997, 157, confidential evidence from woman removed as a baby in the 1940s)

There has been much debate in Australia over the extent to which such practices were well-intentioned and thus less reprehensible. This is a difficult argument to sustain, notwithstanding the considerable variability in how children were treated in individual foster families and institutions. What is quite clear from the evidence is that both pol-

Fig. 10. Point Macleay Mission, South Australia. Courtesy The Image Library, State Library of New South Wales.

icy and practice were founded on essentialist and imperialist conceptions of race and that they contributed to the systematic deculturation of many Aboriginal groups. The separation of children from their social networks prevented the transmission of language, culture, knowledge of traditional responsibilities, and links to land. As such, the report found that

> the policy of forcible removal of children from Indigenous Australians to other groups for the purpose of raising them separately from and ignorant of their culture and people could properly be labelled "genocidal" in breach of binding international law from at least 11 December 1946 . . . The practice continued for almost another quarter of a century. (Commonwealth of Australia 1997, 275)

The invisibility of Aborigines, together with the assumption of their decline, is seen in a variety of forms of public culture. The process was powerfully and perceptively expressed when the noted anthropologist W. E. H. Stanner used the term "the Great Australian Silence" in his 1968 Boyer lectures, in which he argued that the structure of Australian race relations remained virtually unchanged from the early 1800s until at least the 1930s. Stanner is best known anthropologically for his explications of the multiple bases of Aboriginal relations to land and of the Dreaming, based on many years fieldwork in northern Australia; thus, his critique is all the more powerful because he turned it on his own work as well: "What was missing was the idea that a major development of aboriginal economic, social and political life from its broken down state was a thinkable possibility. How slowly this idea came to all of us" (1969, 14). He cites a chapter he wrote for Aughterson's 1953 book *Taking Stock: Aspects of Mid-Century Life in Australia:* "[T]he book opens with a chapter entitled "The Australian Way of Life," written by W. E. H. Stanner, who can safely be presumed never to have heard of the aborigines, because he does not refer to them and even maintains that Australia has 'no racial divisions like America' (Stanner 1969, 23–24).

Historian Tom Griffiths has recently argued that the Great Australian Silence was often in fact "white noise", "[I]t sometimes consisted of an obscuring and over-laying din of history-making. But the denial was frequently unconscious, or only half-conscious, for it was part of a genuine attempt by white Australians to foster emotional possession of the land and was sometimes accompanied by respect for pre-existing Aboriginal associations" (Griffiths 1996, 5). Griffiths' study, focusing on Victoria, is particularly important in bringing to light vernacular and amateur discourses through nature writing, travel literature, local historical societies, and collectors. In contrasting these with professional debates in history and in anthropology, he argues that at the points where the frontier intersected with place, the Aboriginal presence could not be avoided. The history of this intersection continues to haunt in forms such as place names like Slaughterhouse Gully and country town memorials to the "last" local Aborigine. Geographer Jane Jacobs (1996) has also written recently of the haunting legacy of colonialism in Australian cities. Griffiths and Jacobs are among a number of writers to suggest that a reengagement with local knowledge and associations provides a mechanism for both racial reconciliation and a more socially conscious ecological management. (These ideas are explored further in chapter nine below.)

Photography and postcards provide interesting examples of the multiple meanings expressed in local representations of Aboriginal people. In a study of 291 postcards of Aboriginal people from about

1900 to 1920, Peterson (1985) identified two main frameworks within which images were situated, the romantic and the realistic. Romantic images were characterized by decontextualized backgrounds or by recontextualization in the bush (cf. fig. 8), while realistic ones were contextualized in contemporary living situations with European clothing and artifacts. Peterson argues that the latter, dominant in more than 80 percent of the sample, bolstered white ideas of racial superiority and eased consciences concerned about the Aboriginal decline by showing impoverished shanty dwellers, thus implying the inevitability of poverty and demise.

Much of the photography of Thomas Dick fits into Peterson's romantic framework (see, e.g., fig. 11). Working on the north coast of New South Wales in the early years of the twentieth century, Dick was concerned to document the passing of a culture whose "race was run" (McBryde 1985, 146). However, as McBryde identifies, Dick's work shows several layers of meaning: although people are often depicted as Aboriginal "types," there are many strong portraits of individuals. McBryde argues that Dick had three purposes: to correct misconceptions of Aborigines as the lowest race of people; to record in detail activities and technological processes; and to "convey regret for a lost life-style, nostalgia for an Aboriginal Arcadia" (152). In images such as fig. 11, in which people pose on stone flaking floors or middens, there is also the conflation of contemporary people with the fossil past.

Another public locus of Aboriginal invisibility is in the field of geography—which, like anthropology, has an impeccable imperial disciplinary pedigree (Livingstone 1992). It is all too easy to find early-twentieth-century examples that echo the gist of Herbertson and Herbertson's 1914 *Man and His Work: An Introduction to Human Geography* in reflecting the position of Aboriginal people in the life of the nation: "[T]he native tribes of Australia are fast disappearing altogether" (117). There are any number of imperial geographies in which the diffusion of civilization, embodied by people bearing agriculture, is inevitable; although the framework in which the process is presented varies somewhat from anthropological studies, the overall message is almost identical.

The first issue of the *Australian Geographer* included a section on "Some Aspects of the Aboriginal Problem in Australia," being notes on addresses delivered by Dr. W. L. Warner, Prof. A. R. Radcliffe-Brown, and Rev. F. W. Burton to the fledgling Geographic Society of New South Wales (Warner et al. 1928). Dr. Warner argued that the Aborigi-

Timeless and Placeless   73

Fig. 11. Aborigines making stone implements on Aboriginal field, Port Macquarie. Photograph by Thomas Dick, 1905. Courtesy The Image Library, State Library of New South Wales.

nal had no hope of surviving, "but some effort must be made to make his passing easy," for example by the establishment of a Board of Aboriginal Protection and/or reservations of land, "say in eastern Arnhem Land, a soft, marshy country where there are no minerals and not much grazing. Here the aboriginal could continue many years undisturbed, and it would only be giving to him what actually belongs to him" (67). The ensuing discussion reflects the complex and contradictory ideas in circulation. The rapporteur noted that "the Australian aboriginals present perhaps the most difficult task to try and save, because of their nomadic habits. We cannot catch them ... Hence a nomad people can best be helped in a pastoral, and later in an agricultural environment" (68).

With few exceptions, the absence of Aborigines from academic geography persisted until at least the 1960s (for a more detailed overview, see Howitt and Jackson 1998). For example, Meinig's *On the Margins of the Good Earth* (1962) is a classic of historical geography, de-

74 Embedding

scribing the nineteenth-century empirical testing of the limits to agriculture in South Australia. His emphasis on colonization as process rather than event prefigures discussions that would not occur in mainstream history or anthropology for another twenty years: "The agricultural colonizations of the nineteenth century are of compelling geographical interest. Because, on any close view, colonization is by its very nature not a mere event but a complex process" (1). So it is even more striking that the complexity of the overlaying process is implied to occur on a blank, unpeopled slate.

> By definition it [agricultural colonization] involves the radical replacement of one vegetative cover by another, the radical disturbance of the soil, and the alteration of a host of other less apparent but no less important ecological features. Likewise, by definition, it involves the imposition of a new plan of organization upon the land, the creation of new resources out of nature's materials, the spread of a new volume of population unevenly over the surface, the development of a new network of routeways, and the initiation of a new pulse and pattern of circulation throughout the region. In short, it necessarily results in a radically new geography. (1–3)

Functionalism in Social Anthropology

The rise of functionalist approaches in social anthropology, indeed the definition of social anthropology itself, is inextricably associated with the work of A. R. Radcliffe-Brown (1881–1955), foundation professor in the anthropology departments at Cape Town, Sydney, and Oxford. He arrived at Sydney University in 1926—two years before Griffith Taylor left for Chicago.

When addressing the Geographical Society of New South Wales Radcliffe-Brown had reportedly declared himself pessimistic as to the future of the Aboriginals and had distinguished between the role of anthropology as an objective science and its application by policy makers: "A relation such as that of the Pure Chemist to the Chemical Engineer is analogous to that of the Anthropologist and the Administrator" (Warner et al. 1928, 69). Radcliffe-Brown ([1923] 1958) was concerned to distinguish very clearly between both the methods and the results of ethnology and of social anthropology, as applied to the institutions of uncivilized peoples. He saw ethnology as using the historical method to trace the origins and development of phenomena and, where possible, the causal agents; because there is virtually no historical data, only hypothetical reconstruction is possible, unless it can be supplemented where feasible by archaeology.

Although ahistorical approaches are often attributed to Radcliffe-Brown, it is clear that he was aware of a long period of human history: "From written documents we can only learn the history of civilization in its most advanced stages during the last few centuries, a mere fragment of the whole life of mankind on earth. Archaeologists, turning over the soil, and laying bare the buildings or dwelling sites, and restoring to us the implements, and occasionally the bones, of races and peoples of long ago, enable us to fill in some of the details of the vast prehistoric period" ([1923] 1958, 6). However, he saw historical approaches as providing only knowledge of a succession of events, whereas social anthropology—using inductive methods—allowed the discovery of general laws. The social anthropology that Radcliffe-Brown advocated had immediate social applications: in South Africa, for example, to help find a way in which "two very different races, with very different forms of civilization, may live together in one society" (31). This was all the more urgent because the people who were to be the subject of study "have been extinguished, as the Tasmanians, or are approaching extinction, as the Australians and our own Bushmen" (37).

> It is only when we understand a culture as a functioning system that we can foresee what will be the results of any influence, intentional or unintentional, that we may exert upon it. If, therefore, anthropological science is to give any important help in relation to practical problems of government and education it must abandon speculative attempts to conjecture the unknown past and must devote itself to the functional study of culture. ([1929] 1958, 41).

The shift from an evolutionary anthropology concerned with issues of deep time to anthropology as a science with social application is exemplified in the respective presidential addresses to the anthropology section of the Australasian Association for the Advancement of Science by Pulleine and his successor, Radcliffe-Brown. Pulleine's address (1928) was titled "The Tasmanians and their stone-culture"; Radcliffe-Brown's (1930) was titled "Applied Anthropology."

Pulleine was engaged in the debate over how people got to Tasmania: overland via a land bridge, or over sea by canoe; he used his address to present "evidence on behalf of the voyagers" (1928, 296) (an explanation rendered redundant by later evidence). However, the paper is better known today for its classic expression of fossilization that later archaeologists would see themselves as redeeming: "Here the aborigines must have lived for ages, and if any light could be thrown on their culture by excavation, the Rocky Cape talus offers the best deposit in all Tasmania. However, it is to be feared that excavation would be in vain, as everything points to the conclusion that they were an unchanging people, living in an unchanging environment" (1928, 310). There has been some debate about exactly how much stasis Pulleine wanted to imply. Frankel (1995), for example, argues that Pulleine was not saying that the Papuan voyagers would not have to undergo significant adaptations on arrival in Tasmania, particularly to the cold climate, but that they had entered an unchanging *cultural* environment, where there was to be no stimulation from outside.

Notwithstanding the debates over interpretation, there were profound thematic differences between this paper and Radcliffe-Brown's. The latter (1930) saw anthropology as a science, seeking to discover general laws. These could be applied to the task of improving society, particularly by assisting in the administration of colonized peoples. The urgency of such study in Australia was emphasized because the race was rapidly disappearing.

The evolutionary approach to anthropology as presented by Morgan had come under critique from a number of angles (for example by Lowie, Boas, and the German diffusionist school founded by Ratzel), so it would be wrong to suggest that Radcliffe-Brown was the first to criticize it, or that so-called evolutionary anthropology had not moved on. However, contrasting the two extreme positions may allow us to see our present predicament a bit more clearly. In particular, Stocking (1987) argues that the reaction against evolutionism in the United States and Britain led to a "dehistoricization" of the discipline that was the dominant (although not the only) voice between about 1920 and 1960. One influence on this—expressed also in much of the Australian literature—was the feeling that what was under study were "relic" or "remnant" peoples.

> In sharp contrast to the evolutionary period, when the characteristic posture of anthropologists toward surviving primitive peoples was one of progressivist assimilationism, a romantic preservationism with strong undertones of "Noble Savagery" became the attitudinal norm of sociocultural anthropology ... [T]his romantic tendency to view the societies they study as outside the historical processes of modern civilization has continued strong until the present. (Stocking 1987, 289)

In the Australian context, Stanner identified the influence of Radcliffe-Brown and Malinowski on his own early career:

> I had been taught to turn my back on the speculative reconstruction of the origins and development of primitive institutions, and to have interest only in their living actuality . . . Where a society was breaking down (as with most of the aborigines) we thought it our task to salvage pieces of information and from them try to work out the traditional social forms. Such were my interests. They help to explain why an interest in "living actuality" scarcely extended to the actual life-conditions of the aborigines. (Stanner 1969, 14)

The paradox that Stanner identified in the work of anthropologists of his generation—that in the search for living actuality they somehow overlooked contemporary historical processes—is entangled with another. Their modern empirical studies arose in part in reaction to the turn-of-the-century "pseudo-histories" that had made "Aboriginal man" contemporaneous with "Stone Age man": "They were made to appear a people just across, or still crossing, that momentous border which separates nature from culture, and trailing wisps of an animalian past in their human period" (37). In the last two decades critique of ahistorical approaches has occurred in "the hunter-gatherer revisionist" debate, and in Australia by anthropologists and historians reexamining "the essential" Aborigine (developments examined in more detail in chapter eight). However, the preceding period of "timeless" anthropology meant that when modern Australian archaeology, armed with radiometric dating, emerged and flourished (chapter four), it had more in common with the geological heritage of nineteenth-century evolutionary anthropology than with twentieth-century sociocultural anthropology.

The Timeless Land and Australian Cultural Debate

The role of landscape myth in Australian cultural life and the creation of white Australia's sense of national identity has been discussed at great length; for useful recent approaches see Hamilton 1990; Hills 1991; Gibson 1992; Carter 1987; Schaffer 1988; McGrath 1991; Short 1991; Griffiths 1996, chap. 8. Here I want simply to draw out three related points from this literature; the way that the engagement has been with an essentialized land, the theme of the land as inimical to culture, and the ways in which our appropriations are themselves acts of creation.

The essentializing of the landscape has been negative and positive, complex and contradictory, in a range of different contexts. It focuses mostly on the deserts, the "dead heart" of Australia, and on themes of emptiness and alienation. (A slightly different argument would be needed to examine the ways in which the coast, for example, has been essentialized.) The cultural engagement—in art, literature, film, and even history—has been overwhelmingly undertaken from afar, by city-based people. Further, Heyward (1995) shows that a period as an expatriate is common among the creators of this culture, for example by writers Alan Moorehead and Patrick White and painter Sydney Nolan. The notion of pilgrimage is often involved, either in the way that the artists approach the country for inspiration or in the works themselves. By contrast, we get a more densely contextualized view in studies of how Europeans have engaged the desert—and the rest of Australia's environments, for that matter—in everyday life, for example in the works of historical geographers such as Meinig, Heathcote, Powell, and Seddon.

According to Gibson, "Alienation and the fragility of culture have been the refrains during two hundred years of white Australian images and stories" (1992, 64). The harshest parts of the continent, particularly the deserts, are seen as inimical to culture (just as they are quite literally inimical to agriculture). There are three dimensions to this hostility and alienation that need highlighting here. First, Aborigines are either gone completely from this landscape or absorbed completely into it. They are not in a historically constructed relationship to it. Hamilton notes that Aborigines disappeared from serious artistic treatment between about the mid-nineteenth century and the 1930s, "precisely at the time when artists were 'discovering' white Australian rural life as a subject" (1990, 19). They became a figure of fun in more popular artistic forms, after having been the object of serious artistic treatment in the late eighteenth and early nineteenth centuries. She also comments on the absence of Aborigines from Australian films until the 1940s (28).

Second, the land is hostile to white struggles, both spiritual and physical. Lines identifies and challenges what he refers to as a "mythic geographical determinism" propounded by a number of writers: "The spiritual darkness they detect at the heart of Australian civilisation they claim emanates from the land itself—a continent of primeval cruelty sustained by omnipotent sunlight and a dry interior" (1992, 278). Again, such attitudes are of interest not only because they were around in the middle decades of the century but also because in some contexts they persist into the present. The first chapter of Jill Ker Conway's autobiographical *The Road from Coorain* (1989) is a powerful piece of Australian landscape writing. The western plains of New South Wales are presented, with affection, as a harsh, fickle, intractable environment that dwarfs "human purposes" even while a living must be wrested from it. Aborigines were once physically part of this landscape: "The oldest known humans on the continent left their bones on the western plains. Nomadic peoples hunted over the land as long as forty thousand years ago. They and their progeny left behind the blackened stones of ovens, and the hollowed flat pieces of granite they carried from great distances to grind the native nardoo grain" (6–7).

It is probably no accident that Ker Conway's memoir is a 1980s expatriate memory of a thirties and forties childhood. Ker Conway occupies an ambivalent place in Australian cultural life, similar to other expatriate intellectuals. Returning at regular intervals for speaking engagements and to market their books, they engage in ritual media conflicts with an Australia that is at least somewhat different from the one they left behind. In fact, far from having "no settled native people" (Conway 1989, 7), western New South Wales has a number of Aboriginal communities who are actively negotiating joint ownership and management arrangements over national parks valued for their cultural as well as natural heritage.)

The third dimension of the hostility to or absence of culture in the "blank slate" of the Australian landscape is the sense of possibility that it evokes. The nature of this country is expressed in the opening lines to Moorehead's *Cooper's Creek*:

> Here perhaps, more than anywhere, humanity had had a chance to make a fresh start. The land was absolutely untouched and unknown, and except for the blacks, the most retarded people on earth, there was no sign of any previous civilization whatever: not a scrap of pottery, not a Chinese coin, not even the vestige of a Portuguese fort. Nothing in this strange country seemed to bear the slightest resemblance to the outside world: it was so primitive, so lacking in greenness, so silent, so old. It was not a measurable man-made antiquity, but an appearance of exhaustion and weariness in the land itself. (1963, 1)

So, to follow Gibson's argument, we still construe Australia as empty space, devoid of inhabitants. We lack myths of belonging; we can see the land only in natural terms, not cultural ones. Yet in projecting so many of our myths and desires onto the inland, particularly the desert, we fill it, create it and appropriate it (Carter 1987; Gibson 1992; Hills 1991).

> There is a tendency in Australian culture to embrace Romantic notions of the innocent, prelapsarian self, or of pre-human nature and to offer it as a spiritually more rewarding alternative to civilisation. The difficulty with this position is that it denies the role of society in depicting landscape even though the texts are the products of a highly urbanised culture. (Hills 1991, 15)

The inspirations provided by "pre-human nature," "wilderness," and "desert" have been widely discussed, and there are clear parallels across art, literature, and film. The rhythms cross into contemporary conservation debates without missing a beat; most of us are still more interested in protecting the landscapes "out there" than the fundamentally flawed ones in which we spend our daily lives. Bradshaw judges this attitude—including the way that it appropriates Aboriginal relations to land—as escapist, representing "a refusal to come to terms with the environment that European society has constructed, the built environment" (1986, 66). For Hills, Bradshaw's argument is significant because it shows that "the cultural problems are not so much the result of failing to tame a wild and inhuman environment as much as the result of a failure to come to terms with history and with the European heritage" (1991, 24).

I have attempted to show that the "timeless" land and people are the flip side of the "primaeval and inconceivably ancient" coin. The images are infinitely malleable because they are not historicized; they can be at once suspended within yet removed from both time and space. Many writers have drawn parallels between the shallowness of Euro-Australian attachments to land and the short span of their historical association. Fewer have articulated the point that, when a past was created, it related to land rather than to people: 'Australians did not have a distant past until they created the outback myth. The outback is conveniently remote and ancient and so are its original people' (McGrath 1991, 122). These thoughts echo David Lowenthal's analysis of Australian (and, comparatively, American) attempts to find a usable past when faced with recorded histories of "embarrassing brevity."

> To compensate for the absence of a long recorded history, we are prone to stretch history back into the mists of pre-history. The Australian heritage incorporates not only the few decades since the European discov-

ery but the long reaches of unrecorded time comprised in Aboriginal life and, before that, in the history of nature itself, the animals and plants and the very rocks of the Australian continent. Thus the felt past expands, enabling Australia to equal the antiquity of any nation . . .

The Aboriginal past is largely absent from this Australian primordial heritage, partly because Australians and Aborigines are still antagonistic, partly because earlier epochs yield only paltry Aboriginal remains. A few flints and kitchen middens inspire no awe comparable to Mayan pyramids or mid-Western Indian mounds . . . Only if Aboriginal "hallowed ashes" became conspicuous monuments in the Australian landscape could the Aboriginal past form part of the mythic heritage that nature alone now supplies. (1978, 86, 88)

Even as he wrote in 1978, the middens, flints, and hallowed ashes were in the process of becoming such monuments. The antagonisms were decreasing, at least in theory, as Aboriginal expressions of their relations to land were heard and acknowledged more widely. But what sort of history was it to be, and how far would it transform the mythic heritage provided by these people of nature?

All the Children She Had

The tribal area of the Minjambuta of the Ovens River valley in northeastern Victoria covered approximately 6200 square kilometers, including prized Bogong Moth aestivation sites on Mt. Buffalo. In summer the Minjambuta approached Mt. Hotham and Mt. Buffalo from the west, the latter up the Buffalo River valley. "A sort of highlanders' confederacy" of the tribes whose country included such resource-rich sites set themselves in opposition to the coastal tribes; along with the Minjambuta, the "confederacy" included the Jaimathang of Omeo, the Djilamatang of the Murray River headwaters, the Duduroa of the upper Murray, the Ngarigo of Monaro, the Walgalu of the Bogong Mountains, and the Ngunawal of the central Murrumbidgee River (Flood 1980, 72) (map 4).

The Bogong Moths were a communion food that financed large ceremonial gatherings for men only. However, they were not a resource that could be relied upon, being vulnerable to fluctuating winds such as those that in recent years have deflected them onto the walls of Parliament House in Canberra. So what did the men eat for the rest of the time, and what did the women and children eat year-round? The food most frequently mentioned in the ethnohistorical literature is the Yam-daisy, growing in alpine areas in a slightly different form. Indeed, the Yam-daisy is argued to have underpinned the day-to-day economy of these southern highlands (Bowdler 1981).

After Hume's and Hovell's enthusiastic 1824 descriptions of the rich grasslands in the Ovens Valley, the "pioneers" followed quickly. By the 1850s and 1860s, several new families were heading up the Buffalo River valley. In 1862 my great-great-grandfather Hector and great-great-grandmother Jessie Macaulay squatted on a run at the top of the valley, naming it Winterigah (Robertson 1973, app. 2 and 3). They became seasonal nomads of a different kind when they took cattle up to the high country each summer.

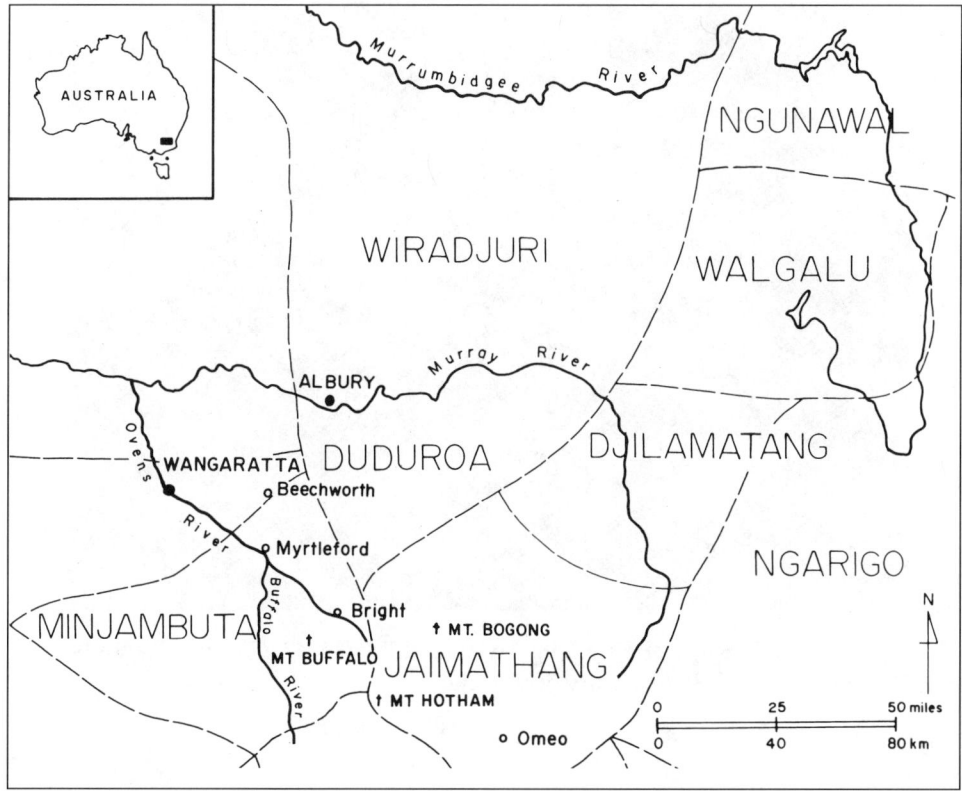

Map 4. The Ovens and Buffalo valleys, Victoria. Tribal boundary locations approximate (after Tindale 1974)

Even in the sections of Australian time that we acknowledge as history, land rights battles have been at the heart of things, and the story of the Buffalo Valley was the colonies writ small. Hector was one of a handful of squatters who held the whole valley, but thousands of disappointed diggers from the Ovens goldfields were by now looking for some pieces of land from which to make a different kind of living.

In 1868 friends William Moore and William McGuffie made their selections on opposite sides of the Buffalo River. Moore chose ten acres at Top Flat, and McGuffie cleared his fourteen acres of virgin bush at Nog Nog Wah (now Nug Nug) and planted potatoes (fig. 12). They helped each other build four-roomed, bark-roofed slab huts, and McGuffie called for his family to join him. Two years later, however, a

84   Embedding

Fig. 12. Buffalo River at Nug Nug Myrtleford, Mar. 1947. Courtesy La Trobe Picture Collection, State Library of Victoria.

great flood struck the valley. Moore lost all of his domestic animals, mostly pigs; McGuffie lost his potato crops and, most significantly, most of his land: "His only plough was recovered later six feet below eroded soil. The erosion resulting from this flood was so disastrous that a portion of that land was to remain uncultivated for the next seventy years" (Robertson 1973, 97).

Moore, a widower with two small children, was looking for a wife, and in 1871 he found one in the person of Janet Gillies, a Scottish lass whose emigration had been funded by her brothers' lucky strike on the Beechworth goldfields. According to their granddaughter—who would later marry the Macaulays' grandson—she called her husband "Mr. Moore" all her life. Notwithstanding this, they managed to produce four more little Moores. Soon, however, another set of invaders followed the farmers into the Buffalo Valley and made life difficult for decades: Rabbits first appeared about 1880, along with wort, blackberries, thistles, sparrows, starlings, rabbits, and foxes (Robertson 1973, 150). The main crops were potatoes, pumpkins, and maize, with hops grown under irrigation from Nug Nug Creek. The area supported other inhabitants as well: "A few Aborigines were still in the valley in 1890, and when ill visited Mrs. Moore for treatment. Their summer hunting ground was at Nug Nug, and one of their ceremonial grounds was the rocky outcrop above the water-hole near the present-day homestead of the Masterton family" (98).

When the alluvial and reef gold started to run out, the gold diggers' dredges started to munch up the river flats, swallow the gold (and any remaining Yam-daisies), sluice the soil downstream, and spit out the stones and gravel. In the absence of any records of the response of the daisy-yammers to the generation before, we could see the opposition to the gold dredges as the first conservation battle fought in the area—one fought by landowners over the preservation of livelihood rather than by distant visitors over the preservation of nature.

> The permanent mutilation of the rich land in the valley of the Ovens amounts to 600 acres of fruitful flats being converted into shingle every year. In all, the 3,000 acres of fecund and hop sustaining land has been destroyed for all time. Productive fields have been hopelessly defertilised. (Harrietville farmer, quoted in Robertson 1973, 80)
>
> We the pioneers of this district have worked under many hardships for the land we love, and the home where we have reared our large families. We have been a peace-loving community, but if you allow our beautiful land to be washed away, we will become tyrants and fight for our land. (Farmers' representative to Minister of Mines, 1911, quoted in Robertson 1973, 84)

Still, the dredges provided employment. Bright suffered a severe economic slump following their demise in the next few years. As with most conservation battles, the greenies probably provided a convenient scapegoat for job losses that were inevitable anyway. The community would have to wait for the next extractive industry—forestry, pine plantations, hydroelectricity, tourism—before economic recovery. These too would ultimately be temporary.

Jessie and Hector Macaulay had nine children, the first in 1856. Seven of their offspring were able to hold a reunion in Melbourne in 1938, at an average age of seventy-six. Within a handful of years—like William and Sarah Head—this branch of a single colonizing family had a fertility rate greater than the surviving Aborigines of the Melbourne area. However, there were two edges to this genocidal sword.

There was disease and violence visited on "blacks"; and there was Aboriginality denied by the policies that stole children who were "not black enough" from their parents.

> 1936 it was. I would have been five . . . We had been playing all together, just a happy community and the air was filled with screams because the police came and mothers tried to hide their children and blacken their children's faces and tried to hide them in caves. We three, Essie, Brenda and me together with our three cousins . . . were put on my old truck and taken to Oodnadatta which was hundreds of miles away and then we got there in the darkness.
>
> My mother had to come with us. She had already lost her eldest daughter . . . because she had . . . polio, and now there was the prospect of losing her three other children, all the children she had. I remember that she came in the truck with us curled up in the foetal position . . .
>
> When I finally met [my mother] through an interpreter she said that because my name had been changed she had heard about the other children but she'd never heard about me. And every sun, every morning as the sun came up the whole family would wail. They did that for 32 years until they saw me again. Who can imagine what a mother went through? (Commonwealth of Australia 1997, 129–30, confidential evidence, South Australia)

Part Three
Unsettling

4

Numbering Deep Time

> There are still living today in Arnhem Land people who know almost no History. They are Aboriginal tribesmen who live in practically the same way as their forefathers and ours did, tens of thousands of years ago. Like them, they have not only no accurate knowledge of past events, but no aeroplanes, motor-cars or picture-shows; not even any books, houses or clothes.
>
> —R. Ward, *Man Makes History*

A story that is becoming increasingly well known to Australians—the archaeological discovery of the antiquity of Aboriginal occupation of the continent—provides an opening to explore the relationships between recent archaeological research and our understandings of Australian history. Besides being interesting in itself, the story is fascinating for the way in which it has undergone a process of mythologization in the public mind. Reflecting on this process requires teasing apart a variety of conversations: between archaeologists, between them and their disciplinary cousins such as historians, and between academic and public cultures.

Epics and Epigraphs

Australian prehistorians of recent decades see themselves as having dispelled the widely held myth that prehistoric Aborigines were an unchanging people in an unchanging land and as having put forward a much more dynamic picture of Australian prehistory, a picture in which people interact with a range of significant environmental changes and themselves contribute to shaping the landscape. The notion of an "unchanging people in an unchanging land" has become modern Australian prehistory's epigraph to its own story; the overturning of that notion is the hook on which we hang many an undergraduate lecture and research grant application.

Historians too have emphasized the importance of "the transformation of 'prehistory' into 'history' " (Griffiths 1996, 94) through the archaeological provision of a chronology prior to 1788. In particular, Griffiths was commenting on the leading role in this process played by John Mulvaney. If my discussion treats Mulvaney as emblematic of his "generation" (a problematic term in itself), it is not to deny the singularity of his contribution nor the significance of other people's; it is simply because, with his recent retirement, Mulvaney's work has been exposed to more sustained historiographic analysis than that of his contemporaries (Bonyhady and Griffiths 1996).

For Attwood, Mulvaney's *Prehistory of Australia*—first published in 1969 and his most well-known work—constitutes a "foundational narrative" of the newly emerging Aboriginal history, a book that challenged conventional Australian history's depiction of European settlement of an empty land (1996, 99). Its signal contributions, Attwood argued, were the assertion that Aborigines founded Australia, the provision of a history for the period prior to 1788, and an attack on the current anthropological emphasis on ahistorical Aborigines. Few would disagree with Attwood's argument that "in attacking the convention of the ahistorical Aborigine, Mulvaney's work also ruptured other important myths that were embedded in the founding narrative of the Australian nation," specifically by "representing Aborigines as a people with a rich and strong culture, who had effectively colonized the continent, both adapting to and changing the environment" (106). (Of course, this attack was not all Mulvaney's work.)

Clearly, the task for the first generation of professional prehistorians in Australia was different than it is for those who will take archaeology into the twenty-first century (and those who are currently teaching them). The social context into which we speak has changed in a number of ways. For one, many of the things Australians now know about Aboriginal people they know through the process of archaeological representation. We therefore need to ask whether archaeology is creating a new set of naturalizations that cohere around the centrality of antiquity (older is better), progress (change is better, complex is better) and material evidence (culture as a package). How do we critique and, where necessary, renounce the myths when we are part of the process of their creation?

To put it another way, why has recent Australian archaeology, for all its considerable achievements, only partially subverted and replaced nineteenth-century views of Aboriginal history? Three reasons may be explored through three intertwining narratives. The first is the narrative of Australian prehistory itself, as constructed mainly by archaeologists; the chronological revolution is built on linear notions of time and teleological conceptions of historical progress that have proven easier to extend than to overturn. The second narrative—the stories that archaeologists and others tell about the process of discovering and (less often) constructing that history—has insufficiently acknowledged parallels with stories of European exploration of the continent. Heroes abound; they push back frontiers, peg out the corners of the room, and fill in blank slates. The third narrative is the increasing exchange between the first two and Australian national or public culture in its many expressions. At one level it is undeniable that the public now has a more dynamic view of Australia's prehistoric past than it had thirty years ago. Murray (1996) explores some of the ways that non-Aboriginal Australians are identifying with prehistoric Australia as part of their own heritage; Lowenthal's "hallowed ashes" are indeed becoming monuments on the national landscape. However, we need to reflect often and carefully on the process by which that is happening: widespread visual and textual metaphors include timelines with numbers, layers of sediment, and ladders of evolution.

The epigraph at the beginning of this chapter is used not primarily to illustrate the profound ethnocentrism of Australian history as taught in primary schools in the 1960s, although it also serves that purpose and thus reminds us of the context into which the archaeological discoveries described in this chapter were received. Rather, it is intended to juxtapose again the two faces of timelessness—an absence of history and an awareness of very long periods of time. In this perspective, history is not just being there, it is *doing* something, preferably something that shows the advance of civilization. This gives us some clues to the range of imagery that people have applied to Australian prehistory and to the coexistence of apparently contradictory images.

Putting Numbers on Australian Prehistory

A number of sources provide detailed overviews of the history of the antiquity question (Bowdler 1993; Horton 1991; Jones 1993; White and O'Connell 1982; Mulvaney 1975; Frankel 1993; Griffiths 1996, chap. 3 and 4); this is not a new story, and I retell only a bare outline here. Deep time—the awareness of the immensity of the past and the quick flash of human history—became accepted among scholars at least between the mid-seventeenth and the early nineteenth centuries (Gould 1987, 3). Among Australian scholars of geological bent, there was quite a vigorous debate over the antiquity of occupation in Australia, couched in numerical terms.

> To sum up, it may be fairly stated:—(1) That up to the present, as at the time Mr. R. B. Smyth wrote, the existence of man's works in any geological deposit above question, has not been shown to exist...
>
> In conclusion, I would distinctly wish it to be understood that I have not lost sight of the bearing the relative antiquity of the Tasmanian aborigines has on this subject. The former geological connection of Australia and Tasmania now appears to be a generally accepted fact. The late Mr. James Bonwick regarded the Tasmanians as an older race than the Australians, although emanating from a common centre, and dispersed over a then existing continent of which our present Australia and Tasmania formed portions. If such be the case, how vast a period of time must have elapsed since then, allowing for the formation of the channel we now know as Bass Straits; and herein lies one of the strongest proofs of man's early existence on the Island Continent of Australia. Notwithstanding this, however, there remains the undoubted fact that we still lack trustworthy geological information of the approximate date of his first advent in Australia. (Etheridge 1890, quoted in Horton 1991, 99)

> I have before said, and desire again to repeat, that the conclusions to which I have been led as to the origin of the Tasmanians and Australians, necessarily demand a vast antiquity on the Australian continent for the former and even a very long period of at least prehistoric time for the latter. (Howitt 1898, quoted in Horton 1991, 109)

> On the whole, then, the evidence is in favour of the Tasmanian aboriginal having arrived in Tasmania between about twenty thousand and one hundred thousand years ago. (Edgeworth David 1923, quoted in Horton 1991, 134)

Gregory's rather disappointed conclusions illustrate clearly the expectation of a long antiquity.

> The tribal distinctions only prove the antiquity of the tribes and not their long residence in Victoria... A general survey of the evidence known to me, therefore, shows that, however ancient the Australian aborigines may be, there is no evidence of the long occupation of Vic-

toria by man. This conclusion is unexpected; it is in opposition to preconceived anthropological opinion; it is opposed, I fully admit, to what are apparently the obvious probabilities of the case. (Gregory 1904, quoted in Horton 1991, 120–21)

Mulvaney (1961, 65) noted that within a year of Pulleine's "unchanging people" comment, "Australian prehistory was based firmly on stratigraphy and a recognition of cultural change" through Hale and Tindale's excavation through twenty feet of stratified deposit at Devon Downs, South Australia (map 5). The presence of layers—differences between them and the order in which they came—was fundamental to this recognition of cultural change. Until the 1950s it provided the only means of dating objects found in deposits, whether stone axes in caves or fossil pollen in lake beds. However, postulating antiquity by correlation with mooted glacial phases inferred from northern hemisphere evidence was of course problematic in the Australian context of an erosional rather than a depositional landscape. Further, tying stratigraphy to any sort of stone tool typology was virtually impossible in Australia, where Neolithic and Paleolithic tools occurred together as well as separately but where a Neolithic culture as conventionally understood never happened.

Hale and Tindale's excavations at Devon Downs formed the basis of a five-stage model of cultural development, based on stone and bone technology and faunal remains (Hale and Tindale 1930). McCarthy (1948) performed a similar task for New South Wales, inferring two cultural phases, the Bondaian and the Eloueran, from his excavations at Lapstone Creek.

The ability to label the layers with specific numbers—and thus to date them not just in comparison with each other but with other layers in distant sites—was first provided by radiocarbon. The first reliable numbers came in 1955 when Edmund Gill (1955a) published radiocarbon dates on charcoal from midden sites in Victoria. The same year he published an overview of archaeological and geological carbon-14 dates for the continent as a whole (Gill 1955b). The oldest firm date presented was 8500 B.P. (years before present) for a fossil hearth in the Keilor Terrace, in the outer suburbs of Melbourne.

It was at this time that the story became one of "pushing back"—like a curtain, or a frontier—the date of human occupation. There were barriers to be broken, just as there had been spatial ones for the residents of Sydney in the early nineteenth century as they struggled to

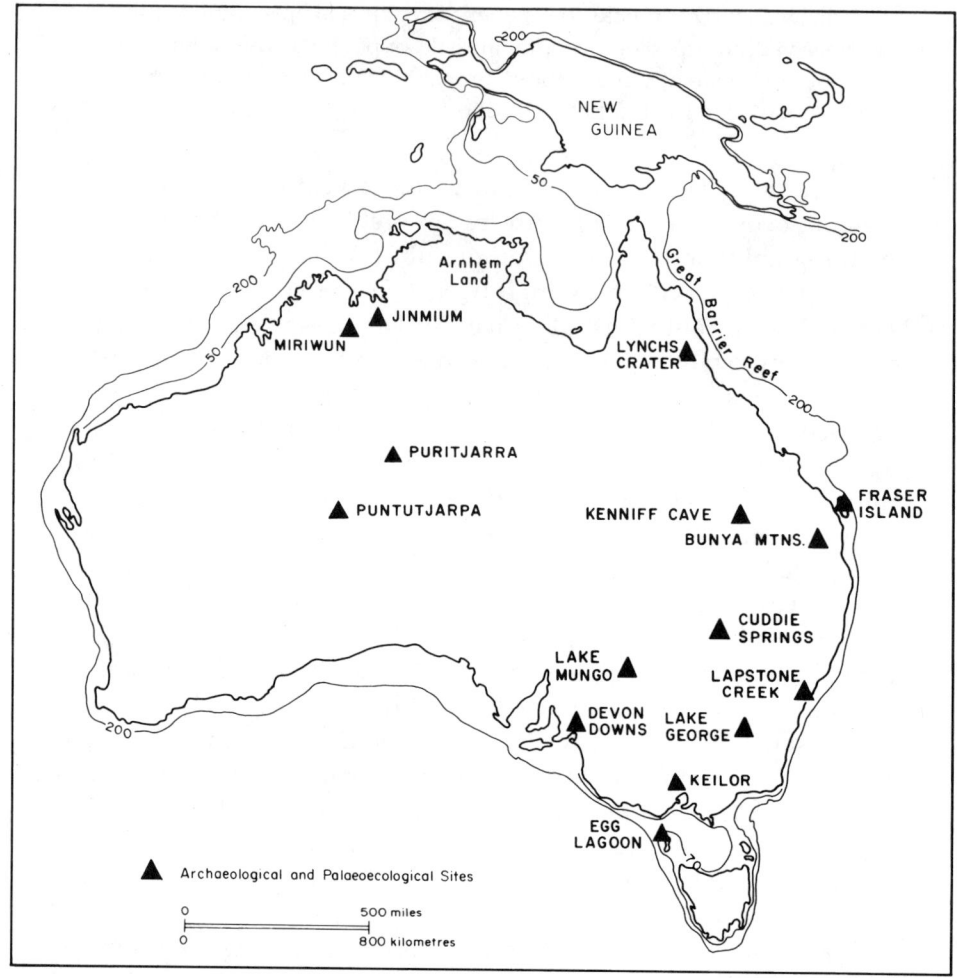

Map 5. Location of archaeological and paleoecological sites mentioned in the text

cross the Blue Mountains and open the door to the western plains. The first temporal barrier was the Pleistocene one, the demonstration that Aborigines had been in Australia during the last Ice Age, at least ten thousand years ago.

The struggle with the Pleistocene barrier provides perhaps the most frequently told story in Australian archaeology. It was first told by Mulvaney and Joyce in their site report on Kenniff Cave and The Tombs.

> Samples collected during the test dig in 1960 were submitted to the National Physical Laboratory, Teddington. On 26 July 1962, the second expedition was at breakfast in Lethbridge Pocket; the temperature was below freezing point. Reg Orr had tuned his transceiver set to the Royal Flying Doctor Base, Charleville, our daily routine for contacting the outside world. In this way, the news of the Pleistocene age of our site was broken, in the form of a telegram from Melbourne. (I suspected a transmission error, with an additional nought; my doubts were dispelled by a second telegram next breakfast-time.) News of this kind is well-timed to get the maximum work from the labour force. (Mulvaney and Joyce 1965, quoted in Horton 1991, 208–9)

Mulvaney and Joyce's recounting of the notification evokes so many themes in a single paragraph that it is to be found in virtually every text on Australian prehistory. An historical discovery has become in itself historic. The story is beloved of university lecturers trying to emphasise the rapid changes that have taken place in our understanding of Australian prehistory over recent decades, its poignancy enhanced by the romance of fieldwork in an isolated setting, the cold morning and the image of intermittent radio contact with the Royal Flying Doctor Base. In her widely used textbook, Flood adds a campfire outside the cave and billy tea to the "characteristically Australian" setting (1983, 95). Moser (1995b) has discussed the importance of fieldwork in the construction of a disciplinary identity for Australian archaeology and has drawn parallels between it and the importance of the "bush" in Australian national mythology.

By the end of the decade the Kenniff Cave dates had been more than doubled by discoveries at Lake Mungo, where an antiquity in excess of thirty thousand years had been established.

> The Mungo site is dated to between 25,000 and 32,000 years old. It is thus the oldest archaeological site so far discovered in Australia . . . The human remains at Mungo, being by far the oldest dated skeletal material from Australia, are of considerable interest . . . [T]he Mungo remains confirm Hiatt's prediction (1969) that cremation has a Pleistocene antiquity in Australia. In these features, it seems possible that a distinctively Australian culture was already established in the region when the Mungo Site was occupied some 25–32,000 years ago. (Bowler et al. 1970, quoted in Horton 1991, 329)

> The new radiocarbon data define the age of the Mungo remains as lying between 24,500 and 26,500BP . . . At 26,000BP this lake con-

tained water to a depth of more than 8m, although like others in the region it has been dry for the last 15,000 years. The "pluvial" environment exploited by its shoreline inhabitants at the time of the Mungo cremation was very different from that today ... The Lake Mungo skeleton suggests that fully sapient populations were present in south Asia earlier than their known presence elsewhere. (Bowler et al. 1972, quoted in Horton 1991, 332–33)

The impacts of the radiocarbon "revolution" differed in the Old and the New Worlds. In the former there were existing chronological frameworks to be overturned, whereas in the latter it was a matter of establishing temporal frameworks for the first time. Renfrew (1973) describes how the two radiocarbon revolutions (the second ascribed to the adjustments required by the publication of tree-ring calibration curves) led to the collapse of diffusionist frameworks for the relationship between European and Middle Eastern traits and societies. The concept of independent invention in different areas of developments such as farming had to be confronted.

On a world scale, the chronological relationships between events on different continents could be established for the first time, although it is important to note that the dating did not of itself overturn the thematic frameworks previously used to conceptualize New World prehistory. Terms such as "developmental stages" and dating the "upper paleolithic" were still used in relation to Australia and the Americas (Renfrew 1973, 62). The length of human occupation in Australia also put the continent into the mainstream of world prehistory in another way, by locating it in the timespan (approximately the last 40,000 years) when modern *Homo sapiens* was thought to have evolved. Throughout the 1970s and 1980s a number of sites provided carbon dates between 30,000 B.P. and 40,000 B.P. but there was increasing suspicion that the apparent 40,000 year was not real but methodological.

Since at least 1975 (and possibly earlier), there has been a parallel debate about the possibility of an anthropogenic signal being present in paleoecological evidence, independent of the archaeological record. These mooted dates have consistently leapfrogged the archaeological ones. For example, discussing his work from Lynchs Crater, in northeast Queensland, Kershaw argued:

It is difficult to imagine that natural fires created by lightning strikes should suddenly become critical after having had little influence on the vegetation for many thousands of years without some kind of concomitant climatic change, but fires made by man would be a different proposition. The earliest dated evidence for the existence of man in Australia is 32,000 yr, BP (Barbetti and Allen 1972), and it is probably reasonable to suppose that he could have been present by 38,000yr BP, the beginning of this transitional period [from vine forest with *Araucaria* to sclerophyll vegetation]. (1975, 184)

Six years later, and more controversially, Singh attributed the expansion of *Eucalyptus* at Lake George (near Canberra) around 130,000 years ago to Aboriginal burning (Singh et al. 1981). More recently, offshore cores from the continental shelf of northeast Queensland provide a record of environmental change interpreted as due to Aboriginal burning about 140,000 years ago (Kershaw et al. 1993). (The ecological dimensions of these arguments are discussed further in chapter five.)

These paleoecological discoveries have never been widely accepted by archaeologists, however, for two main reasons. One is that the mooted dates have always been considerably older than the established archaeological evidence of the time. Secondly, many archaeologists have difficulty with the notion that nonarchaeological data might provide independent evidence of human activity. Further, paleoecologists themselves tend to use anthropogenic causes as a last resort explanation. There is no more agreement over the criteria against which such evidence might be assessed than there is over the evidence itself (Head 1994a).

In 1990 Roberts, Jones, and Smith argued on the basis of thermoluminescence dates for occupation in northern Australia between 50,000 and 60,000 years ago. The debate that followed, and which still continues, relates partly to technical questions over the differences between radiocarbon and luminescence dating and, within the latter, between thermoluminescence (TL) and optically stimulated luminescence (OSL). The relative applicability of TL and OSL is contentious at Jinmium, where TL ages indicate human presence prior to 116,000 years ago (Fullagar et al. 1996).

In such a context, is it inevitable that we get caught up in superlatives: oldest, biggest, best? After Lake Mungo, Australia had the oldest continuous culture in the world (based on comparisons between economic findings in Mungo middens with records of nineteenth-century Aboriginal lifestyles in the Darling Basin); the oldest cremation in the world (26,000 years ago at Mungo); the oldest edge-ground axes in the world (Arnhem Land). More recently we have the oldest evidence of artistic activity, ochre at Malakunanja (Roberts et al. 1990), and the oldest grindstones with evidence of seed processing, at Cuddie Springs (Fullagar and Field 1997). Any such findings are now likely to attract front page coverage in Australia.

In confining my review to the influence of temporal frameworks in Australian prehistory, I run the risk of overemphasizing the aspects that I want to critique. There have been many important debates within the discipline in recent decades; in particular, engagements with the wider society, particularly through Aboriginal demands over heritage, have transformed its practice. Arguably, however, the shadow of the timeline has been cast over all these. The power of this image is illustrated by two developments: the interchange between archaeological research and public culture, and an archaeological debate that focuses not on the time of human arrival on the continent but on the last few thousand years.

Before discussing these developments, however, further reflection in the meaning of those timescales is in order. Harvey's analysis of the totalizing power of the map and the chronometer over Enlightenment space and time respectively provides an insight into the power of the frameworks that are still with us:

> The conception of past and future as linearly connected by the ticking away of the clock allowed all manner of scientific and historical conceptions to flourish ... And even though it took many years for geological and evolutionary time scales to be accepted, there is a sense in which such time scales were already implicit in the very acceptance of the chronometer as the way of telling time. (Harvey 1989, 252)

The paradox of radiometric timescales is that they are being developed and extended at precisely the historical moment when, in other dimensions of life, absolute conceptions of space and time are breaking down under what Harvey calls "time-space compression," "processes that so revolutionize the objective qualities of space and time that we are forced to alter, sometimes in quite radical ways, how we represent the world to ourselves" (240). Revolutions in physics have enabled us to project backwards conventionally linear understandings of time. Central both to the compression and to the representation are the high technology media in which public understandings about prehistory are now developed. In examining the social contexts of production of three 1980s "high-technology mediated images of human unity and diversity," including the holographic portrait of the Taung child on the cover of the November 1985 *National Geographic,* Haraway comments that these images "stimulate a repressed uneasiness about the narrative apparatus of late twentieth-century technologies, in their power to reconstruct 'human' unity" (1989, 193). The creation of a South African icon for a story of human unity at a time when apartheid still prevailed was problematic for many scientists.

Public Perceptions of Time and Change

The uneasiness of which Haraway speaks has parallels with an Australian reaction to the Tandberg cartoon with which I introduced this book (Fig. 2). In the Australian context the powerful leitmotif is not human unity but antiquity.

Current wisdom has it that Australian archaeology is providing a history for two peoples without history: for white Australia, who valued measurable antiquity but had only a measly two-hundred years of their own, and black Australia, the timeless people. The cultural need for such a sense of history is illustrated by the ways in which Australian prehistory is being incorporated into popular and institutional culture; more systematic research is needed on the complexity and ambivalence in the ways this information is used. These examples show how Australian prehistory has gained value in the public currency in recent decades because of its demonstrated antiquity: the older, the better. (That this has also lent support to the claims of Aboriginal people for land rights, at least intellectually if not in practice, is discussed in more detail in later chapters.)

Among Aboriginal people there have been a variety of responses. The concept of ka B.P. (thousands of years before present) is not necessarily the way Aborigines see themselves or their past; the "Dreaming" encompasses both a distant time before the world as we know it existed and another dimension of the present reality (Jones 1991; Hiatt and Jones 1988), and thus is very different than the white preoccupation with linear time. Nevertheless, it is linear time that sets the parameters of the debate—or the auction—in which Aborigines are compelled to participate in order to gain credence in the wider community.

A 1992 newspaper advertisement for Toyota LandCruiser has a large color picture of a lonely vehicle kicking up red dust on a long straight track through an outback plain (fig. 13). The heading reads, "After 20,000 years, Herbie Laughton Antjalka has no doubt Toyota are

Fig. 13. Toyota LandCruiser advertisement, *Weekend Australian*, 9–10 May 1992. Courtesy Saatchi and Saatchi Australia.

here for the long run." The small print at the side says, "The Arrernte people were walking around the Red Centre at least 22,000 years ago. Now, for them, there's only one way to cross Australia's harsh and unforgiving heart. By Toyota LandCruiser." This followed the dating of human occupation at Puritjarra rockshelter as at least 21,950 +/−270 years old (Smith 1987).

In a 1993 advertisement for Aboriginal-operated tourism in the Northern Territory, the Northern Territory Tourist Commission asks, "Where in the world can you find a guide with 60,000 years of local knowledge?" (see e.g. 24, no. 5). In the accompanying booklet available from the Commission, the introductory blurb says that "over 60,000 years Aboriginal people have developed a unique understanding of the interplay between the physical and spiritual world. Now many are working professionally to share their knowledge with visitors" (Northern Territory Tourist Commission 1993). Other Northern Territory Tourist Commission literature invites people to "visit the world's oldest art gallery" in Arnhem Land, and "See the world through 40,000-year-old eyes." In 1996 the Australian Museum, Sydney, advertised its exhibition of the work of two of West Arnhem Land's senior Kunwinjku artists with the line, "See the exhibition that has been thousands of years in the making" (*Sydney Morning Herald*, 10 Feb. 1996). In the wake of the Jinmium research (in which its scientists were involved), the Museum publicized its new Indigenous Australia gallery with the caption "Hear 100,000 years of Australian history in the words of those who lived it."

Further, there is evidence that elements of an archaeological consciousness are being incorporated into official nationalisms. This was expressed by Prime Minister Paul Keating in his November 1993 address to the nation on the Native Title Bill.

> The Bill will necessarily be complex, but this evening I want to cut through the complexity to some of its simple principles. First we need to get the background straight. Over tens of thousands of years Aboriginal people had developed a complex culture built on a profound attachment to the land ... Yet this most remarkable fact about Australia—this oldest continuous civilisation on earth—has until now been denied by Australian law. (Keating 1993)

Although archaeology is not mentioned, the priority accorded by antiquity is implicit in the Preamble to the Native Title Act of 1993: "The people of Australia intend ... to ensure that Aboriginal peoples and Torres Strait Islanders receive the full recognition and status within the Australian nation to which history, their prior rights and interests, and their rich and diverse culture, fully entitle them to aspire" (2). In a multicultural environment, as Beckett (1992) argued, the Aboriginal movement needed a past giving it priority over those who came after.

For some Aboriginal people this was irrelevant—even offensive—information, because they had always been here, since the Dreaming. Williams quotes Burrumurra, a leader at Elcho Island, Northern Territory, demanding to know "where, in what museums, were the rafts in which Aborigines had arrived" from southeast Asia: "He asserted that spirit-beings had bestowed the land on Yolngu in the distant past, and that he spoke for all Aborigines when he affirmed, 'This country was always ours' " (Williams and Mununggurr 1986, 29). For others, archaeological dates became a source of pride and a tool of cultural negotiation in issues such as heritage management. For some, of course, they were both irrelevant *and* useful. (This issue is discussed further in chapter eight.)

The point is that a radiometrically dated prehistory is challenging in particular ways, both for Aboriginal people and for others. As Haraway points out in relation to the narratives of human evolution, the huge spans of time now under discussion make it harder, not easier, to historicize humanity:

> If biblical calendars flattened time by allowing too little depth to see difference, the extreme depths of modern evolutionary calendars make a mockery of mere historical experience; humanity's real time is measured without reference to ordinary experience. It should also be clear that these imagined, timeless theatres of origin could only be produced through the lived social experience and advanced technologies of late industrial peoples. (1989, 195)

Even within the apparently broad range of current possibilities, the timespan of human occupation of Australia is an order of magnitude less than those discussed by Haraway for *Australopithecus* and relatives, but her argument is still relevant. Our efforts to situate people historically are mocked not just on temporal grounds, but spatially and socially as well. How do we discern people's interactions with the landscape and with each other from the fragmentary and intractable evidence that constitutes the archaeological record?

Narratives of Change

Of course, we can hardly expect the public absorption of Australian prehistory to be other than simplistic as long as archaeologists themselves continue to struggle with this question—and even with the very idea of "non-linear systems of social transformations" (Cosgrove 1995, 118). The narrative of "intensification," as originally proposed by Lourandos (1983) and extensively debated during the 1980s, exhibits the range of ways in which archaeologists have sought to explain temporal change.

As the body of research in Australian archaeology expanded in the 1960s and 1970s and radiocarbon dating was increasingly applied to individual sites, it became clear that "something on a continental scale happens in the mid-Holocene" (Beaton 1983, 96). Manifestations of this "something" included apparent increases in numbers of sites and intensity of occupation; the appearance of new types of stone technology; changes in resource use such as more intensive grass seed use in arid areas and processing of toxic cycads; and more regionalized patterns of rock art (for overview see Dodson 1992). Lourandos proposed that these changes were driven by sociocultural rather than by environmental factors.

Lourandos and Ross argued that the contribution of the debate was twofold. First and most widely recognized, it challenged environmentally deterministic views about hunter-gatherer societies. Second, it questioned the dichotomy between hunter-gatherers and agricultural societies: "This new debate demonstrated the *similarities* between these societies, with respect to social organisation, economy, demography and change, in both the long- and short-term" (1994, 54–55). In challenging the static stereotypes of Aboriginal people as aimless nomads, the discussion tended to emphasise these similarities.

This emphasis was by no means confined to Lourandos' work or to people who agreed with all aspects of his theory; rather it was widespread among practitioners of diverse perspectives. It is also characteristic of overviews written for general readerships (Flood 1983; Blainey 1975). Nomadic hunter-gatherers had had such a bad press that it seemed necessary to show how like agriculturalists they were.

Both in the original expression of the intensification theory and in the way that it was taken up by others, the similarities identified between hunter-gatherers and agriculturalists led to an implicit (or, less often, explicit) shift towards a temporal determinism. Aborigines were seen to have been on the way to becoming agriculturalists; "incipient agriculturalists" became a widely used term. For example, "[I]ntensification of social and economic relations would appear to have been increasingly taking place during the Holocene period on the Australian mainland, the process being nipped in the bud by the coming of the Europeans" (Lourandos 1983, 92). Indeed, this interpretation was not confined to Australia; the Australian material was often tied into broader debates about "complex" as opposed to "simple" hunter-gatherers (Price and Brown 1985).

Criticisms came from several directions; two are of note here. First, Horton discussed "the feeling that hunter-gatherers are somehow second class citizens in comparison to farmers and that we must therefore see them as being more like farmers" (Horton 1982, 248). Although he was specifically criticizing Jones' (1969) fire-stick farming model and the reaction against hunter-gatherers being seen as "in harmony with the environment," Horton's sentiment was reflected in a number of other works written during this period. Frankel discussed the way Aboriginal environmental management (for example fish traps and fire use) was "seen by some as still reflecting an attitude that farmers are 'better' than foragers, and that it would be good to establish that Aborigines were, to some degree, farmers, thereby raising them a step on the ladder of social evolution" (1984, 14). (On the other hand the Aborigines' embodiment as environmental damagers also had a political dimension, as will be discussed in chapter five.)

Second, because of the way that the Holocene changes were being portrayed, the Pleistocene came to be characterized as something of a dark age when nothing much happened. The first call for a Pleistocene revisionism came from Horton (1986), who suggested among other things that the megafaunal hunting of the Pleistocene would have required large, well organized, and territorial groups. Allen puts forward a related view: "[A]lthough now we like to scoff at the notion, derived from the 1920s but held current into the 1960s, of Aborigines as an unchanging people in an unchanging land, the 'unchanging people' view is not far removed from the still widely held template of Pleistocene people in Greater Australia—dispersed and mobile groups operating within the constraints of a basic and basically similar technology" (1993, 203).

Attention in the nineties has shifted firmly toward the Pleistocene, with a large conference devoted to the issue (Smith et al. 1993). Once again Tasmania has been the focus of particularly intensive study (Kiernan et al. 1983; Cosgrove 1989; Cosgrove et al. 1990; Murray

1992a) (see also map 6). On the one hand southwest Tasmania in the Pleistocene fulfilled most of the archaeological criteria that Lourandos had laid down for late Holocene intensification. On the other, the apparent "extinction" of regional economic systems at the end of the Pleistocene emphasized what Murray called the "spurious progressivism of intensification" (1992a, 740). In the most detailed exposition of this argument, Cosgrove (1995) demonstrates the parallels between linear views of Australian prehistory and nineteenth-century social evolutionism. Such views are problematic because they obscure regional variability (among other reasons).

Whatever the revolutions of the 1960s, Murray argues, not much has happened since, because ethnography is trying us to the timeless Aborigine:

> On the face of it, the idea of the essential Aborigine should have died in the 1980s under the twin assault of Aboriginal history . . . and prehistoric archaeology . . . Historians of Aboriginal Australia have played their part in this process of historicising (or denaturalising) Aboriginality, as have anthropologists, but there has been very little movement from the prehistoric archaeologists. Unlike Aboriginal history or anthropology there has been no revolution of opinion in prehistoric archaeology since the early 1960s. Indeed, much Australian ethnoarchaeology implicitly assumes that the present is a reliable guide to the past, and there is a growing fear that writing the history of Aboriginal people recorded at contact, and of Aboriginal groups surviving over the last 200 years, may well be at odds with the goal of making sense of 60,000 years of Aboriginal history. (Murray 1992b, 18–19)

Moreover, there is an explicitly political context to this debate. Allen, Murray, and Cosgrove were putting forward arguments about discontinuities at the same time as they were in dispute with the Tasmanian Aboriginal Land Council over rights to cultural heritage (Murray and Allen 1995). It is not yet clear to what extent their archaeological views are a cause of their dispute.

In a converse view to Murray's, Pardoe argues that it is the conceptual separation of prehistoric and contemporary Aboriginal people that has ossified the past.

> One of the greatest crimes committed by anthropologists and archaeologists has been the reification and "ossification" of Aboriginal culture into a changeless, timeless, glorious past that has denied

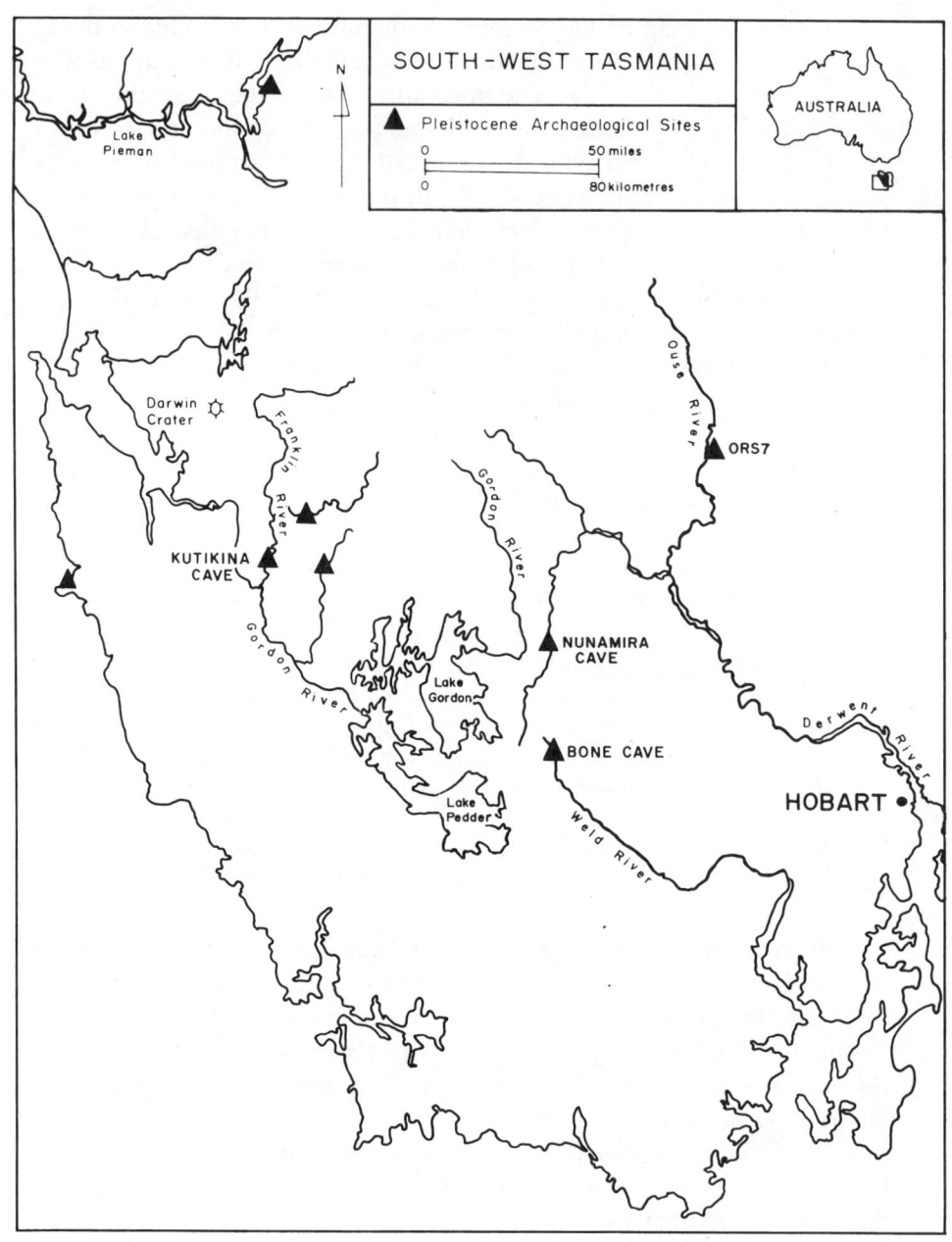

Map 6. Southwest Tasmania (simplified after Cosgrove 1995)

contemporary Aborigines a valid present or a cultural future. Negotiating archaeology and the Aboriginal past is assisting both Aborigines and archaeologists to define a cultural future that may be able to include us both and accommodate a range of points of view. In that sense, archaeology is at the cusp of culture change and it is an exciting place to be. (Pardoe 1992, 139; see also Pardoe 1993)

Discussion by Murray, Pardoe, and others (e.g. White 1994; Frankel 1995) of the relationship between prehistoric archaeology and ethnography is a contemporary manifestation of a much older problem. Earlier solutions were to fossilize the Australian Aborigines between the Lower Palaeolithic and the Aurignacian Age, as Sollas did; or to suspend them as relict peoples, outside history, as early sociocultural anthropology did. Radiometric dating provided a certain sort of rescue, but it was one grounded in the geological heritage of Australian archaeology, as identified by Horton (1991). The scholars who had the earliest perceptions of change and of the long term had such perceptions in stratigraphic terms, and their images are still with us—layers, ladders, and timelines—as are their developmental views of evolution. Despite their many differences, there are clear parallels between the stratigraphy of Sollas' chapter structure, Taylor's Zones and Strata theory, and the notion of intensification. All of these theories also include a certain sort of stranding, of contemporary Aboriginal people as separate from their past.

It is not time that we need to come to terms with but change, continuity, and the nature of historical process. The archaeological record creates a particular set of problems in this regard, hinging on the relationships between material culture and the rest of society. For example, does the invention or adoption of a new type of stone tool connote a profound change or a trivial one? What sorts of social transformations might have no material manifestation at all? The spatial and temporal patchiness of the available evidence provides problems for any attempt at fine-grained analysis. These are dialogues that archaeologists must have primarily with each other (and are thus beyond the scope of this book), but they spill over into the wider debates.

In a society where two hundred years of occupation is seen as an achievement, a cause for celebration, it is not surprising that people have seized on such measurable antiquity as provided by the radiometric timescale. Practitioners for whom tens of thousands of years have become such second nature that they refer to them as "ka" are prone to forget the revolutionary qualities of the numbering of deep time. Writing in 1971, Mulvaney emphasized the radical aspects of these discoveries: they put Australian (pre) history on the world stage and stimulated a rethinking of the concepts of primitivism. They also helped to create a public consciousness amenable to cultural heritage management and legislative protection of sites. In giving due recognition to those whose efforts so profoundly altered our understanding of Australian history, and in summarizing their work for an enthusiastic lay audience, scholars need to be vigilant about what we replace terra nullius with. We need to continually articulate the colonial heritage of archaeology and the ambiguities this brings with it, both within the discipline and in conversation with the broader society. Otherwise, we risk becoming part of a newly naturalized landscape, as reified as the nineteenth-century stereotypes that we pride ourselves on having overturned.

A History for the People Without History

On New Year's Day 1989, with my father (the great-great-grandson of William and Sarah Head), my mother (great-granddaughter both of Hector and Jessie Macaulay and of William and Janet Moore), my nine-week-old son (the youngest offspring of them all), and several hundred others, I went to a picnic to commemorate the 150th anniversary of the arrival of William and Sarah. Her death certificate described Sarah as "relict" of her husband. The babies were seventh-generation Australians, and the valley of Gardiner's Creek had long since been appropriated for a freeway. The only thing that has saved some of the redgums from concrete is that the area farmed by William and Sarah for John Gardiner is now the site of one of Melbourne's wealthiest boys' schools.

In the shade, there was talk of the updated family tree, of the statistical view it allowed us of the total descendants of William and Sarah (2454) and their generational distribution across the fertile branches (seven of the original fourteen children had offspring). There was sombre reflection on the prematurely foreshortened stumps on the trunk: Henry 1842–1844, Elizabeth 1852–1854, Mary Ann 1854–1855, Emma 1858–1859, Hannah Maria 1859–1884 (in childbirth), and John Thomas 1861–1863.

5

Landscape

PURE AND PRIMORDIAL?

> *The new ideas about natural disturbance, succession and the relatively ephemeral composition of contemporary ecosystems deprive environmentalists of the scientific grounds to construct hard and fast distinctions between human and natural disturbance on the landscape and thus between natural and disturbed landscapes and geographies.*
>
> —P. Demeritt, "Ecology, Objectivity and Critique in Writings on Nature and Human Societies"

Revisionist approaches to ideas of stability and balance in ecosystems have been influential in recent decades. The evidence of long-term environmental change derived from the broad range of methods that come under the umbrella of paleoecology was also significant. Of importance for our study, both ecological theory and paleoecology have unsettled our understandings of the Australian landscape as "pristine."

This work raises challenges to both dimensions of pristineness, primordiality and purity. The notion of pristine in relation to physical landscapes is often associated with primordiality and ancientness. Australia is labeled as New World in terms of culture, but its nature has always been synonymous with antiquity. Although there is much geological truth in this image, it is only part of the story; as might be expected on a continent with considerable bio- and geodiversity, there are many ecological examples of newness and change. The idea of purity has much in common with blank slates and emptiness—"a land untouched by human hands or footsteps." While rock art galleries, fish traps, shell middens, and artefact scatters all attest in very visible ways to the prehistoric human presence in Australia, there are also signatures of human activity other than explicitly archaeological ones. In recent decades the landscape itself has been made to speak of its peopling, albeit somewhat ambiguously.

In some ways it is artificial to separate the archaeological and paleoecological histories. They have depended on many of the same technical advances, for example dating techniques, and there has been a long-term dialogue between the practitioners. Many of the debates are by necessity interdisciplinary; the question of megafaunal extinctions is a case in point. It is then all the more useful to explore differences in the ways in which the measurement of temporal change has affected explanatory frameworks in archaeology and in physical geography—more specifically, frameworks that center on human agency—as compared with broader ecological ones. Why, for example, has paleoecology found it easier than archaeology to unshackle itself from linear progressivist explanations for change? To try to answer such questions I explore the cultural use of environmental narratives in two contexts: within the broader science of ecology and within conservation debates.

A number of factors impinge on our ability to work out what was going on in the past, let alone to discern any anthropogenic signature. The record is being derived from proxy and patchy data, with a heavy bias towards the well-watered parts of the continent where evidence is better preserved. These layers were found not in rockshelters but in sediments drilled from the bottom of crater lakes, still wet; salt lakes, now dry; swamps, a bit of both; and coral reefs, to name a few. Sometimes the whole landscape was recognized as a fossil, witness to a time not so long ago when the desert center was fuller of water or when dunes were active in northern Tasmania. Moreover, as with archaeological sites, the heritage of post-European land use differentially affects what is discovered and what is preserved. Explorer Hamilton Hume—for whom the main highway between Sydney and Melbourne is named—could not have guessed when he left his pastoral run at Lake George on the way to Port Phillip that part of the explanation for the abundant grazing country he was to encounter lay locked in the dry lake sediments supporting his sheep. For here was one capsule of deep time suggesting that the main reason open eucalypt forests were so abundant in Australia was that Aborigines had regularly burned them. At Lynchs Crater in northeast Queensland, the pollen-rich sediments are now quarried for peat to be used in potting mix. They have by now scraped off at least the top twenty thousand years.

Patchy as the paleoecological record is, it forces a reassessment of the wilderness in two main ways. First, whatever we think of now as wilderness has not always been there in its present form. Second, people have been transforming it in a variety of still poorly understood ways for much longer than originally anticipated. These have been well established academic understandings for several decades now; in what contexts have they escaped into the broader social consciousness?

We Live in Atypical Times

One of the first things to become clear as researchers explored deep time and space was that we live in atypical times. At the timescale of many millions of years, the Australian continent left its Gondwanan family of Antarctica, India, Africa, and South America and drifted north. The story of the next few million years is essentially one of increasing aridity, with the more tropical flora becoming stranded as relicts like the brown coal deposits of the La Trobe Valley or as living fossils like the rainforests of eastern Australia. As the children of Gondwana inched away from the motherland, the great Southern Ocean opened up and its strong circumpolar circulation became established. This cut off the transfer of warm water currents from equator to poles, which previously had contributed to relatively uniform conditions. The new rearrangement of land and sea meant a consequent rearrangement of moisture-bearing air—or, more crucially for Australia, dry air. For as the continent moved north it was overtaken by the subtropical high pressure belt going in the same direction but slightly faster. By a million or so years ago that dry subsiding air had taken up its position as the primary desert-maker of Australia, assisted by the sheer distance of most of the land from the oceans (Bowler 1982; White 1986) (map 7).

Within the last million or two million years there was a shift from gradual change to more rapid oscillations between cold and warm, wet and dry. The pattern of the past one hundred thousand years was probably foreshadowed four or five times in the last half million years (Bowler 1982). Survivors, whether plant or animal, would have to be able to respond rapidly to these changes. Within this so-called Quaternary period, the warm, wet times have been short interludes—usually lasting only ten thousand years or so—between the longer, harsher ice ages. We have been in a warm period now for ten thousand years. (For the most recent summaries of these changes see Dodson 1992; AGSO 1996) (map 8).

In many other parts of the world (including the island of New

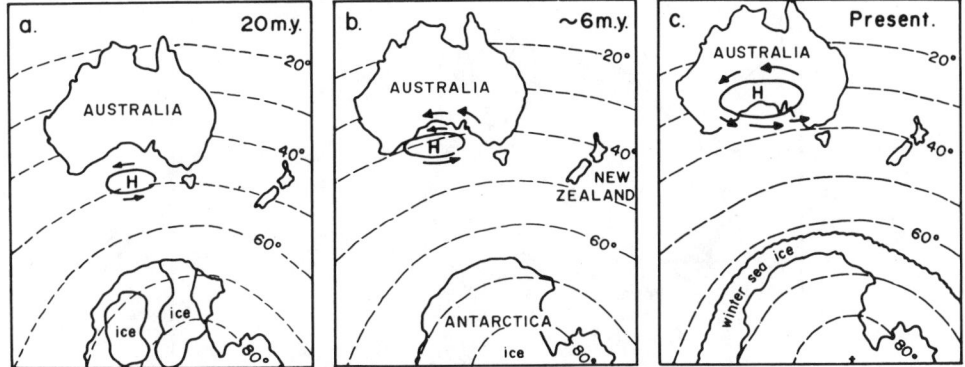

Map 7. Latitudinal position of Australia relative to path of high pressure cells, 20 million years ago to present (simplified after Bowler 1982)

Guinea, to which Australia remains joined under a risen sea), this present interglacial spawned agriculture in all its variations—but not in Australia. Here, vegetation communities such as rainforest and forest, which had been beaten into submission by the cold dry conditions, recovered and flourished in the mid-Holocene. Conversely, communities more adapted to the harsh conditions, many of whose country was flooded by the rising seas, have shrunk in area—shrubland, grassland steppes, alpine herbfields (Dodson et al. 1992). In turn, new ecosystems were created as the sea level stabilized in the last six thousand years (fig. 14). On some new landforms, such as the coastal plains of Arnhem Land, rainforest patches were actively expanding in the last few thousand years (Russell-Smith and Dunlop 1987; Russell-Smith 1991).

It is thus important to understand the climatic, geomorphological, and biotic processes under discussion as operating at a range of overlapping temporal and spatial scales. Although notions of ancient land, eroded land, or isolated land are all true at the timescale of millions of years, there have been very significant changes in the last one hundred thousand years or so, especially at the scale that makes a difference to people. For example, rainforest decline is a long-term process that commenced in the Tertiary, long before people got here; debate continues over the extent to which it was accelerated by humans. Similarly, fire was an important environmental variable before people arrived. Without attempting a comprehensive review, I identify here (with examples) some of the factors that people now hold to be significant.

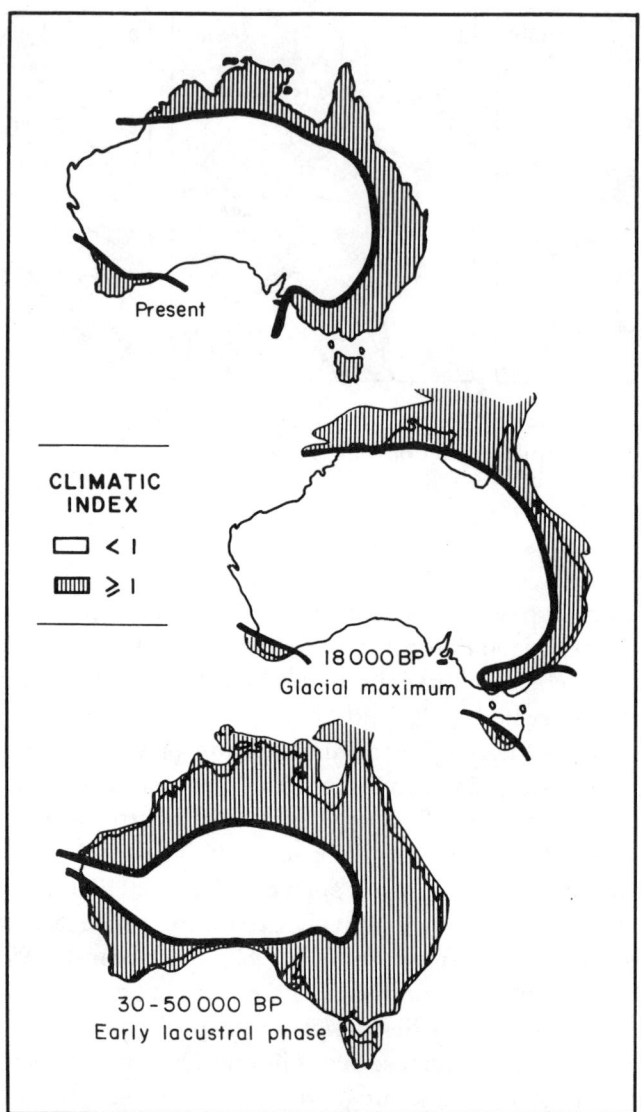

Map 8. Climatic index showing the contraction of the arid zone during the period 30–50,000 B.P. and the subsequent expansion at the last glacial maximum; the higher the index the greater the effective precipitation (simplified after Bowler 1982)

Landscape: Pure and Primordial? 115

Fig. 14. An example of a new ecosystem within the last few thousand years: the estuarine flats of Cambridge Gulf, Western Australia. At the last glacial maximum this area would have been several hundred kilometers from the coast. Photograph by author.

As in most fields where researchers struggle to discern patterns and trends, the exceptional example has problematic status. For example Nanson et al. (1996) have argued that Lake Eyre, which drains a large part of the continent through the Coopers Creek system, was full of water at the last glacial maximum, about twenty thousand years ago. Most other lines of evidence suggest this to have been a time of aridity. Are the dates perhaps wrong? Is there another explanation? Was the hole dug in the wrong place? Rigorous approaches to the issues of spatial and temporal scale are crucial given the range of processes operating, from the catastrophic tsunami to the long-term evaporation regime.

Very different records can be derived from different parts of Australia at the same time; even though global processes might be operating, responses can be very different in, for example, northern (tropical) and southern (Southern Ocean–influenced) Australia. A striking example of this comes from Hidden Lake, on Fraser Island (Longmore 1996a), where the indications are of a mid-Holocene dry period—in contrast to many other parts of Australia, which are thought to have been substantially wetter than present between about six and eight thousand years ago. Additionally, there are differences between east and west: the lake full phase of about 60,000–25,000 years ago, such as that which produced high lake levels at Lake Mungo, is not apparent in the evidence from southwest Western Australia, where lakes remained saline (Bowler 1996).

There now appear to have been spatial and temporal lags between significant climatic parameters such as temperature and moisture; for example, there was an arid period right at the end of the last glacial (15,000–11,500 years ago), when temperature seems to have risen much faster than precipitation, producing arid, dune-forming conditions in parts of southeastern Australia (Crowley and Kershaw 1994; D'Costa 1996a). Moreover, there are often considerable lags between changes in climatic parameters and the biotic response. Vegetation in particular may be insensitive to aspects of climate change. Pearson argues that animals responded more sensitively than vegetation in the arid zone, but they also might be responding to nonclimatic factors (Pearson 1996).

Pollen evidence provides some long-term insights into old debates about Clementsian versus Gleasonian succession (discussed in more detail later in this chapter). A plant community is shown to be an opportunistic association of species at a particular place and time rather than an entity that all migrates together. This has been best demonstrated in the United States, but Australian examples include the lack of present analogues for vegetation communities from the not so distant past, for example the steppe grasslands that covered much of southeastern Australia during glacial periods. Conversely, while present communities have long heritages, they have only existed in their present form recently. Forest expansions are extremely brief episodes in an era typified by more open vegetation formations (see for example diagrams in Heusser and van der Geer 1994). Further, the composition of forests differs greatly between the last interglacial (125,000 years ago) and the present one (the last ten thousand years). At Egg Lagoon, King Island, pollen in the sediments provides abundant evidence of the cool temperate rainforest elements *Phyllocladus* and *Nothofagus* at the last interglacial (D'Costa 1996b). This could have been because it was cooler and wetter in the last interglacial period than the present one, or because of the influence of fire: "[A] sustained rise in charcoal particles recorded from the middle glacial period suggests a more frequent fire regime which may have prevented a return or expansion of some taxa in the Holocene pollen record."

This has obvious parallels with the situation from Lynchs Crater and Lake George, where similar changes in forest composition are attributed to Aboriginal burning. Clearly the question of disentangling anthropogenic and climatic influences is now not as simple as just separating the glacial and interglacial cycles; there can be a range of climatic cycles operating.

With the better development of long records and the means to establish a chronology, there are now suggestions from a number of different lines of evidence that the glacial cycles are increasing in intensity and that the arid periods are becoming more arid. For example, in a core record spanning 400ka from perched dune lakes on Fraser Island, Queensland, Longmore (1996b) has argued that a range of indicators (pollen, carbonised particles, chemistry, and chironomid head capsules) show an overall increase in aridity: "The increasing aridity may be a continental feature of Australia and perhaps more extensively as part of a lower frequency cycle such as the 413ka theoretical variation in orbital eccentricity." The suggestion also comes from aeolian and fluvial records in central Australia (Nanson et al. 1996), where each fluvial cycle seems to have become less fluvially effective. Dust records from marine cores in the Tasman sea show an increase in size of dust peaks towards the present (Hesse 1996).

There are now some elements of a history of ENSO (El Niño/Southern Oscillation), a phenomenon that influences cross-Pacific climates at the approximately decadal scale. McGlone et al. (1992) suggested that ENSO did not really become active until the last five thousand and particularly the last three thousand years. This was based mainly on increased variability within pollen records and increases in charcoal within the latter period. There is some independent support for this scenario from isotopic and trace element records from corals on the Great Barrier Reef; Gagan et al. (1996) argued that their mid-Holocene episode showed "weaker ENSOs and more dependable but moderate rainfall, rather than the warmer conditions and higher rainfall that are generally associated with the mid-Holocene 'climatic optimum.'"

In summary, the dynamism that is expressed is seen to be on a long-term downward trend. Biologically, Australia is characterised as an ark, supporting isolated remnants; geomorphologically, it is old and worn down, with no active source of sedimentary renewal such as glacial or volcanic activity; climatically, it is arid and unpredictable, at scales that still defy rhythmic characterization (for example El Niño). The images of these changes collide with one face of timelessness, that of frozen stability. However, the idea of exhaustion—of a continent gradually being drained of its lifeblood—is in another way quite consistent with the face of great antiquity. At the same time, vegetation communities are in fact constantly reinventing themselves to cope with changing conditions.

A Landscape Transformed by Human Action

At the broadest landscape level, the issue of Aboriginal impacts on the environment is a debate that focuses on the role of fire (particularly its influence on vegetation) and the question of the extinction of the megafauna. The ubiquity of Aboriginal fire and its role as an agent of transformation has been commented on since Europeans first arrived in Australia (for historical reviews see Merrilees 1968; Hallam 1975). Moreover, the early colonists also seemed conscious of land management through fire use as a symbol of ownership and possession (see also Jones 1980). As late as three decades after the arrival of the First Fleet, convict painter Joseph Lycett was depicting the Awakabal people of the Newcastle/Lake Macquarie area using fire to hunt kangaroos (fig. 15). Hoorn argues that this is one of a series of paintings showing "a people in possession and full enjoyment of their land" and prepared to defend it against invaders (1993, 78). In this respect it differs from other colonial art of the time which, although it initially showed Aboriginal control and use of the land, had removed them to the margins by about 1815. Most works after 1815 "show Aboriginal people as an exotic element located at the edges of compositions. In these works Aboriginal people have been transformed from a people in control of their land and culture to powerless and passive observers of European culture in Australia" (80).

Like many other aspects of Aboriginal land use, the use of fire was widely assumed to have disappeared very quickly in most parts of the country, as its disappearance from colonial art exemplifies. The rediscovery of fire as an issue in the 1960s and 1970s brought to light a range

Fig. 15. Joseph Lycett, "Aborigines using fire to hunt kangaroos," ca. 1817. Courtesy National Library of Australia.

of unrecognized evidence about situations that were argued to be very traditional. Postcontact changes in fire use have not been comprehensively researched, but available case studies suggest that in situations of social and ecological flux, the most resilient aspect of fire use continues to be the ethic of "cleaning up the country" (Head 1994b). That is, even when Aboriginal people have no practical rights to burn under current tenure situations, the thing that disturbs them most is not the loss of economic opportunities as such but rather the inability to impress a human signature on the landscape (fig. 16). This is not just a question of physical transformation.

Although the question of fire gradually became less visible in the national historical record, Australian evidence came to be utilized in international debates. For Carl Sauer, the Tasmanians provided one of his examples of hunters and collectors using fire: "Even the obtuse Tasmanians helped their food gathering by burning over the ground. A little-explored subject is the use of fire to change the character of the vegetation deliberately ... In not a few cases, fire became a deliberate instrument of land management by deliberate deformation of the plant association" (1952, 11–12). Around the same time Tindale discussed the

Fig. 16. Unburnt country, Ningbingi, Western Australia. Photograph by author.

Australian evidence, arguing that perhaps "man has had such a profound effect on the distributions of forest and grassland that true primaeval forest may be far less common in Australia than is generally realised, as indeed it is relatively rare in all lands where man has intruded for lengthy periods of time" (1959, 43). He also extended his argument to the megafauna:

> [T]he lands and forests were in an age-old state of balance with a Pleistocene fauna of large and small marsupials and giant flightless birds. It can be assessed that in process of developing a state of equilibrium with this Australian flora and fauna the newcomers must very quickly have eliminated many of the more vulnerable animals of the Pleistocene period and by firestick and digging stick must materially have altered the flora. (42)

The evidence that Tindale presented in support of his argument about fire was ethnographic, including his own research. As for Sauer, there is a moral dimension to Tindale's argument, but in contrast to Sauer he is quick to use the term "destructive," describing for example the "waste" of half-cooked lizards on newly burned ground (42). Although he acknowledges that many birds "appeared from nowhere to feast" on the lizards, the possibility that that might have been part of the Aboriginal rationale for firing seems not to have occurred to him.

A second aspect of Tindale's argument worth noting—because it affects the way that the debate about the prehistoric period developed—is his emphasis on Aboriginal burning as an agent of grassland creation: "[I]ndeed much of the grassland of Australia could have been brought into being as a result of his exploitation" (1959, 42). Although he referred also to altered forest dynamics, the grassland question allowed him to tie his argument more closely to international debates. For example, he compared upland savannahs on the Bunya Mountains with the grassland "balds" of the Great Smoky Mountains of Tennessee, suggesting that both were anthropogenic. The concept of humanly created savannah grasslands in Australia became a bit of a red herring, although it took several decades of pollen and charcoal analyses before Clark could argue that "it is likely that Aborigines neither created nor maintained vast areas of grassland, although their burning may have been responsible for the continuation of patches of grassland or woodland within larger forested regions" (1983, 35). Most debate over human influences now focuses on the rainforest-savannah boundary question or on more subtle compositional questions within vegetation communities.

The debate about human impact on megafauna has a more explicit history in Australia, again through the influence of geologists. In 1979, Horton noted that the debate over the relative influences of climate and people in the extinction process had been going on for over a hundred years. He cites Richard Owen (1879) as the earliest exponent of the overkill hypothesis, with dingoes as possible accessories to the crime. Horton, by contrast—who has been a strong proponent of a climatic explanation for extinctions—argues that "it is difficult to see why the climatic change model for megafaunal extinction was ever questioned" (1979, 14). He situates this in the context of nineteenth-century thought, stressing the differences between Australia and Britain. Four reasons are emphasized (22); First, the climate model "was an evolutionary theory proposed in a society to which Darwin was anathema." In this respect Owen, one of Darwin's most vocal opponents, typifies for Horton a number of scientists who underwent changes of heart. In 1843 he had canvassed the possibility of a climatic cause for megafaunal extinctions (Horton 1979, 15–16), and there is ambivalence in his writings on the subject in the following decades. Second, the climate model "was a theory which provided no convincing biological mechanism for the link between climatic change and extinction"; proposals such as water balance, reproductive impacts, and competitive exclusion were not made until the 1970s. Third, "it was a theory which provided no hope of success to scientists searching for concrete evidence of ancient man in Australia." Because Australia lacked clear-cut glacial deposits, the paleontological approach was seen to be the most profitable: "Europe has megafauna known to be old; Australia has megafauna; find man in association with Diprotodon et al. and the problem is solved" (Horton 1979, 18–19). Finding humans and megafauna in association, and proving that association meant agency, continue to be problematic issues in Australian archaeology (see e.g. Furby 1995); Horton argued that it was a search that should never have begun. Fourth, "the Australian environment emphasized continuity, in contrast to the European experience where glaciers, mammoths and Neanderthal Man were figures from a radically different landscape." Moreover, in Australia "Owen's 'australoid wielders of club and throwing sticks' " (Horton 1979, 18) could still be observed in action, albeit without the megafauna.

Although Horton's work clearly shows a long heritage for the climate vs. human impact debates, they are often considered to have been reignited in Australia by two papers published in the late 1960s, which also bear examination in some detail. Rhys Jones' paper (1969) on fire-stick farming is one of the most cited papers in Australian prehistory, and the term itself has entered the Australian lexicon. Jones challenged the idea of the prehistoric environment as "natural," drawing on ethnographic evidence that showed bushfires to have been "systematically and universally lit" (225) across the continent. He also drew on the arguments of botanists such as Jackson, who had argued that the coastal sedgeland of western Tasmania was a fire-maintained artefact. Jones' early arguments on fire were also developed in two other papers (Jones 1968, 1973), where he suggested that the arrival of fire-bearing humans contributed to megafaunal extinctions.

Merrilees (1968) hypothesized that Aboriginal fires leading to habitat modification (as opposed to overpredation by humans) was the likely reason for megafaunal extinctions. He argued against the then-widely-accepted concept of a "Great Australian Arid Period" between about 6000 and 4000 years ago. Many of the details have changed in the intervening decades; the mid-Holocene is now more often seen as a period of climatic optimum, and most extinctions probably predate this in any case. Most advocates of human over climatic influences prefer overpredation as an explanation over fire, which may have actually assisted grazing herbivores. Nevertheless, the controversy is as deeply etched today as it was in 1968.

Another notable thing about Merrilees' paper—which was given originally as a presidential address to the Royal Society of Western Australia—is that he tied his argument explicitly into contemporary conservation debates. While leaving open the question of whether Aboriginal people were aware of their ecological impact (and ignored it) or were unaware to start with, he spoke out for conservation: "European man may have dispossessed Aboriginal man of a biological system already much impoverished, and he appears bent on continuing this impoverishment for narrow 'economic' ends" (1968, 20).

If these debates have always been infused with the moral dilemmas of the colonial society, so have they affected global perspectives on hunter-gatherer land management skills and techniques. From the more detailed regional fire studies (e.g. Hallam 1975; Haynes 1985, 1991) to Jones' incorporation of Aboriginal perceptions and taxonomies into his work (1985, 1990, 1991), the notion of Aboriginal hunter-gatherers as active and knowledgeable land managers became established (e.g. Williams and Hunn 1982). The Tasmanians were apparently not as obtuse as Sauer thought.

The Pollen and Charcoal Evidence

Merrilees had flagged the issue of charcoal deposits and pollen evidence, and such evidence came to prominence in the next decade or two.

The pollen and charcoal records from Lake George and Lynchs Crater were the first to be interpreted as evidence that Aboriginal burning had dramatically changed the Australian vegetation, in each case because a signature separate to the climatic cycles of cold glacial periods interspersed by warmer interglacials could be discerned. At Lake George, Gurdip Singh argued that prior to the last interglacial (ca. 130,000 years ago) *Casuarina*-dominated forests, in association with some fire-sensitive rainforest taxa, had dominated interglacial vegetation for at least half a million years. *Eucalyptus*-dominated forests began to expand from 130,000 B.P. onwards, at the same time as charcoal abundances increased considerably. Singh attributed the expansion of the relatively fire-tolerant *Eucalyptus* to Aboriginal burning (Singh et al. 1981; Singh and Geissler 1985). For Lynchs Crater, Kershaw suggested a similar transition from fire-sensitive (in this ecological context, drier araucarian rainforest) to more fire-tolerant (*Casuarina* and *Eucalyptus*-dominated) vegetation, but about 38,000 years ago (Kershaw 1976, 1985, 1986), which he argued could only be accomplished with the assistance of fire.

These two bodies of work were subjected to a range of criticisms over the next few years. Lake George was particularly problematic because the suggestion of people in Australia at 130,000 B.P. predated the then available archaeological evidence by eighty to ninety thousand years (Horton 1982; Clark 1983). This was not the only argument; a range of other technical points were advanced. In later developments, offshore pollen evidence from northeast Queensland has been interpreted as evidence of Aboriginal burning about 140ka (Kershaw et al. 1993), and the site of Cuddie Springs, New South Wales, shows coexistence of humans and megafauna for at least several thousand years (Dodson et al. 1993).

As suggested above, resolution of the argument has rarely been separated from what people wanted to believe about Aborigines and about natural man. As part of his 1982 paper, Horton suggested that people were interpreting the evidence over fire-stick farming according to what they wanted to believe about Aborigines. He argued that in order for land rights to be widely recognized by non-Aboriginal society, Aboriginal ways of "using" the land had to appear as much like farming and as little like hunting and gathering as possible (see also Frankel 1984). My point here is not to resolve the debates but rather to examine the terms on which they have been constructed.

Micro-scale Anthropogenic Landscape Changes

Situated between the paleoecological debates over long-term human impacts and the ecological discussions of the nature of change in ecosystems is a relatively small body of writing with relevance to both. Both anthropologists and biologists have recognized anthropogenic influences on plant distribution and adaptations, at much smaller scales than that of continental biogeography. These influences relate to the effects both of the gathering of tuberous plants and of fruit tree utilization:

> Next to the firestick the woman's digging stick was probably the most effective instrument in altering the patterns of plant growth, removing a considerable portion of the more edible forms of vegetable life. (Tindale 1959, 43)

> If murnong [*Microseris scapigera*, Yam-daisy] was gathered in such large quantities, does it follow that this resource would have become exhausted over the years? An examination of gathering practice and its effect on the plant indicates that its abundance and productivity would probably have been increased by Aboriginal activity. (Gott 1983, 11)

> The effect of this digging on the soil would be to aerate it, loosen it for seed germination and root penetration, and to incorporate litter into the soil. Plants would be propagated by scattering and breaking-up of the underground parts. (Gott 1982)

A number of workers have documented examples of plant management strategies and practices that must have considerably affected vegetation communities at the local scale. These include planting, particularly of yams (Hynes and Chase 1982: 40), the description of areas as "all the same gardeny" (Jones 1975, 24; Lucas and Russell-Smith 1993), and protection and ownership of fruit and shade trees (Hynes and Chase 1982, 40–41).

Although such evidence is regularly discussed within anthropology and archaeology, particularly in relation to the origins of agriculture, it has made minimal impact on the theory or practice of ecological biogeography. There are very few ecologists who analyze Australian vegetation with the assumption that there is an inbuilt, if residual, legacy from thousands of years of Aboriginal interaction. It is much more common for researchers to construct sampling and analytical procedures with a default assumption of no human signature.

The Ecological Conversation

Again, treating geological and ecological narratives separately here is somewhat artificial, because they interact in many ways—perhaps especially through climatic processes, which themselves combine relatively predictable temporal cycles with others of apparently stochastic variability. However, the ecological conversation of recent decades shows some distinctive features that help us to understand the way that Australian biotic changes have been interpreted. In turn, the ecological conversation is seen by Barbour (1995) as part of the broader scientific story of holism yielding to reductionism. It was played out, he argues, in the debate between the ideas of vegetation ecologists Frederic Clements and Henry Gleason and in the revolutionary shift by 1960 to majority acceptance of the latter's view.

> Clements argued that groups of species living together in a given habitat were highly organized into natural, integrated units called communities. Gleason countered that such communities were only constructs of human thought and that in reality the distribution and behavior of every species were unbounded by imagined holistic bonds to all the surrounding species. (Barbour 1995, 234)

Drawing on the oral histories of American plant ecologists who experienced the so-called revolution, Barbour argues that the revolution was the product not of an accumulated weight of new evidence but of cultural factors conducive to the idea of fragmentation. His survey

> identifies widespread American cultural themes of fragmention [sic] of norms, the celebration of the individual, and rebellion against convention. Impermanence and uncertainty replaced predictability, and individual competition displaced group cooperation. At the same time there was an expression of anxiety at the loss of past certitude and stable social organization. (250)

In fact, Barbour argues, few ecologists were in complete agreement with the details of Clementsian orthodoxy. Particular successional paths, or the number of climaxes in a single climatic region, were always issues for debate. In Australia at least the notion of disturbance as something outside the system under study and relatively infrequent had long been problematic. Fire was too frequent, too necessary to the lifecycles of many species, and thus too integral to most vegetation communities to be considered abnormal. The question in Australia was not whether a single climatic region could support one or several possible climax communities but whether such a state is reached often enough for it to be conceptually useful. Even the concept of neat and tidy zonations gives way in the Australian context to the mosaic, where spatially variable patterns of soil and fire interact with temporally variable climatic processes. More often than not, Australian biogeography lecturers use northern hemisphere textbooks only to show the inappropriateness of such frameworks for interpreting the Australian evidence. (This is not to say that there is agreement among such lecturers about the extent to which those fires have been caused by people.)

For Barbour, the central question is whether Clementsian plant communities are objective reality. Are plant species "organized into natural, recognizable units of vegetation called formations, associations, or communities, and [are] these entities . . . steady-state balance points in nature that exhibit stability and constancy over time" (1995, 236)? He recognizes (244) that paleobotanical evidence on past species movements had some influence on the changing views of ecologists, but sees this—like other types of evidence—as minor in influence by comparison with cultural factors.

I am not in a position to argue against Barbour's American "cultural ecology" of the 1950s, nor would I wish to downplay the importance of broader cultural influences on scientific thought. It is interesting, however, to note how comprehensively the actual evidence from paleoecology (mainly pollen) has demolished essentialist ideas of vegetation communities in the decades since 1960. This is less the case in Australia than in North America, where three factors have facilitated mapping of species movements in considerable spatial and temporal detail (see e.g. Delcourt and Delcourt 1987): first, the wide distribution of sites with conducive preservation conditions; second, the detailed work generated by the larger research population; and third, the fact that northern hemisphere forest formations are represented palynologically by a useful number of distinctive tree genera. By contrast, Australian forests and woodlands are dominated by *Eucalyptus*, whose more than seven hundred species span enormous ecological variability yet are not distinguishable palynologically.

Significant progress is now being made in providing the rigorous and quantitative comparisons between the pollen production and distribution of modern vegetation and its antecedents that will enable paleoecology to move beyond its traditional work of descriptive natural history and towards more precise hypothesis testing. Davis (1994) argues that this brings paleoecology closer to the spatial and temporal scales used by ecologists and predicts that the two will soon be part of the same mainstream enterprise.

The meeting of ecological and paleoecological timescales in terms of the Australian fire debate has so far produced divergent interpretations (Head 1996). For example, in contrast to Kershaw's pollen evidence, biogeographer David Bowman argues that Aborigines have always had a conservative impact on fire-sensitive components of the northern Australian vegetation. His evidence shows that fire-sensitive types such as *Callitris* were being maintained at European contact by Aboriginal burning and have declined since the demise of traditional fire regimes (Bowman and Panton 1993; for a review of this debate, see Bowman in press). Resolution of apparent discrepancies between different sources of evidence depends partly on more rigorous consideration of spatial and temporal variability in both social and ecological processes.

Utilizing the Narratives

A number of characteristics make these research findings fluid and malleable sources of myth and inspiration in contemporary environmental debate. One factor is that because we lack agreement even on the criteria for separating anthropogenic and natural processes (Head 1994a), a range of views are still tenable among researchers. Continental-scale explanations seem to be easily confounded by local variability, yet the small scale changes exemplified above are paleoecologically invisible with the scientific tools currently available. Added to these issues of spatial scale are ones of time. Ethnographically observed burning patterns, for example, operate over at most several years, whereas the core records usually encompass much more than this within a single sample. The cycles of aridity that need to be teased apart may operate over hundreds of thousands of years.

Moreover, the often implicit confusions between intention and outcome, between emic rationales for burning and their variable impacts on vegetation, infuse much of the debate with a moralism that is too rarely made explicit. The moralism, however, is ambiguous, with different groups finding empowerment in different parts of these stories.

Government agencies responsible for environmental management deal ambiguously with the scientific legacy of uncertainty about the human role. For example, in an overview published by the Biodiversity Unit of the Commonwealth Department of the Environment, Sport and Territories, the following summary is presented:

> Since the late Tertiary, Australia has been subject to the dramatic climatic fluctuations associated with global glacial-interglacial cycles. Fire, which has always been a component of the Australian sclerophyll vegetation environment, also became more prevalent . . . Rainforest and other fire sensitive communities became largely restricted to isolated wetter east coast areas and to fire-free stream valleys and rocky outcrops . . . These trends accelerated because of the burning activities of Aboriginal inhabitants after their arrival at least 50 000 years ago . . . It is also probable that Aboriginal people were involved in the massive phase of megafaunal extinction within the late Pleistocene. (Commonwealth of Australia 1994, 13–14)

The report emphasizes living fossils—such as kauri pines, cycads, and crocodiles—and Australia is characterized as a biological ark.

For many physical geographers and others researching past environmental change, there has been a pragmatic move to situate themselves for funding. Concern over projected future environmental changes has affected the rationale for funding research that looks back at the long term. The best example of this is research that can be cast in a framework that relates to projected greenhouse-induced change, for example by arguing that past interglacial changes provide an analogue for greenhouse-induced warning (see papers in Bishop 1988). What is too rarely addressed in the literature is how the scientific research articulates with the political and cultural realities; exactly how is this information going to help solve environmental problems?

Two important because widely known and quoted popular histories provide interesting examples here, both for their similarities and for their differences. William Lines' *Taming the Great South Land: A History of the Conquest of Nature in Australia* (1992) and Tim Flannery's *The Future Eaters: An Ecological History of the Australasian Lands and People* (1994) are both oppositional in the sense that they challenge the heroic and triumphalist versions of Australian history, replacing them with tragic sagas of ecological catastrophe. (David Suzuki's foreword to Lines's book says that it "puts the lie to the myth of the heroic history of modern Australia and reveals it as the sordid tragedy it really was." [xviii]), Both Lines and Flannery start their epics with the prehuman saga of the continent. This is not surprising for Flannery—who as an ecologist wants to make explicit the point that we need to understand the reality of the long-term ecology in order to manage the present—but it is notable that even historians such as Lines now routinely, if with varying degrees of skill, acknowledge the importance of factors such as isolation, evolution, aridity, fire, climatic change, variability, and extinction.

How do these authors deal with Aboriginal interactions and impacts? For Lines, Aborigines provide examples of people who have learned to live appropriately in the Australian environment: "All over Australia Aborigines regularly and ingeniously manipulated their environment... Nevertheless, 60 000 years of Aboriginal occupation only lightly touched the environment and did not fundamentally alter the natural fecundity of the land, nor greatly disturb relationships within the community of plants and animals living in Australia." By contrast, Flannery creates parallels between the first Aboriginal and first European settlers—each group wrongly perceives a land of plenty and proceeds to overdo things destructively. The Aborigines, however, hewn into shape by the harsh land, learn to live with things and become conservationists; white Australians need to be on a much steeper learning curve than them and should take note quickly of what science is telling us about ecological reality. Although Lines is more concerned than Flannery with the ways in which landscape is socially constructed, neither of these writers is self-critical of the (contrasting) Aboriginal images they use. (For more detailed critiques of the two works see Powell 1994; Head 1995.)

Conservationist depictions have focused on the ark part of the story, but without Noah. For example, in their coffee table journey through Australian wilderness, Moult and Meier (1983) call their chapter on Kakadu "The Untamed North." Rock paintings are presented among natural wonders, and there are no people in the pictures: "The pink devastation of fire... is reflected in the harmless setting of a sunset in this wilderness in the untamed north" (caption 130–31). In fact, most fires in northern Australia are lit by people, and most are required by the vegetation. These authors are not alone in the apparent contradictions of their interpretations and in airbrushing Aboriginal people out of the picture; Rhys Jones (1985) has noted that the original plan of management of Kakadu National Park talks of this "untamed wilderness" in the same breath as its (then) twenty-five thousand years of human occupation.

To be sure, there are signs of a transition in the conservation movement in the last decade, stimulated by a range of factors. However, because this is such a recent shift—and one seen much more among the leadership than at the grass roots level—it is worth dwelling on the foreword to Moult and Meier's book, by Bob Brown (now a Green senator in Federal Parliament):

> Two hundred years ago Australia, the world's smallest continent was all wilderness. Its people lived in wilderness. They were part of it. Australia was the same as it had been ten thousand years ago when, before the advent of agriculture and industry, the whole world was wilderness and everyone lived in wilderness.
>
> Now only a few small patches of this vast Australia remain wild and unchanged . . .
>
> We are, after all, part of nature ourselves. We come from wilderness. Except for a few dozen generations at most, all of our numberless ancestors were children, women and men in wilderness. Wherever our origins, whether we be black or white, we were designed for life in the wild. (Moult and Meier 1983, 12–13)

In contrast, prodevelopment forces have been quick to co-opt and utilize the notion of environmental change. In the 1980s the Queensland Forestry Department, for example, argued that it is acceptable to log rainforests because—on the evidence of Kershaw's pollen cores—they have recovered from dramatic climatic change before (Head 1990). The Public Lands Council of Victoria (PLCV)—a coalition comprising the Victorian Association of Forest Industries, the Victorian Farmers' Federation, the Chamber of Mines, the Association of Four Wheel Drive Clubs, the Field and Game Association, the Mountain Cattlemen's Association of Victoria, and the Australian Deer Association)—in 1991 opposed the Victorian government's wilderness legislation (National Parks [Wilderness] Act of 1992) using the idea that "wilderness" is a culturally relative concept. They argued that the preservation of "natural" areas made little sense if Aborigines had been changing the Australian landscape for at least sixty thousand years (Mercer 1993).

Alliances and conflicts between green groups, Aboriginal groups, and prodevelopment groups such as mining representatives are shifting and fluid. As with their view of prehistory, Aboriginal people have expressed a variety of responses to their depiction as part of nature or as the original conservationists (these dilemmas are discussed further in chapter eight). Many white environmentalists would still be shocked to realize that some Aboriginal people see national parks as just the next wave of colonization, after squatters and missionaries (Birckhead et al. 1992). There have been a number of examples of cooperation between Aboriginal and conservationist groups, but there are also ongoing conflicts. Marcia Langton challenges the perceptions of members of The Wilderness Society: " 'Wilderness' as a partial construct of nature is husbanded in the institution of the national park in contemporary Australia. The national park is an institution of power which governs and commodifies 'nature' and thereby culturally constructs an imagined 'wilderness' " (Langton 1995–96, 16). On all sides, there is a need for more understanding of the ways in which Aboriginal people themselves have culturally constructed the land.

No Dams

When, in the summer of 1982–83, thousands of Australians fought to save the Franklin and Gordon Rivers in southwest Tasmania from being dammed for a hydroelectric scheme, we did so under two banners. "THINK GLOBALLY, ACT LOCALLY. SOUTHWEST TASMANIA—WORLD HERITAGE," proclaimed one. It was jostled by another: "YOU HAVE ENTERED ABORIGINAL LAND" (fig. 17).

The media campaign spearheading what was widely regarded as the most significant conservation victory in Australian history brought the rivers and the rainforest to the national television news. Politically, the battle was to persuade the federal government to intervene in a land management issue—historically in Australia the province of state governments. So it is not surprising that the tensions implicit in the simultaneous proclamation of world heritage and indigenous ownership did not immediately surface.

The claim of Aboriginal land could be made because archaeologists had discovered the time before the wilderness. "The most southerly human beings on Earth" called this place home when there were glaciers in the back yard and rainforests cowered in riverine refugia (Kiernan et al. 1983). The rainforests of southwest Tasmania had long been thought to be unoccupied by Aborigines at the time of European arrival, but Kiernan and his colleagues showed that people had occupied Fraser (now called Kutikina) Cave through the height of the last glacial maximum, apparently abandoning it when the rainforests began to return about fourteen thousand years ago.

December 1982. While the pageant is played out on the river, the annual conference of the Australian Archaeological Association meets in Hobart. Ros Langford presents a paper on behalf of the Tasmanian Aboriginal community entitled "Our heritage—your playground," in

Fig. 17. The Franklin blockade, 1983. Photograph by R. Fullagar.

which a claim to control over cultural heritage is staked: "We are the custodians. You can either be our guests or our enemies."

> Kutikina cave in the Southwest is a good example of manipulation by archaeologists for their own ends. Archaeologists have held press conferences over the "finding" of this cave (among others) in support of the conservationists' effort to prevent the flooding of the area. The manipulation of that issue by scientists has been made without recognition of the rights of Aborigines to preserve their own culture. Delegates would be aware that the Aboriginal Movement is in conflict with the Tasmanian Wilderness Society on this issue and there has been a stony silence by them on our claims whilst much mileage has been made by them on the importance of the sites (Langford 1983, 5–6). Michael Mansell, one of the first four Aboriginal people known to enter Fraser Cave in 14,500 years, expresses the power of the site to his people: "You can sense the spirit here. This is the sort of stuff we

need to get the dreaming back. We have been cut off from the past . . . If anything in Tasmania is a sacred site, this is it." (*The Age* [Melbourne] 23 Dec. 1982.

Yet the role of archaeology in this reclaimed sacredness is profoundly paradoxical, as Allen identifies:

[T]his reunion of past and present has added a profound dimension to the nature of Tasmanian Aboriginal identity. The TAC [Tasmanian Aboriginal Centre] has now identified Kutikina as a sacred site . . . It is true to say that some Aborigines have been upset by the 0.5m sq test pit in the deposits, which, because the deposits were wet-sieved, is now backfilled with river pebbles. Were it not for this excavation, however, the reunion of Kutikina and Aborigines would not yet have occurred. (1983, 9)

February 1983. Launchloads of greenies are still coming down the river in police custody. Rafting traffic increases as people flock to see the wilderness before it goes under. Laden with equipment, archaeologists chug upstream under horsepower that can glide up the rapids like spawning salmon. "Technogreenies," "mind merchants," comes the abuse, some good-natured, some not, from the launches.

A photo of the archaeologists would probably show them sweaty and frustrated, entangled in the detail of the forest in their systematically slow search. The intertwining mass of horizontal scrub, *Anodopetalum biglandulosum,* knits itself around their limbs. They can't see each other at fifty metres, let alone easily see the evidence of people who lived there thousands of years ago. They too are making history—the history of a distinctive regional economic system involved in long-distance trade. Later analysts consider that this factor was pivotal in saving the wilderness from the flood—the evidence of "hearth and home in a populated landscape" (Griffiths 1991, 96).

Tuesday, 8 February 1983. While large areas of southeastern Australia suffer their worst drought on record, Melbourne is enveloped in a dustcloud blowing parched soil in from the west. Its worst recorded dust storm and highest February temperature produced a dust cloud spanning five hundred kilometers from Mildura to Melbourne, extending one hundred fifty kilometers from east to west and varying between 350 meters and 3500 meters in height (*The Age* (Melbourne), 9 Feb. 1983).

It is a profound but disturbing meeting between country and city, and one of those moments when everyone remembers what they were doing. The city-dwellers have heard about overstocking, land degradation, erosion—all the result of activities carried out on their behalf—but it has never been thrown in their faces like this. There is a sense of community embarrassment when we hear some days later that most of it has landed in New Zealand. Jokes about land rights claims, reclamation, mining. How many layers of southeastern Australia have headed east since the arrival of Europeans?

Sitting under the summer track of the subtropical high pressure systems, the southeast is used to the hot dry northerlies sucked down by the rear ends of the anticyclones. When traffic banks up in the Tasman Sea, they can sit there for several days, to be relieved only by the cool southwesterlies fed in by the arrival of the next system.

Wednesday, 16 February 1983: Ash Wednesday. The northerlies blow ahead of a cold front bringing gale force southwesterlies. There are numerous ignition sources, some of them deliberate. Dozens of people die in bushfires in Victoria and South Australia. The number will rise into the seventies in the next few days. The prime minister, Mr. Fraser, interrupts his election campaign to visit affected areas.

As usual, comparisons are made between southeastern Australia and the two other most fire-prone areas in the world, California and the French Riviera. They share long hot summers, low humidity, abundant and flammable vegetation, and strong winds under certain weather conditions. Less often do people ask whether they also once shared hunter-gatherers who kept fuel levels low by burning regularly.

Saturday, March 5 1983. Australians elect a consensus prime minister, Bob Hawke, whose victory speech begins: "The dam will not be built."

> On Friday 1 July 1983 the High Court of Australia ruled that the Commonwealth Government had the power to stop the Gordon-below-Franklin dam. Within days the bulldozers and trucks were being dragged back to Strahan on barges that had, only months earlier, forced their way through our fragile lines of protest. (Wilderness Society 1983, 120).

Bob Brown reflected on the role of the people in this process:

> Three thousand people, spurred by the knowledge of ancient beauty falling beneath the bulldozers, put their energies into the national election. Thousands more gave their money and encouragement. Maybe

most of all, an untold rank of voters broke their allegiance of a lifetime to vote for an ideal and against the pro-bulldozer government.

Meanwhile, the few kept a presence for the many who cared, in the forest by the rivers. The world will never be free of troubles but one day we will sit on a verandah, rocking in the afternoon sun, and hark back to these times and break out in a little smile. (Brown 1983)

Heavy rain had begun to fall on March 21. With a new government, the breaking of the drought, and a legal victory, there may have been a sense around the country that things really were changing. Against such a villainous opponent as the Hydro-Electric Commission and the arrayed forces of an erstwhile police state, it was easy for archaeologists, greenies, and Aborigines to appear united and to share success. The dam proposal was a dinosaur whose time had been and gone. But what of the terra nullius view of wilderness? And of national land rights, which was also part of the policy that Hawke's Australian Labor Party had brought to the election?

6

Peopling the Wilderness

The landscape is redolent with memories of other human beings.

—H. Morphy, "Landscape and the reproduction of the Ancestral past"

Having examined issues surrounding the physical peopling and transformation of Australia, I move here to the way that land is brought conceptually into the human domain among Aboriginal people. Virtually every Australian would now be aware that there is something "special" about Aboriginal relations to land, but few could articulate what it is. In the attempt to express that "special relationship," two themes stand out. The first is that Aboriginal land is a densely humanized set of spaces, as full and busy in their own way as is the center of Sydney. There is rich irony in appropriating Aboriginal images as inspiration for the ways in which Euro-Australians use "empty," "desert," or "wilderness" lands. The second theme is the increasing role of Aboriginal voices over the last few decades in the dialogues discussed here. A focus on land provides a good example of this because it allows us to examine issues (such as native title) that are at the heart of contemporary public debate. (The other main example which could be used, and which deserves a full treatment, is the way that these issues are expressed in Aboriginal art, literature, and drama.) The difficulties involved in translating cultural concepts involved in land ownership help to explain why Aboriginal voices have been differentially heard in Australian society.

In seeking here to argue that Aboriginal voices are themselves part of the process of transforming our understanding, I am only too aware that I have chosen to present those voices mainly through the intermediary ones of anthropologists. The main reasons for this are the complex problems of linguistic and cultural translation and the context-dependent nature of revealed information; the authors cited have gone to great pains to explain both information and context. (For an anthology of Aboriginal voices see for example Rose 1996c.) I have also chosen to concentrate on a particular group and region—the Yolngu of northeast Arnhem Land—both because of their influential anthropological heritage and because of their unique role in Australian legal history, highlighting the differences between Aboriginal and white Australian relations to land.

In reviewing the main features of Yolngu relations to land, I concentrate on concepts of space and place, with the acknowledgment that the temporal dimension can only artificially be separated from these. In choosing the Yolngu example there is a risk of reifying a particular set of relations to land as archetypal; this is explicitly not my intention. However, such reification is arguably one outcome of the Yolngu influence on the Australian legal system's dealings with wider Aboriginal land relations. We need then also to ask, in what ways do the various pieces of legislation dealing with land rights and Aboriginal heritage require Aboriginal people to articulate their relations to land according to externally imposed frameworks?

One of the best ways for nonanthropologists to understand something of complex Aboriginal relations to land is through descriptions of how Aboriginal people respond not to their own land but to country in other parts of Australia that they visit for the first time. As the first English tried to make sense of the land around Sydney Harbour within their own cultural referents, so Frank Gurrmanamana of Arnhem Land interpreted the landscape around Canberra, as related by archaeologist Rhys Jones.

> There was a calm acceptance of the various gadgets and machines of our technological world, which one might at first have assumed to be potentially rather intimidating or confusing to a man who hunts with a spear and spins string on the side of his thigh ... The questions that Gurrmanamana wanted to ask most were what was the moiety of the land on which we were staying and did the block next door have an opposite moiety, the boundary being marked by the fence line? ... Here was a land empty of religious affiliation; there were no wells, no names of the totemic ancestors, no immutable links between land, people and the rest of the natural and supernatural worlds. Here was just a vast *tabula rasa*, cauterised of meaning ... This land and its people therefore were analogous to the state of all the world once in some time before the Dreaming, before the great totemic Ancestral Beings strode across it, naming the places and giving it meaning. Viewed

from this perspective, the Canberra of the geometric streets, and the paddocks of the six-wire fences were places not of domesticated order, but rather a wilderness of primordial chaos. (Jones 1985, 205–7).

Aboriginal Relations to Land: The Yolngu Example

My discussion draws mainly on Morphy 1995; Williams 1986; and Williams and Munungurr 1989. Because of the importance of precision in some of the distinctions being drawn, I have chosen to quote their work in detail. The Yolngu live in an area of about eight thousand five hundred square kilometers in northeastern Arnhem Land, including the adjacent islands (map 9).

> For Yolngu as well as other Aborigines, the charter that establishes and validates all categories of rights in land is first of all religious. It is also historic. Thus, for example, Yolngu may use past residence as an argument for continued residence or even stronger rights of tenure, along with or even instead of a founding myth. The charter is also economic. But for Yolngu, "religious," "historic," and "economic" are not mutually exclusive categories; they are complementary and reinforcing modes of perceiving and using land and natural resources. (Williams 1986, 18)

I have noted often in this book the close relation between Euro-Australian relations to land (even in urban contexts) and the pastoral/agricultural settings from which they derive. It is appropriate then to quote, as Williams does, Stanner's observation that "[t]he fact that hunters and foragers developed a zoomorphic and phytomorphic imagery was as appropriate to men in the Australian environment as that nomadic shepherds developed a pastoral imagery in the environment of early Judea and Israel" (Stanner 1965, 237).

According to Williams, "for the Yolngu, travels of spirit-beings through the land, the sea, and along rivers established the framework of people's relations to their land" (1986, 37). Particularly important in this process was their bestowal of names. Like other types of knowledge, names are ranked, and access to that knowledge is regulated; thus words, especially names, are a form of property.

> [T]here are some names of sites that Yolngu regard as the exclusive property of one group, and asserting that a particular name is the

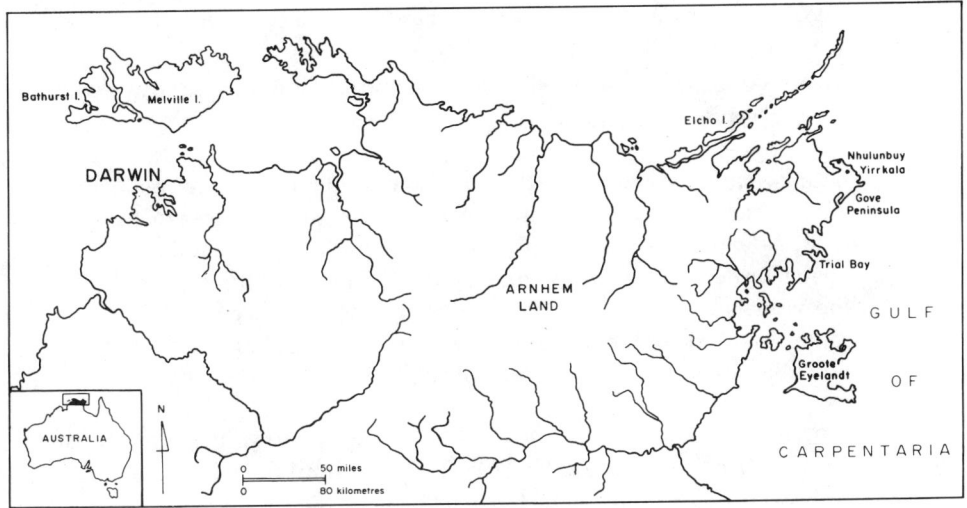

Map 9. Arnhem Land

property of a certain group conveys the information that the group holds title to the site and all other interests are contingent. Identical names of sites or areas that are geographically separate or distant signify that those sites or areas and the groups that own them are linked by a common myth of bestowal. (42)

Morphy explores relationships between landscape and the ancestral past in ways that help us make sense of the relationship between the religious and economic dimensions, explaining that "the resilience of the network of linkages between ancestral beings and places is a reflection of the fact that the attachment of people to place through the mediating process of the ancestral past is part of the core structure of Aboriginal society" (1995, 186). Noting that the links between landscape and Aboriginal conceptions of the world have been central in Australian anthropology since Spencer and Gillen (at least), Morphy argues that "it is not simply that landscape is a sign system for mythological events, as is now well understood. Rather, the landscape is the referent for much of the symbolism. Too often landscape has been seen as an intervening sign system that serves the purpose of passing on information about the ancestral past. I would like to argue that landscape is integral to the message" (186). An important part of this message is the human role, for "the landscape is viewed simultaneously as a set of spaces for people to occupy" (186).

Moreover, names—as well as succession to rights in a name—can be given to others or exchanged.

> Because names may be shared, they also provide the basis for maintaining continuity in ownership of land through time. Yolngu use them as expressions of the jural basis for the claim of continuous ownership of land by successors, "the same people," through time. Individuals, or individuals on behalf of their patrilineages, are "the same" by virtue of the names and other property that are associated with the names that they share. (Williams 1986, 73)

The process of naming as a means of the European appropriation of the land is discussed by Carter (1987). Other symbols of land ownership important to Yolngu include rituals and ritual property.

Both patrilineal and matrilineal interests in land coexist. When a spirit-being animates a fetus it appears in a dream to the father explaining where it has come from: "The spirit is most likely to come from a site in territory owned by the father's patrilineal clan or from that of a group to which the father is closely linked by some form of agnatic tie. A child thus acquires certain rights in the site from which his spirit came, rights that he or she may exercise during his or her lifetime" (Williams 1986, 32). Female symbols are more related to the body than to the spirit; one is tied matrilineally to one's place of birth. Individuals are also tied into their mother's and father's inheritance in land. Williams summarizes it thus:

> [T]hrough women as mothers, as sisters, as wives, and as daughters, the substance of connection to land is created and transmitted. Through men as fathers, as brothers, as husbands, and as sons, the animation of substance and of relationships ... by means of spiritual forces and particular spirit-beings is maintained ... Matrilines endow one with the substance of rights. Patrilines give these rights political expression and spiritual force. The *mari-gutharra* relationship [a reciprocal relationship with, for example, mother's mother's brother] provides the means of fusing them so that validation of continuity is temporal and spiritual at the same time. (55)

Yolngu principles of land allocation include the following (see Williams 1986, 76–80). Adjacent areas belong to groups of opposite moiety and alternate areas to groups of same moiety ("The Yolngu con-

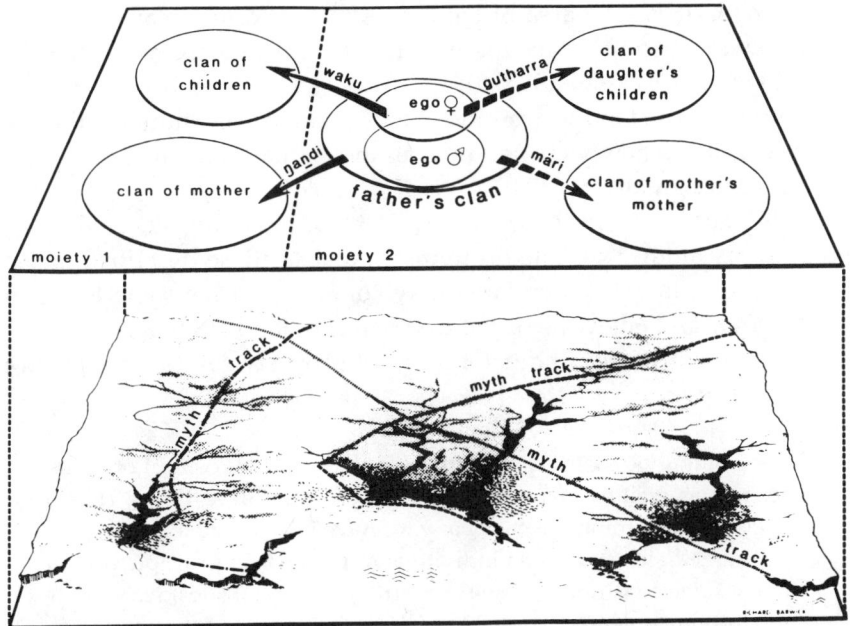

Fig. 18. The relationship between clan structure and land ownership among Yolngu, as illustrated by Williams (1986, 77): "The top portion of the diagram shows kin terms used to express the relations of individuals to groups and also of relations among groups. The landscape below shows how these kin labelled groups are related to each other in terms of the estates they own.... The stippled circles on the landscape indicate focal areas of clan estates." Courtesy Aboriginal Studies Press.

ceptualise their universe in terms of a complementary opposition labelled and often expressed by the named moieties, *Dhuwa* and *Yirritja*" [21]) (fig. 18). Estates of land-owning groups are made up of noncontiguous lands, usually one major coastal and one inland area; together these furnish most of the available resources. At the same time, "Small bounded areas, sometimes very small indeed, within the estate of a land-owning group may be held by a member or members of another land-owning group" (78). These subsidiary rights can be allocated on any of the following rationales:

Religious: "Sites of some degree of sacredness are tangible evidence of the link in myth between the owners of the large estate and the holders of the encapsulated areas or sites, which are generally called *ringgitj*" (79).

Spirit origin: "An area of land may be vested in a man of another land-owning group for his lifetime, if his spirit came from a place outside his father's clan land" (79).

Affinal link: "On the grounds of a long-standing connubial alliance, or to confirm a newly created one, an individual or a patriline may be given such a small site" (79).

Relationship to female land-owners: "A man may be allocated a portion of his mother's estate on terms similar to those described above, and his patrilineal descendants may continue, on the same terms, to 'look after' and enjoy the use of that parcel of land" (80).

Along with these understandings of property comes a sense of responsibility.

> The Yolngu view of responsibility for land includes control of its resources as well as maintenance of its territorial integrity ... Thus a decision concerning the use of any resource in an estate for more than the immediate needs of an individual or family is in principle subject to the same constraints as one concerning a grant of subsidiary rights to land. In contemporary terms, such a decision might involve a request to harvest bark for use in the commercial production of bark paintings, or a proposal to establish a commercial fishing venture, or to allow mining. (75, 93)

Resource conservation is a conscious issue, manifest in a variety of ways, and burning of the country is part of stewardship.

Collisions with European Perceptions

Because of the centers of bureaucratic and academic power in Canberra, the country that Aboriginal people from northern Australia are most likely to engage as visitors is the temperate woodlands and grazing lands around the national capital, extending south into the Australian Alps. Another evocative description of an Aboriginal person's response to this country comes to us via Howard Morphy, who travelled in the Snowy Mountains with Narritjin Maymuru, a Yolngu from northeast Arnhem Land, "a continent away to the north."

> We came to a place where the river opened out to form a shallow, oval lake, tapered at one end, with sharp pebbles strewn on either side. We sat down beside the lake and Narritjin began to interpret its mythology for me. It was, he said, land of the Dhuwa moiety connected with

the Marrakulu and related clans of the Trial Bay area of the Gulf of Carpentaria. It was land connected with Ganydjalala, an ancestral woman who, with others, hunted kangaroos through the forests with stone spears. Ganydjalala is associated with the origin of stone spears as well as with one of the great regional ceremonies of Arnhem Land, the Djungguwan. The ancestral women cut down trees in the inland forests as they looked for honey. In different places, where the trees fell, they created water courses and lakes, or ceremonial grounds, or stone-spear quarries.

I asked Narritjin how he knew it was Dhuwa moiety country since neither of us had ever been there before. Moreover, little was known of the mythology of the people who had once lived in the area, before their lives had been so rudely interrupted by European colonization in the middle of the last century. Narritjin pointed to the sharp pebbles that lay beside the stream that were Ganydjalala's stone spears, and he pointed out the trees that were similar to those in the forests through which Ganydjalala hunted, and finally he reminded me of how the lake she created was represented in paintings on the *djuwany* posts made for the Djungguwan ceremony by his brother Bokarra, and how its shape resembled the shape of the lake by which we were sitting. Yes, we were in Dhuwa moiety country. (Morphy 1995, 184)

A number of themes in the foregoing material need highlighting because they collide so strongly with stereotyped views of the nature of Aboriginal land ownership. They also help to explain how patterns of ownership can survive the colonial process. This is particularly true of the social rather than (or as well as) the ecological dimension of relations to land, artificial as it is to separate them. Many Euro-Australians conceptually equate Aboriginal land ownership with hunting and gathering. The point is not that ecological interactions are irrelevant but that they need to be understood in the context of the social relations that authorize them. Chase's (1989a) teasing apart of *domus* (a hearth-based area of exploitation), *domiculture* (localized packages of interaction between people and resources), and *domain* (following Stanner, the geographical area of legitimized use) is useful here.

For some reason disputes between Aboriginal people over ownership are often seen by outsiders as proof that the system is being "invented" on the spot. As with Euro-Australian ownership, the existence of detailed procedures for dealing with disputes and changes in circumstance attests rather to the resilience of the concept of ownership. It is this outside perception that real Aboriginal rights to land are "given" and "sacred" rather than mediated through the social system that has given rise to a reified, frozen stereotype of "traditional" ownership. Williams explains Yolngu clans as groups made corporate by their ownership of land: "Corporate groups do not search for land to own; Yolngu groups are made corporate by their ownership of land ... Defining a group as corporate with respect to the ownership of land facilitates the understanding of how stability and continuity can be maintained while change occurs" (1986, 95–96). The successional procedures for transfer of ownership thus facilitate change by emphasizing continuity: "In a sense the new group takes on the clothing of the old group so that, from an ancestral perspective, nothing has changed" (Morphy 1995, 190). All of these processes are open to negotiation and dispute, again according to due process.

Collisions with European Law

In June 1992 the High Court of Australia decided in *Mabo v. the State of Queensland* "by a 6:1 majority that pre-existing land rights ('native title') survived the extension of British sovereignty over Australia, and may still survive today, provided that the relevant Aboriginal and Torres Strait Islander people still maintain sufficient traditional ties to the land in question; and that the title has not been extinguished by governmental action" (Nettheim 1994, 55). In doing so they overturned the underpinnings of Justice Blackburn's 1971 decision in *Milirrpum v. Nabalco and the Commonwealth* that "as a matter of law Australia was vacant, uninhabited land belonging to no one, that is, *terra nullius*" (Bartlett 1993, 64–65; see also Hocking 1993, 68). Mr. Justice Blackburn had decided against the Yolngu people in the so-called Yirrkala land case. In reaching this decision Blackburn "considered what the Australian historical material in the evidence before him revealed about Aborigines' proprietary interest in land ... In the end he found it revealed none" (Williams 1986, 141). Despite having "unequivocally found a system of law" among the Yolngu, Blackburn then said that it did not provide for any proprietary interest in land (158).

The reasons for this finding are discussed in considerable detail by Williams. It is worth highlighting some of them here, partly to consider how a different decision could be made twenty years later. Williams situated some of the problems in the terms in which the Statement of Claim was couched; for example, the relationship between the religious connection to land and the economic use of it, and the relationship of band and clan to land over time, were problematic. Williams quotes an unpublished statement by Stanner: "Possibly the greatest single handicap which the Yirrkala aborigines face in making their case will be to counter the widespread but erroneous idea among Europeans that the day-to-day usage of land was itself the system of ownership and possession" (1986, 163–64). Although the spiritual relationship of the clan to its land was considered by Blackburn to have been "well proved," the clan was "not shown to have a significant economic relationship with the land" leading to his famous statement that "it seems easier, on the evidence, to say that the clan belongs to the land than that the land belongs to the clan" (Blackburn in Williams 1986, 270).

Indeed, "One of Blackburn's critical findings on the disputed facts hinged on the definition of the clan, since clans were specified as the land-owning claimants, and since particular clans claimed to have owned particular lands 'from time immemorial' " (Williams 1986, 166). Williams referred to this as "a vexed intersection: groups reified by anthropological concepts clashed with Yolngu attempts to simplify explanations so that the English-speaking court could comprehend them" (166). The question of succession in ownership over time, particularly in the period 1788 to 1935 (the time of establishment of the Yirrkala Mission) was a crucial one in the failure of the case: "The changes in rights that result from succession correlate with changes in role, and so succession entails re-adjustment of role relationships in which property is a pivotal feature. It is further useful to distinguish between presumptive rights of succession, which depend on patrifiliation, and subsidiary rights of succession, which are based on a number of other principles" (175).

Blackburn had also found that "no permission was required for a band to go anywhere" (Williams 1986, 173). Williams discusses extensively the complex negotiations involved in the process of permission.

> Blackburn's decision in the Yirrkala land case affirmed the principles underlying the rights of the citizen isolate as individual economic man, principles basic to assumptions of Australian law in 1970 . . . Because it lacked concepts of property that existed in contemporary common law, Yolngu ownership by right of title was found to be a matter of religious belief and not of economic significance. It was therefore not law. (202; see also Williams 1982)

Land Rights after Blackburn

The loss of the Yolngu case contributed to the passing of the Aboriginal Land Rights (Northern Territory) Act (1976) (referred to simply as the Land Rights Act), which provides for grants of inalienable freehold title to Land Trusts comprising traditional Aboriginal owners or Aboriginal people living on the land granted or both" (Tehan 1994, 36). In reviewing literature that analyses the operation of the act, Povinelli notes that "traditional Aboriginal owners" are designated in the act as

> a local descent group of Aborigines who—
> (a) have common spiritual affiliations to a site on the land, being affiliations that place the group under a primary spiritual responsibility for that site and for the land; and
> (b) are entitled by Aboriginal tradition to forage as of right over that land. (1993, 29)

In distinguishing between land-holding and land-using groups, following Berndt and Stanner, the Land Rights Act has overcome some of the constraints of the Blackburn decision, but many authors believe that this "orthodox model" does not do justice to the dynamism of land-holding relationships (Povinelli 1993, 29). More problematic for Povinelli is the "Act's subtle contrast between totemic/cultural and economic sides of Aboriginal life. At the surface this is not apparent; after all the act makes specific reference to Aboriginal foraging. But the contrast is found in how cultural beliefs and economic practices are disarticulated as categories" (30). She suggests that "it is, perhaps, deeply ironic that in order to present the proprietary interest of Aborigines, Stanner felt he had to demonstrate that economy and culture could be unhinged and that each differently influenced the shape and function of the social group" (10), reminding us that Stanner was arguing in an environment where the four stages theory of human development was still influential. Thus the complex Aboriginal social and conceptual systems were portrayed as existing almost in spite of what were seen as relatively basic economic practices; these days we would tend to see greater complexity in the economic strategies of hunter-gatherers than acknowledged in ladder-of-evolution depictions. More to the point, however, for Povinelli, is the false dichotomy between "culture" and "economy" (explored in more detail in chapter eight below).

Aborigines outside the Northern Territory have had even lesser protection of their rights to land, partly because of a particular "political and legal tension" (Tehan 1994, 34) within the Australian federal system. While the commonwealth government has power to make special laws in respect of Aboriginal people, the individual states—with their powerful mining and farming lobbies—have responsibility for land management. As a federal territory the Northern Territory, although it has been given self-governing status, is ultimately under the control of the federal government; the territorial legislature has a limited ability to act in relation to Aboriginal land owned pursuant to the Land Rights Act. In general, land rights—whether legislated or not—vary in different states (Tehan 1994); notably, there is no land rights legislation in Western Australia, a state with a large Aboriginal population and covering a large area of Australia.

When it came to power in 1983, the Hawke Labor government, along with promising to protect the wilderness of southwest Tasmania, had promised to use the constitutional powers of the commonwealth to legislate a uniform national land rights scheme. By 1986, under sustained pressure from the mining industry (particularly in Western Australia), the government had backtracked to the extent that it was prepared to "leave land rights to the States" (Goot and Rowse 1994, 1). The issue was not to go away, however, as a case which had been in the courts for a decade would show.

> Since *Mabo*, although Australia remains a settled colony, it is now regarded as one that had prior owners like New Zealand, New Guinea, Canada and the United States. It is now decided that, when an inhabited colony has been settled rather than ceded or conquered, those principles of land law relevant to vacant land are inapplicable ... *Mabo* correctly interprets and applies principles of the common law concerning constitutional and property titles that stretch as far back as Roman law and which have recently been confirmed anew in the civil law world by the ICJ [International Court of Justice] in the *Western Sahara* case. (Hocking 1993, 70)

There were a number of issues not resolved by the *Mabo* decision (Nettheim 1994), including the question of whether titles issued since 1975 (the date of the Commonwealth Racial Discrimination Act) were valid. In October 1992 Prime Minister Paul Keating announced his intention to legislate a response to the decision by the end of the following year, triggering a protracted series of negotiations between the natural resource industry lobbies, Aboriginal groups, and state and federal politicians (Rowse 1994; Nettheim 1994). The Native Title Act, passed just before Christmas 1993, among other things

> • recognises native title rights and sets down some basic principles in relation to native title in Australia;
> • provides for the validation of past acts which may be invalid because of the existence of native title;
> • provides a process by which native title rights can be established and compensation determined. (Attorney-General of Australia 1994, 271)

Although the majority of Aboriginal Australians can claim no land under *Mabo*, their title having been long ago extinguished, the process has offered a cultural challenge to all Australians (Pearson 1994). The legal and political complexities of the issue are explored in detail in the references given in this section and are beyond the scope of this discussion, except for one point relating to the relationship between native title and property rights. In the aftermath of the High Court decision a number of conservative commentators, most notably Hugh Morgan of the Western Mining Corporation, called for legislation to overturn the decision on the basis that it had "plunged property law into chaos" (Bartlett 1993, 59). Bartlett explores in some detail the relationship between the common law and the protection of property rights; far from overturning these rights, Bartlett argues, common law continues to protect property rights and—as in the 1823 American *Johnson v. McIntosh* decision by Chief Justice Marshall—"effects a compromise between the rights of settlers and aboriginal people" (61).

The broader social discourse in which *Mabo* was played out is analysed in an important recent study that provides further insights into the reversing of the Blackburn decision in *Mabo*. Ritter argues that terra nullius is not a legal doctrine but a discourse of power, that prior to *Mabo* it "had never been identified as a barrier to the recognition of Aboriginal people's land rights under the common law" (1994, 7). The discussion that identified a nexus between native title and the abandonment of terra nullius is found not in case law or statute, Ritter argues, but in wider legal commentary, history (especially the work of Henry Reynolds), and anthropology.

> It is the operation of the "discourse of *terra nullius*" which explains why the common law failed to recognise Aboriginal rights to their tribal lands. In a society in which the dominant discourse defined Aboriginal people as "wandering tribes living without certain habita-

tion and without laws," the absence of Aboriginal land rights was not a matter for judicial decisions, it was a truth that was self-evident, and the development of the law was predicated upon that truth. (36)

The aftermath of *Milirrpum v. Nabalco* was a "crisis of truth," in which the law was seen not to conform to social reality. This crisis was only temporarily averted by legislation, for example the N.T. Land Rights Act.

Why then did the High Court express its decision in *Mabo*, albeit ambiguously, in terms of terra nullius? Ritter argues that it was "a symbolic legitimation ritual" (1994, 89):

> [B]y doing something like "rejecting" a "doctrine of *terra nullius*" in Mabo, the High Court resolved a long-term discursive crisis in Australian legal discourse in which the law had been seen to be inequitable and unjust because it no longer conformed to the relevant "truths" in Australian society. Thus, the "rejection of *terra nullius*" provided a rhetorical explanation for why Aboriginal land rights had historically not been recognised; it re-legitimated the rule of law in Australia; it allowed the Australian judicial system to once again appear to reflect the relevant "truths" in Australian society; and it realigned truth and power to reinforce the legitimacy of the white Australian nation. If the "rejection of *terra nullius*" as such marked a judicial revolution at all, it was a stage-managed one: things were changed in order for things to remain the same. (96)

As Ritter notes, these new "truths" were not of course universally accepted, and the decision created a new discursive crisis for many on the right, for example Hugh Morgan (as mentioned above) This may be even more the case with the High Court *Wik* decision of December 1996, which found that the grant of pastoral leases did not necessarily extinguish any native title that may be held in respect of those areas (Attorney-General's Department 1997), though where the two are inconsistent, the rights of the pastoralist are to prevail. Our apparent inability to live with coexisting tenure systems in some of the most extensively settled areas of Australia has, by the late 1990s, led to attempts by the federal government to amend the Native Title Act to extinguish native title in certain contexts.

Aboriginal Relations to the Past

Another important context in which Aboriginal voices have been heard—albeit with just as many constraints and external constructions as in the land rights debate—is in debates about the past. These relate to both perceptions of the past and the authorization of its telling. We return then to an argument (introduced in chapters two and four) that Aboriginal people view the past very differently than the way that archaeologists and the broader Australian community do. Of course, "It is not just archaeologists who value knowledge of the past" (Layton 1989, 1); there is a large body of work that now challenges the assumption that oral cultures have neither interest in nor means of recording the past. Layton sees Malinowski's theory of myth as existing "almost entirely to validate contemporary behaviour" as an example of functionalist dogma in anthropology (1). Layton argues that an us-and-them approach simply perpetuates the notion of the other: "Not only . . . do such dichotomies obscure equally interesting differences between the diverse cultures in the 'other' category, such simplistic thinking tends to attribute opposed functions to oral art forms and written literature" (4).

A Yolngu accounting of the past shows the complexity of this situation. Williams and Mununggurr start by emphasizing that the Western view of time as "natural, real, moving . . . precise and accurate" is problematic, in terms both of the physics and of the social context. Following Landes (1983), they argue that the link between clocks and the development of modern capitalism led to time being associated with change: "As Europeans came to value change in itself, and for its association with the idea of progress in their own societies, they attributed to non-Western, non-capitalist societies the opposite: that is, those societies were not only unchanging, they resisted change" (Williams and Mununggurr 1989, 72).

However, argue Williams and Mununggurr, all cultural systems show aspects of supposedly mutually exclusive dichotomies such as timeless/time based, cyclic/linear, and changeless/changing (see also Gosden 1994). In fact, Yolngu often express linear temporality; for example, message sticks were not just mnemonic devices for verbally delivered messages but contained information about the precise timing of planned ceremonies and the number of people invited: 'The devices used include representations of the Moon in specific phases, and lines and circles that conveyed number" (Williams and Mununggurr 1989, 77). They also locate events in time according to synchronicity, for example with a specific ecological event or combination of events, especially when signaling the most appropriate time to gather particular resources. Thus, for example, "the flowering of a certain tree occurs when yams are fully mature at a particular place" (77). Similar examples to this are often quoted as evidence of Aborigines' detailed ecological knowledge; Williams and Manunggurr's linking of that to time concepts shows the close interconnections between time, space, and land that pervade this book. Morphy argues further that "the subordination of time to space is reflected pervasively in the syntax, morphology, and semantics of Yolngu languages. For the most part temporal markers are derived from . . . the languages' devices for describing spatial relations" (1995, 189). Although the time it took ancestral beings to complete their journeys is expressed in spatial rather than in temporal terms, nevertheless there "are certain identifiable strata of time or bands of synchronicity" (188).

In particular, "For Yolngu there is a far-distant past about which no living person can have direct, therefore sure, knowledge" (Williams and Manunggurr 1989, 77). The term *Wangarr* refers to this past, "in which the spirit-beings travelled through the land doing many of the things that Yolngu on whom they bestowed land would continue to do" (78), and also to the spirit-beings themselves. The greatest authority claimed by Yolngu is continuity: "[O]ur fathers taught us, as their fathers taught them" (78).

As they travelled through the country, Wangarr left signs of their activities, both objects such as digging sticks and marks or impressions at places where they stopped; at the most sacred places, they even left parts of their beings. Thus, "It is because the Yolngu landscape is saturated with signs that bear meanings that are still immensely important to Yolngu that they regard it as potentially dangerous to disturb the features of the landscape. Furthermore, Yolngu perceive the land as themselves in some respects, and their most sacred religious objects are the bones of the land" (Williams and Manunggurr 1989, 79). In terms of the archaeological possibilities of excavating a midden, Manunggurr says that "that was a very long time ago. And that place, where we see the evidence of people living there, we are not allowed to dig up. We must leave it like that" (80). (Aboriginal attitudes to archaeology and excavation vary considerably; see Moser 1995a for an overview.)

"Perhaps the most useful guides to understanding Yolngu signs of the past are found in Yolngu procedures governing the keeping of standing accounts, including the protocol of access—the assignment of rights to know and to reveal knowledge that Yolngu value highly" (Williams and Manunggurr 1989, 82). Specifically, "the more important that Yolngu regard a category of knowledge to be, the more precisely they express rules of access." This relates particularly to the "religious myth narratives of land bestowal"; the safest place to store such knowledge is still considered to be "inside the heads of the oldest clan leaders" although, or perhaps because, written forms of information storage are becoming more common within the community. Williams and Mununggurr argue that because Yolngu have the means of making the past available to present experience, it should not be taken to imply either "conflation of perceptions nor dichotomous barriers of time" (81), any more than it might among Christians taking the body and blood of Christ during communion.

Related arguments have been made by other workers among Aboriginal communities in northern Australia. Tacon argues that people's relationship with stone, through painting, engraving, and assembling boulders, "is associated with a sense of permanency for all peoples." He argues further that the "rise of rock art has more to do with the development and importance of the concept of time than it does the rise of language . . . I argue strongly against ideas that certain indigenous peoples or ancestral populations had no sense of time, or that time is solely a Western construct" (1994, 126).

Converse to the assumption that historical consciousness is the prerogative of the West, Layton reminds us of Hobsbawm's argument that the past has become much less relevant as a basis for human behavior in the West, particularly in private life.

> In the private lives of most people . . . even the invented traditions of the nineteenth and twentieth centuries occupied or occupy a much smaller place than old traditions do in, say, old agrarian societies. "What is done" structures the days, seasons and life-cycles of twentieth-century western men and women very much less than it did their ancestors', and very much less than the external compulsions of the economy, technology, bureaucratic state organization, political decision and other forces which neither rely on nor develop "tradition" in our sense. (Hobsbawm 1983, 11)

In his analysis, Hobsbawm distinguishes between "tradition" and "custom": "The object and characteristic of 'tradition,' including invented ones, is invariance. The past, real or invented, to which they refer imposes fixed (normally formalized) practices, such as repetition." Custom, on the other hand, which dominates so-called traditional societies, "cannot afford to be invariant" (1983, 2). Because I am retaining (while critiquing) the concept of tradition in later chapters, it is worth pursuing this further. Tradition, as used by Chase, "rather than being a largely fixed entity across time and space, relates to authorization for current routine actions in terms of maintenance or order and power structures; it can thus consist of quite recently created mythologies as well as those from a more distant past" (1989b, 170).

Chase tells of aspects of Aboriginal perception of the past in northeast Queensland, focusing on the complexity of contacts during the European period. From the perspective of many Europeans the incursions—by luggers, trepangers, missionaries, and government officials—were such that "traditional" Aboriginal society must no longer exist. However, Chase emphasizes that among local Aboriginal people, the various transformations are viewed retrospectively within a sphere of normality precisely because they were not "massively destructive in terms of people-land relationships" (1989b, 174). Because many of the incursions were from the sea, they were not only intermittent but did not involve the appropriation of land that happened in many pastoral areas. Thus each set of relationships becomes accepted and routinized, and "the normative or authoritative base for society remains relatively untouched in the view of later members of the society" (175). The centrality of the links to land is the currency by which the degree of historical change is measured.

Chase (1989a) has put forward a similar argument in explaining why agriculture as a total system was never adopted by Aboriginal hunter-gatherers, despite their contact with agricultural peoples across Torres Strait and the widespread use of procedures to enhance plant growth and productivity. It is similar in that it allows us to understand how social and ecological disruption (or potential disruption) is dealt with in the context of overriding relationships to land and processes of authorization that thread through the whole society (see more detailed discussion in chapter eight). It also helps to clarify some of the sources of potential conflict between environmentalists and Aborigines over rights to practice "traditional" land use (discussed further in chapter nine).

Yothu Yindi

Yolngu people, if not relations to land, are now known to an international audience through the pop group Yothu Yindi. In this respect they exemplify a broader trend for Aboriginal symbols to be incorporated into Australian popular and public cultures, paralleled by changes in the commercialization of Aboriginal art.

According to Morphy, "The systematic nature of the association between landscape, ancestral being, and social group is reflected clearly in the artistic systems of the Yolngu. Place, ancestral being, and social group are encoded precisely in the content and the form of paintings and song" (1995, 191). Magowan (1994) discusses the ways that the pop music and its expression stem from these ancestral connections and also engage with the wider political context. She depicts the *yothu-yindi* or mother-child link as an organizational feature of traditional song, stemming from the clan identities and relationships discussed above. It thus affects things such as the ownership of songs, the order in which clans sing at a funeral, and the right to sing certain names. Magowan argues that the yothu-yindi concept has been incorporated into the organization of the band Yothu Yindi and into the meaning of their song texts. Most of the songs are performed in a mixture of English and Yolngu dialects, and they combine both Western and Aboriginal musical styles and instruments. Magowan interprets this as part of a politics of resistance that works together with the explicitly political message of many of the songs.

> This land was never given up
> This land was never bought and sold
> The planting of the Union Jack
> Never changed our law at all.
>
> (M. Yunupingu et al., "Treaty,"
> from the album *Tribal Voice*)

The technicalities of Yolngu clan relations to land and their expression in song must be lost on most of the audiences who have made this group so popular, but the political statements that relate so clearly an attachment to land are very clear. It is not just a question of lyrics; Magowan argues that "the ethnoaesthetics of display through performance content and structure create an atmosphere that evokes feelings of what it means to be Yolngu" (1994, 153). Thus European audiences who are excluded from the textual symbolism can engage with the "stylised use of dance space, the energy of the visual display and the articulation of instruments and voices as if in conversation with one another" (151).

The political context in which Yothu Yindi music is used has now become much wider than its Yolngu origins. As Yunupingu (1994, 115) recognizes—and his high public profile attests—the Yirrkala land rights case and Yothu Yindi's songs are both features of a process in which Australian society is grappling with Aboriginal ways of seeing.

New Australia

Land and tenure have been at the heart of Euro-Australian history independent—if that is possible—of Aboriginal-white relations. In traditional histories where the appropriation of Aboriginal land barely rates a mention, struggles between "squatters" and "free selectors" are to the fore. Squatters were pastoralists and stockmen who, in the first decades of the nineteenth century, pushed outside the limits of settlement from Sydney and colonized the Port Phillip district from Tasmania. The empires that were built up in these years formed the basis for the nearest thing Australia has had to a landed gentry. In the aftermath of the 1850 gold rushes there were demands from the growing population to "unlock the lands" for closer settlement.

A hundred years ago, many who had not managed to be the children of squatters were already disillusioned with the great Australian dream and preparing to repeat the exercise on yet another southern continent. In the wake of the 1891 shearers' strike and the drought and depression of the 1890s, a group of people led by William Lane made plans for establishing a utopian socialist settlement in South America. It was to be a particular kind of utopia—an agrarian one, with no place for alcohol, colored skin, or dissenters. Treasurer and later secretary of the New Australia Co-operative Settlement Association was Walter Head—secretary of the Shearers' Union at Wagga, poet, newspaper editor, and grandson of Sarah and William Head.

Wearied of their battle against landed capital, they prepared to journey to another land seen as a remote, distant wilderness. Lane had argued that remoteness would be an advantage and that thousands of drovers and shearers, professional nomads, would have no trouble with the travel. He responded to critics: "You would know, if you were going to do it yourselves, that you could not do it here with anything like the same prospects. We have free land, fertile land, watered, timbered" (Souter 1968, 59).

Walter would never make it to Paraguay, but what motivated him to be so involved? Perhaps it was a hunger for land, frustrated by the small-time farming of his parents and grandparents and stimulated by the squatters' spreads he visited as a shearer's rep around Wagga. Or perhaps his political commitment was fired by what he saw as his family's bondage to subsistence agriculture and wage labor. Or was it the poet in him, prepared to cross the globe in search of the best of all possible worlds?

A small advance party, sent to find suitable land, were enthused by the abundance of eastern Paraguay (map 10), with its characteristic landscape of grasslands or *campo* (field) surrounding islands of *monte* (forest).

> Seen from outside, the *monte* is splashed according to season with the pink blossoms of the lapacho-tree, the mauve of the jacaranda, the red of the flamboyant, and the white blossoms of wild oranges. Inside, there is often a bridle path or oxen track which takes the rider between tall guadyavi-trees hung with vines and set about with ferns; the path emerges briefly into an open forest glade, where the air flickers with acid-yellow butterflies, crosses a brook, and then leads once more into the green dusk of the *monte*. (Souter 1968, 35)

Although this description seems a long way from the landscape of the Australian outback, there were to be several echoes of the Australian situation. The monte would have to be cleared so that its rich soil could be used to grow crops such as tobacco, sugarcane, cotton, maize, mandioca, fruit, and vegetables. And even once this was done, there were problems in the lack of a local market (43–44).

The plan had generated a number of critics at home. *The Bulletin*, an important national paper at the time, commented: "There will be a few hundred people digging and fencing in a dreamy, hopeless fashion out in the great loneliness, and living on woe and unsaleable vegetables and dreams of home. And, meanwhile, the founder of the settlement will be foaming at the mouth and uttering poetry beneath a tree, and wildly asking the damp ferns, 'What is life?' " (Souter 1968, 60). *The Bulletin* also disapproved of "white upstanding Australians" settling among "dusky Dagoes."

Far from pioneering an uninhabited wilderness, the New Australians were embroiled in a land rights dispute as soon as they ar-

Map 10. Paraguay and New Australia (after Souter 1968)

rived. Several hundred Guarani people had been ordered off the land by the Paraguayan government when it gave the land to the Australians, but implementation of the order was left to the newcomers. Local newspapers had much to say:

> *La Democracia:* If the Government hands this land unconditionally to the Australians, the local settlers would be placed in a very difficult position. From the lease contracts it is known that in this area there are more than 300 settlers in danger of being expelled.
>
> *El Centinela:* Let the Australian Gringos come! Let the whole world come to cultivate our soil and sell sweet potatoes! But do not let them come asking for justice when they have need of it, for consideration when they deserve it, or for public freedom, because these things are not produced by the soil. They may only ask for sweet potatoes, because that is the only thing that is produced in the soil. (Souter 1968, 81)

Things did not apparently come to confrontation.

On Thursday morning, 28th September, the *carretas* jolted through heavy forest, with monkeys chattering overhead, and emerged shortly before noon into several hundred acres of rising grassland bounded by *monte*. It was in this place, known to the Guaranies by the Spanish name of Puesto De Las Ovejas (The Sheep Station) that New Australia was founded. The *campo* was uninhabited, but an orange grove in the centre of the clearing showed that someone had once lived there . . .

Work parties felled timber for houses and fences, cut grass for thatching, scoured the *monte* for fruit trees (in addition to oranges, which were about to go out of season, they found peaches, limes, figs, lemons, and guavas), found good clay about four miles away and made bricks for an oven, and cleared land for gardening . . . The first crops planted were sweet potatoes, mandioca, French beans, melons, and Irish potatoes. All but the potatoes did well. (Souter 1968, 83)

It could have been Gardiners Creek, or the Buffalo Valley. Change the trees, the soil each time; keep the aspirations of people who expect to wrest a living from the land by planting and husbanding, who hope to make a better life for themselves in new country. They somehow do not perceive it as country belonging to someone else; they do not have eyes to see the daisy-yammer. In the Amazon basin, the open areas called *campos* are rare in the forest: "They are interpreted as being agricultural clearings of earlier times" (Sick 1969, 451–52).

Ten-year-old Wally Head had sailed with the first batch of New Australians. His parents Walter and Carrie were to have come later with their other children, but they never made it. On a trip to Gippsland with his mother to farewell relatives, Wally's four-year-old brother Rowland was lost in the bush and never found, despite weeks of searching by many people. Walter was called to the search from his preparations in Sydney, and he later returned there without the rest of the family.

Henry Lawson was to mythologize this event in his story "The Babies in the Bush" (1900):

He was one of those men who seldom smile. There are many in the Australian Bush, where drift wrecks and failures of all stations and professions (and of none) and from all the world . . . His name was Head—Walter Head. He was a boss drover on the overland routes. I engaged with him at a place north of the Queensland border to travel down to Bathurst, on the Great Western Line in New South Wales, with something over a thousand head of store bullocks for the Sydney market . . .

"Wally was five and little Maggie three and a half when we lost them. Weren't they, Walter?"

"Yes, Maggie," said the boss—cheerfully, it seemed to me—"I was away."

"And we couldn't find you, Walter. You see," she said to me, "Walter—Mr. Head—was away in Sydney on business, and we couldn't find his address. It was a beautiful morning, though rather warm, and just after the break up of the drought. The grass was knee-high all over the run. It was a lonely place; there wasn't much bush cleared round the homestead, just a hundred yards or so, and the great awful scrubs ran back from the edges of the clearing all round for miles and miles—fifty or a hundred miles in some directions without a break; didn't they, Walter?"

"Yes, Maggie."

"I was alone at the house except for Mary, a half-caste girl we had, who used to help me with the housework and the children. Andy was out on the run with the men, mustering sheep; weren't you, Andy?" "Yes, Mrs. Head."

"I used to watch the children close as they got to run about, because if they once got into the edge of the scrub they'd be lost; but this morning little Wally begged hard to be let take his little sister down under a clump of blue-gums in a corner of the home paddock to gather buttercups. You remember that clump of gums, Walter?"

"I remember, Maggie."

" 'I won't go through the fence a step, mumma,' little Wally said. I could see Old Peter—an old shepherd and station hand we had—I could see him working on a dam we were making across a creek that ran down there... The little ones toddled off hand-in-hand, with their other hands holding fast their straw hats. 'In case a bad wind blowed,' as little Maggie said. I saw them stoop under the first fence, and that was the last that anyone saw of them."

"Except the fairies, Maggie," said the boss quickly.

"Of course, Walter, except the fairies."

...

"And you never tried telling her that the children were found?"

"Yes; the boss did. The little ones were buried on the Lachlan River at first; but the boss got a horror of having them buried in the Bush, so he had them brought to Sydney and buried in the Waverley Cemetery near the sea. He bought the ground, and room for himself and Maggie when they go out. It's all the ground he owns in wide Australia, and once he had thousands of acres." (Lawson 1984, 774–83)

Rowland was stolen by the Gippsland monte while his family was preparing to move to the Paraguayan one. Ingredients of the drama were all there: The bush—anywhere—as thief of children, enemy of civilized people trying to carve out a living in the wilderness. Father, scrub-clearer and leader of men, was too drunk to be found while the search was underway. Mother, prisoner in the house in the clearing, went off with the fairies when she lost her children.

Within a few years New Australia fell victim to both nature and human nature. The community split in two; there were fights over assets and questions over the propriety of Walter Head. Disease attacked the wheat, and the cattle refused to stay in the campo paddocks. And, of course, there was racism: "The assumption that Anglo-Saxons were inherently superior to Hispano-Indians was as much a part of the colony's creed as teetotalism, a principle which had also been made explicit in the New Australia articles of association" (Souter 1968, 157). The colonists' attitudes towards nature and towards the existing inhabitants of Paraguay were scarcely different from those that their grandparents had taken from Britain to Australia. It should be easy for us, with hindsight, to see their blindness to the created landscapes that they occupied, to see in fact that it was their createdness that made them so attractive for new settlement. But we work towards our own utopias, which may be just as blinkered.

Walter Head later started a new life in Tasmania as Walter Woods, helping found the Tasmanian Labor Party and sitting as a State M.P. for seventeen years, including two terms as Speaker of the House. He worked for land reform: "[T]he Labor movement must become the land restoration movement" (Ritchie 1990, 566). The concept of land restoration—to whom? for what?—had a different meaning in the early years of the century than now. Was Walter battling to restore land to its original owners? to restore it to its pre-European condition? Undoubtedly not. By this time the indigenous Tasmanians were generally considered to no longer exist, and the magnificent forests would seem to have offered an endless supply of resources. It would be a number of decades before people started to ask questions about the open patches within the scrub and the trackways through the heath—and about the same time before people thought seriously of damming the rivers to oversupply themselves with electricity.

Part Four
Reworking

7

The New Colonizers

There are no recorded sites of historical significance.
—Phillip Island Penguin Reserve Management Plan

Although we like to believe otherwise, the processes of colonization and appropriation are complex and ongoing. Colonization of land and people was not simply an event that happened in 1788, with a new order being instantly implanted on Australia; rather it is a continuing process, albeit reworked for the late 1990s. This reworking is influenced by globalization, environmentalism, expanding tourism, and increased although still circumscribed Aboriginal power within Australian society.

I will explore these dynamics through three case studies. The first explores the notion of colonizing the past through the history of environmental management associated with the Penguin Parade at Phillip Island, one of Australia's premier tourist attractions. Representations and management strategies at Phillip Island have in recent years embraced the concept of renovating and restoring a "natural" environment; part of this process involves removing artefacts and buildings that attest to a history of European presence. A central contradiction of this program of environmental restoration is that an historically inaccurate ideal of human absence underpins a commodified tourist industry that is actually increasing human impacts in the area. The second example involves environmental and Aboriginal heritage issues associated with the Ord River Irrigation Scheme, a major development project in northwestern Australia. I compare the treatment of these issues between Stage I of the project (1960s and 1970s) with the current Stage II expansion; the intervening twenty-five years allow us to consider the extent of change. Colonial themes of an empty landscape, invisible Aborigines, and the idealization of agricultural land use persist to the present. Moreover, there are consistent attempts to naturalize the inevitability of the development process itself. The policies of the Australian Tourist Commission, the third case study, provide a broader context for discussion of the way that Aboriginal people and landscapes are incorporated into Australia's attempts to find a place through tourism in a restructured global economy. In discussing the apparently theoretical issue of conceptualizations of nature and the human place therein, I aim to show how myth and imagery are woven into very grounded environmental and social processes and outcomes.

Phillip Island: Land Rights for Penguins

The houses perch on the clifftop and dot the plateau behind. Most are ugly rectangular boxes, by turns craning their necks for a glimpse of the sea or huddling against the wind behind the tea tree. They face obstinately in one direction, often the wrong one in the changeable regimes of wind, rain, and sun. They have names such as Aqua Vista, White Horses, Sea Shanty. Electric wires sing and gardens struggle in the wind. Fibro, galvo, and weatherboard are all stained by the weather. By any modern understanding of the concept, they do not belong in the landscape.

The putative deflowering of Summerland Peninsula began in the nineteenth century with the McHaffie brothers, who cleared the whole of Phillip Island for "pasturage and cultivation": "On their first arrival the brothers cleared the island by setting fire to its scrub, a fire that enveloped the whole island. Its extent and density attracted attention for several days and nights on the adjacent continent and far out to sea" (Gliddon 1958, 169).

In a scene to be reenacted around Victoria, there was a ballot of applicants when the island was opened for free selection in 1868. Whether the Melbourne *Argus* was as mindful of the heritage values of other parts of the state as it was of Phillip Island is not known, but there was a clear awareness on Monday, 3 November 1868, that something had been lost in the ballot two days before:

> Although it is to be regretted for more reasons than one, that the island is not to be retained as national property, there is this much to be said—nearly the whole of the land selected yesterday has undoubtedly fallen into the hands of persons who intend to settle upon and cultivate it. Nearly the whole of the applicants were farmers, farm-labourers and hard-working men. (Seddon 1975, 70)

What was it that had been balloted? A buffer of land between the rhythmic violence of Bass Strait and the quiet waters of Westernport Bay, calm enough in many places for mangroves to colonize the mud flats (map 11). An intersection of rough and smooth, sand and rock, grass and tree that encouraged an unusual diversity of animal life. Seals basked on the rocky outliers; penguins came from ocean waters home to sandy burrows; koalas grunted in the inland gum trees; mutton birds traveled annually from Siberia to their nests in the grassy dunes. These, anyway, were the animals that later humans noticed and valued and built a tourist industry around. The snakes, the limpets, the march flies, the spoonbills, the herons, and the land snails never made it onto the postcards. At the southwest corner lay the Summerland Peninsula, an even smaller area in which this diversity was focused: a southern edge of basalt rock platforms, pounded by waves from out Tasmania way; the north side, gentler, a bit sandier, its rocky points deflecting the waves as they come around the corner.

By 1872 three of those "hard-working men" had settled the Summerland Peninsula; J. W. Syme, P. McGrath, and P. Phelan. Chicory, for many years Phillip Island's most valuable industry, was grown by Phelan and McGrath, protected by tea-tree fences (Gliddon 1958, 232). With the brush woven between uprights one and a half meters apart, these acted as windbreaks against the salt-laden southwesterly gales. Other agricultural activities included grazing, mustard cropping, and oats as fodder for the horses (Mrs. A. Reith, personal communication Aug. 1977).

The 1920s and 1930s saw quite marked changes on the peninsula, through the agency of several strong individuals and their projects. One such was Mr. A. K. T. Sambell, a civil engineer and president of the first Phillip Island Shire Council. He had a yen for islands and bought up land on Phillip Island, where he spent as much time as possible. Believing that the island should be developed to cater to more people, he was responsible for the building of the Cat Bay jetty (fig. 19) when the Cowes-Stony Point ferry ceased running temporarily. He opened the tea rooms at Summerland House—and was forced to extend this venture to include accommodation when visitors collapsed on the front step and refused to go home.[1] Between 1929 and 1940 there was a nine-hole golf course on what is now the Penguin Parade Carpark, and jonquils that once lined the fairways now grow wild: "Yards upon yards

---

1. Account of Mr. Sambell's activities based largely on personal communication with his daughter, Mrs. A. Reith, August 1977.

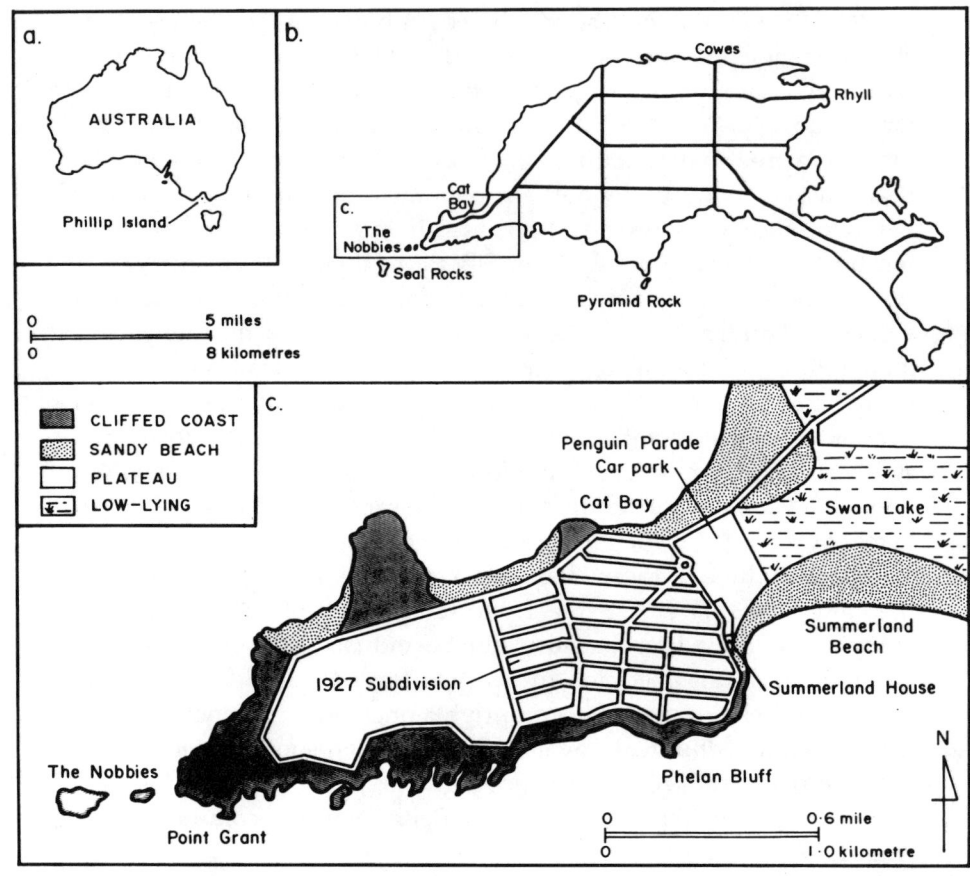

Map 11. Phillip Island, Victoria

of Merri Creek soil were imported to complement the existing sandy terrain—an ideal base for the fairways" (Cutter 1987, 89).

Mr. Sambell also drew up the first subdivision at Summerland, consisting of approximately twelve blocks. It was recognized at the time as an unusually good subdivision, the blocks being extremely large; features such as a roundabout and planted cypress trees are still evident today. Further subdivision by a Mr. Spencer Jackson created 227 new blocks between 1927 and 1931, and in 1950, 437 further blocks were added. Two smaller areas closer to the Nobbies were subdivided in 1958 and in 1961.

Perhaps fortunately for the Victoria government—which is currently in the process of buying back the land and removing the houses—this extensive subdivision was related much more to the spec-

Fig. 19. Cat Bay jetty, Phillip Island. Photograph by K. Head.

ulative investment market than to any real demand for building (Town and Country Planning Board 1971, 29). By 1974 only 11 percent of Summerland's 986 lots had been developed, in the sense of being cleared or built on (Seddon 1975, 169).

There are many so-called developments around the Australian coast that are considered by experts to be blights on the landscape, and in this respect the Summerland Estate is no exception (PIPRCM 1989, 16). It is unique, however, in that the presence of a bird that many first-time visitors find disappointingly tiny has provided the impetus and the means to effect a significant modification of the landscape, in two directions. On the one hand, the built landscape has reflected increasing demands for tourist infrastructure and visitor facilities in the last few decades; on the other hand, towards the end of the century, selected aspects of the human occupation of the area are in the process of being obliterated. The experience of the little penguin *(Eudyptula minor)* illustrates well the assertion that a natural resource is a cultural achievement.

Little penguins nest at many places around the southeastern coast of Australia, but the colony at Summerland is the largest. Several thousand birds, watched by equivalent numbers of humans, cross the beach at dusk after their search at sea for food; parents return to feed spouses and chicks, to moult, and to rest. There is much to-ing and fro-ing, with something happening every night of the year. In the early hours of the morning, unwatched by people, the reverse process occurs. This is a more diffuse "parade"; single penguins tend to scuttle down the beach in a businesslike manner as they head off to work.

The 1920s and 1930s were also the decades when small numbers of people with torches began to go in through the dunes behind Summerland Beach to watch the penguins returning to their burrows. At this time the dunes moved visibly every year, because there was no vegetation on them (Mrs. A. Reith, personal communication). Air photos taken in 1939 show blowouts behind Cat Bay and Summerland Beach; however, after this time vegetation made a marked recovery, aided by fencing, rabbit control, and the penguin reserve (Bayly 1973, 42), the latter originally managed by the shire after a donation of land from the Spencer Jacksons. Further research would be required to establish whether the sparsely vegetated and shifting dunes were a result of the early agricultural land use or, just as likely, a more enduring phenomenon. Nevertheless, efforts to "restore" the environment can be traced to this period.

> There are few things more pleasing than the contemplation of order and useful arrangement, arising gradually out of tumult and confusion; and perhaps this satisfaction cannot anywhere be more fully enjoyed than where a settlement of civilised people is fixing itself upon a newly discovered or savage coast. The wild appearance of the land entirely untouched by cultivation, the close and perplexed growing of trees, interrupted now and then by barren spots, bare rocks, or spaces overgrown with weeds, flowers, flowering shrubs, or underwood, scattered and intermingled in the most promiscuous manner, are the first objects that present themselves. (Governor Phillip in 1789, quoted in Smith 1984: 177–78)

To many western minds of the late twentieth century, there are few things more pleasing than the possibility of reversing this process—removing the civilization and allowing the tumult and promiscuity of nature to do what it will. Whether one is more ordered and less chaotic than the other is still debatable; whether something can be considered a weed just for growing in the bare spaces available to it in its native habitat might also stir an argument in an academic tea room. In any case, as the savage coasts shrink still further, the possibilities of renovating the landscape become as desirable as the renovation of inner-city terraces. Moreover, by 1992 definitions of wilderness had started to acknowledge the history and legacy of Aboriginal presence by removing references to environments untrammeled by human footprints. They also had begun to cope with the realities of continued depredation and declining stocks by including a concept of restoration and renewal:

> A wilderness area is an area that is, or can be restored to be, of sufficient size to enable the long-term protection of its natural systems and biological diversity; substantially undisturbed by colonial and modern technological society; and remote at its core from points of mechanised access and other evidence of colonial and modern technological society. (Robertson et al. 1992, 26)

Something of these attitudes had informed decisions about the Summerland Peninsula a decade or so previously, although those developments had much more to do with removing the ugly aspects of the European presence than with acknowledging an Aboriginal past. In 1974 the National Trust had argued that the southern coastline of Phillip Island between the Nobbies and Pyramid Rock was "essential to the heritage of Australia and must be preserved."

> The aesthetic values of the whole landscape are already lessened by poor quality housing which could encroach onto headlands, poor siting of tourist facilities at the Nobbies and Summerland Beach, and poor quality, unimaginative facilities such as the stands for spectators at the Penguin Parade and the Fisheries and Wildlife seal observation tower on Seal Rocks. There are scattered mutton bird rookeries along this coast and pedestrian traffic is eroding and destroying these. Pedestrian traffic needs management to prevent further deterioration of cliff tops as many vantage points have an unsightly maze of tracks connecting them. The coastal road from the Nobbies to Summerland Bay produces problems of traffic congestion and is a hazard to walkers. The aesthetic quality of this road is also poor. (National Trust of Australia 1974, 37)

The theme was repeated in the 1989 management plan for the Penguin Reserve: "The plateau unit currently suffers from total visual exposure.

Every car, building or structure in this area is visible over considerable distances. The Summerland Estate is a major blight on the landscape of this unit" (PIPRCM 1989, 16).

The original Phillip Island road system is an interesting example of the imprinting of a perception of one landscape onto another, quite different landscape. The road system was determined by the grid survey system of the nineteenth century and so has scant regard for the inland contours of the island; however, this means that the roads almost always meet the coast at right angles. In fact this is "an enormously valuable accident from a conservation and management point of view" (Seddon 1975, 80). An unfortunate exception is the Summerland Peninsula, where a clifftop road runs parallel to the coast around the entire perimeter; thus, the road that was originally most in tune with the environment now poses the greatest threat because it funnels large numbers of people and vehicles onto the coast.

To remove the blight, the short/medium-term management strategies for the reserve are removing "all existing buildings within the Summerland Estate ... as land is acquired and the site restored and revegetated with appropriate native species. Penguin breeding boxes will be selectively placed at restored sites" (PIPRCM 1989, 13) (fig. 20).

> In reviewing the long-term future of the Summerland Peninsula, The Summerland Peninsula Study [1985] proposed a road along the centre of the Peninsula to the Nobbies, with spur roads to the major coastal recreation sites. Closure and revegetation of the present road alignments would follow ...
>
> With the acquisition of the Summerland Estate and the construction of a central peninsula road in the long term, parts of the Reserve will offer feelings of remoteness. These recreation opportunities are not experienced elsewhere on Phillip Island to any large extent, and will greatly add to the overall enjoyment of the Reserve. (23)

That the process is rather schizophrenic is indicated by the overall management objectives:

> a. to protect and enhance the colonies of Little Penguin and Short-tailed Shearwater.
> b. to preserve and protect the natural environment including the flora and other fauna and the landscape, geological and geomorphological features.
> c. to provide the opportunity for public viewing of wildlife to the extent that this is consistent with objectives (a) and (b) above.

Fig. 20. Revegetation program, Summerland Peninsula, Phillip Island. A penguin nesting box is seen at front left, cypress trees from the 1927 subdivision at center rear. Photograph by author.

> d. to provide for the public use, understanding and enjoyment of the Reserve to the extent that this is consistent with objectives (a) and (b) above through the provision of appropriate facilities and to monitor and where necessary control the recreation use of the Reserve.
>
> e. to record and preserve sites of archaeological and historical importance. (PIPRCM 1989, 9)

Although they would never use the term wilderness, this is clearly to be a re-creation of a natural environment that offers a saleable commodity, and "feelings of remoteness" are part of that commodity. Just as clearly, the rights of the wildlife are secondary to the economic resource.

> The Penguin Reserve is now a substantial commercial operation that should be regarded as a medium sized business enterprise . . . without limits and controls on the use of the Reserve, the very resource the visitors come to enjoy will almost inevitably be lost . . . Generating revenue is one of the major means of protecting the existing penguin population and restoring penguin habitat. (2, 19, 35)

Unimaginable, of course, that they could need protection from the present and projected visitor numbers of 475,000 people per year—up to 850 cars, 50 buses and 3800 people per night! To be sure, "crowds of this size can only be accommodated when the tide is low and the two beach viewing areas are in use" (24, 26, 30).

The rights of penguins, seals, and mutton-birds to undisturbed habitat would never have been recognized in public policy had not the economic health of Phillip Island—and increasingly the tourist industry of the entire state—been dependent on them. The program to buy back all private land on the Summerland Peninsula was commenced under shire administration in the 1970s and continues now that the Penguin Reserve is managed as a park under the National Parks Act. By September 1988 $5.5 million had been expended on less than a third of the remaining lots (PIPRCM 1989, 1), with completion of the program projected to take ten to fifteen years.

If the health of the wildlife alone was the issue, it is unlikely that a visitor rate of nearly half a million humans per year would continue to be encouraged. As it is, the revenue to protect the penguins from increasing numbers of visitors is generated by encouraging more visitors to come and spend more money.

It is important to emphasize that I have no argument with the general direction of the Management Plan. By today's environmental standards the subdivision of the Summerland Estate should never have taken place. By the mid-1970s the impacts of tourism had clearly outstripped the capacity of existing management structures and policies to deal with them effectively. The landscape degradation, such as that described above by the National Trust, would have been appropriately dealt with as a management problem. What interests me here is how and why a management problem was recast within a rhetoric of restoring nature, in such a way as to efface some aspects of the human presence and enhance others. That the contradictions of this process have been little remarked on tells us something of how deeply the environmental debate, broadly understood, has naturalized certain categories of human impacts as desirable or undesirable.

The Ord River Irrigation Scheme, Then and Now

Since early this century, plans to develop agriculture in the seasonal tropics of northwestern Australia have been an important part of white Australia's attempts to possess the landscapes of the north. The Ord River Irrigation Scheme (ORIS), in the East Kimberley region of Western Australia (map 12), has been dogged by controversy since it was mooted in the 1920s, particularly following its establishment in the 1960s and 1970s. The scheme is currently in a phase of expansion that involves the extension of the irrigated area onto more extensive areas of alluvial plain, including the lower Keep River area of the Northern Territory. The intervening quarter-century has seen significant social and economic changes in Australia; in theory the plethora of supporting legislation should have ensured that both Aboriginal and environmental justice are central to land use decisionmaking in ways that did not happen twenty-five years ago.

The history and politics of Stage I of the scheme has been thoroughly critiqued by Graham-Taylor (1978) and its agricultural economics by Davidson (1972). Stage II is still in the preparatory phase, and the way that it proceeds depends partly on the outcomes of native title claims currently in progress. In this context it may seem peripheral to offer a discussion that draws more on myth and imagery than on precise economic or environmental indicators; however, if a historical perspective on Ord Stage I shows anything, it is that attitudes to and images of nature have been at least as powerful in driving the process as have any rational or quantitative assessments. These conceptualizations have sometimes been explicit, but more often implicit, albeit fundamental. The empty landscape; the centrality of agriculture as the highest form of land use; and the invisible Aborigine are all present both in Stage I and in Stage II. In general there is increasing recognition of the need to further understand the cultures of development as well as its economic and political underpinnings; Trigger (1997) for example discusses the cultures of mining in terms of development conceived as moral progress, as civilizing and domesticating the unfamiliar, as knowing and naming the landscape, and as male agency releasing the fertility of a landscape.

In a semi-arid monsoonal climate with a nine-month dry season, the Ord River Irrigation Area (ORIA) was made possible by the creation of Lake Argyle. Flooding of the lake followed a long gestation period. Agricultural experiments were undertaken by local pastoralist Kim Durack, and the permanent Kimberley Research Station was established in 1945. Two years after the prime minister opened the dam, however, cotton growing in the area was abandoned due mainly to the prohibitive costs of pest control, with no viable alternative crop. After a period in the doldrums in the late 1970s and early 1980s, the ORIA experienced a resurgence in the late 1980s with attempts at different crops such as specialized horticultural produce (fig. 21). At the same

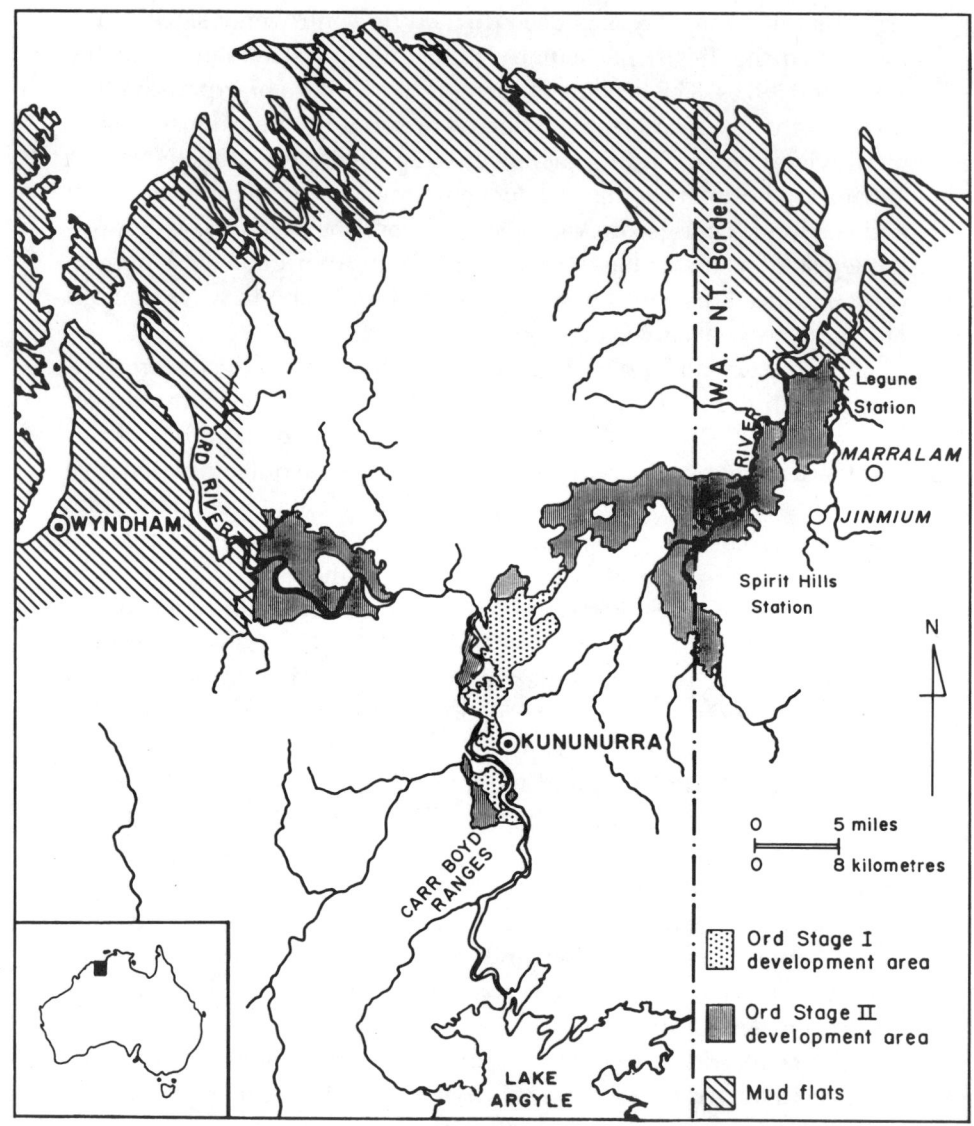

Map 12. The Ord River area, Western Australia and Northern Territory

time the mass market for tourism in northwestern Australia was increasing, following for example extensive publicity given to the "discovery" of the Bungle Bungles. The town of Kununurra, originally built as a service and administrative center for the ORIA and the associated research station, became the service center for this tourist mar-

Fig. 21. Irrigated agriculture on the Ord River floodplain. Photograph by author.

ket. The growth of the town was also facilitated by the establishment of the Argyle Diamond mine through the 1980s.

The economic context of Australian primary industry has also undergone profound changes in recent decades, including the impacts of globalization and the recognition of Southeast Asia as a market for expansion. In 1994 the Western Australia government decided to expand the project onto other low lying alluvial plains serviceable from the irrigation network (Western Australia 1996, 4). Because appropriate land crosses the Northern Territory border, it became a joint project of Western Australia and the Northern Territory. Eventual development of this area was planned during the investigations associated with Stage I (Western Australia and Northern Territory 1997, 14).

In general, "A substantial expansion of the Ord River Project is possible because of the availability of the two key resources of land and water" (Western Australia 1996: 14). To a large extent this expansion is seen as not only possible but necessary because these "resources" are perceived as being wasted in their present state. In fact, the land in question is mostly held under pastoral lease, and there are also substantial Aboriginal interests.

Legislation for environmental and Aboriginal site protection post-dates all the significant decision making related to Stage I, but it is constantly referred to in the public documentation for Stage II. For example, "[t]he Aboriginal Heritage Act 1972 . . . provides for the protection of sites and areas of significance to Aborigines" (Coombs et al. 1989, 49); environmental impact assessment (EIA) legislation dates to 1980 in Western Australia (53). The terms of reference for expressions of interest in Stage II include requirements for Aboriginal involvement, addressing social impacts of development and minimal environmental impact (Western Australia and Northern Territory 1997). Relevant legislation with which Stage II must comply includes at least nine Western Australia laws, thirteen Northern Territory laws, and two commonwealth laws (see Western Australia and Northern Territory 1997). The context in which all these laws, and environmental management generally, operate has changed significantly with the Mabo and Wik High Court decisions recognizing native title, and the Native Title Act of 1993 (Ross et al. 1994). The full implications continue to be worked through.

The major mooted crop for Stage II is sugar, involving the construction of a sugar mill just outside Kununurra in 1995. Cotton has also been resurrected as a potential crop, with the hope that the development of pest resistant strains will obviate the need for heavy pesticide applications. Promotional literature about both sugar and cotton emphasizes environmental issues among other things. Ord sugar is not available on the domestic market except in souvenir bottles for tourists but rather is all sold to markets in southeast Asia; the Ord sugar industry is keen to emphasize its advantages over its Queensland competitors, including a higher yield per hectare. Ord cotton, still a potential rather than a viable crop, is even more explicit in promoting a green image, for at least two reasons: to overcome its image as a historical victim to poor environmental and pest management in the region, and to position it as greener than its competitors in northern New South Wales and southern Queensland, who are causing severe environmental problems through their irrigation practices.

Neither Aboriginal nor environmental issues are conceived of as serious enough to stop Stage II; the decision having been made to go ahead, in the government and promotional literature those issues are portrayed as hurdles which must be cleared before development can proceed. Although the outcome of native title claims currently being heard may change the situation, there is a widespread expectation that at most the process will be delayed or its trajectory modified slightly. Thus for example the commissioning of heritage surveys are expressed in terms of "clearance before release," presuming that nothing of significant heritage status will be found; indeed, the recently released terms of reference state that "[c]learance in the NT under the Aboriginal Sacred Sites and Heritage Conservation Acts has already been obtained" (Western Australia and Northern Territory 1997, 5). This is despite the fact that no systematic archaeological survey of the area to be affected had been undertaken at that time. This is not to suggest that there is no Aboriginal support for Stage Two; rather I am interested in following the lines of continuity in official attitudes toward the land and its indigenous inhabitants between Stages I and II.

An Empty Landscape—The Long History of "Develop and Fill the North"

The rhetoric surrounding attempts by various governments to fill the empty landscapes of northern Australia has a history as old as white colonization of the continent (Clement 1991). By 1912, when land administration in the Northern Territory was being discussed in the wake of commonwealth control, the issue had become one of developing and opening up an uninhabited wilderness, at least for the distant decision makers, as Riddett (1990) shows. That is, it was deemed uninhabited because the people were not agriculturalists.

> Australia has been built up by men who came here from the Old Country, and established here new homes for themselves, and it is our desire that the Northern Territory, where there is plenty of land, and but few people should be settled with people of our own race . . .
> As [to] the question of land tenure, honourable members are aware that I favour the freehold system. In the case of the Papuan lands we were confronted by a wholly different problem. There we had to deal with a large native population of whose habits we knew little, and whose rights had to be respected. We had to be careful in dealing with the land which this race had owned for ages; but the position in regard to the land of the Northern Territory—that uninhabited wilderness—is different. There we should have, perhaps, not more than a couple of thousand aborigines, and there should be no difficulty in doing justice to them, while at the same time dealing with the land in a businesslike way. (Sir John Forrest, Commonwealth Parliamentary Debates, 1912, quoted in Riddett 1990, 22, 56–57).
>
> What is to be the future of Northern Australia? Many persons who have had no personal experience of that great territory hold the

wholly erroneous view that it is a land of waste and wilderness, of sand and spinifex. Such a view is wholly wrong. For a distance of 200 miles from the coast it has an average rainfall of 30 to 40 inches a year, and in places much greater than that; there are many thousands of square miles of plateau covered with luscious Mitchell, Flinders and blue grass. The very richness of Northern Australia makes it a danger to Australia while it remains unoccupied . . . (Brisbane *Courier* 9 May 1933, quoted in Riddett 1990, 16–17)

In parallel to the commonwealth parliamentary debates on the Northern Territory, Graham-Taylor writes of the Western Australian debates:

The empty North was often described as "the weakest link in Australia," "a serious menace to the whole Empire," and we continually read that it was necessary to people the north so as to "complete the chain of defence essential for the protection of Australia against the thousand millions of coloured people adjacent to Western Australian shores." (1978, 38)

The first suggestion of a dam on the Ord, in 1921, came from Kimberley pastoralists concerned about salt water intrusions from tidal activity. Commissioner for the North West Drake-Brockman had plans drawn up in anticipation of being able to use the water for irrigated agriculture, but things went no further at that time (43). According to Graham-Taylor, in the wake of World War II the Commonwealth Rural Reconstruction Commission reported that it

felt that the emptiness, and present primitive stage of development in the north of Australia were a reproach in the eyes of the world, and claimed that "Australia would be in a much better position to face the assembled nations in conference if she were able to state unequivocally that she was committed to a scheme of this kind as a genuine endeavour to utilize the empty north." (84)

This tradition is continued in the Western Australia brochure for Stage II, which continues to frame the expansion potential of the scheme in terms of empty land: "The Ord River Irrigation Scheme in Western Australia's far north is a unique agricultural and horticultural area unmatched by any other growing region in Australia. What sets it apart is an abundant supply of reasonably-priced land and water and an excellent climate" (Western Australia 1996, 3).

It is important to remember that alongside the long history of "develop the north" rhetoric, there has also been a long history of critique. This has come from geographers (for example Griffith Taylor's public arguments against the concept of Australia Unlimited) and from agricultural economist B. R. Davidson.

> Seven years of cropping experience on the Ord have simply demonstrated that it would be cheaper to pay people to live in the area and do nothing, than to subsidize farming in the region. Although this was apparent after four years of cropping on the pilot project, the Commonwealth government in 1968 decided to proceed with constructing the main dam and completing the project. It is possible that this decision was made on political rather than economic grounds as it was made immediately before the Senate election in 1968 in which the Liberal government had every reason to expect a loss of votes in Western Australia. (Davidson 1972, 279)

Today we often tend to set environmental critique against the forces of economic rationalism, but in this debate they have been on the same side, with Davidson's powerful arguments based on the economic inefficiencies of the scheme: "Using existing techniques it would be cheaper to allow water stored on the Ord scheme to flow into the sea than to attempt to use it" (286). It remains to be seen whether the changed economic circumstances since Davidson's study facilitate the kind of "productive" agricultural activity necessary for the massive public investment in the Ord to be recouped.

The Invisibility of Aborigines and Their Interactions with the Land

In their review of the social impacts of development in the East Kimberley, Coombs et al. argue that

> Aborigines have been generally excluded from any significant role in the development process and their contribution to development and its effects on them have been largely ignored by the enterprises concerned and by governments ... Only in the pastoral industry were Aborigines integral to the enterprises as the main workforce and source of local knowledge ... Aboriginal influence on the managerial conduct of pastoral stations, urban enterprises, or mining enterprises has been peripheral. They had absolutely no say in major decisions

such as the construction of Lake Argyle, building the town of Kununurra or establishing the Argyle diamond mine. (1989, 110)

There is a widespread perception that white colonization of northwestern Australia, based on extensive pastoralism and mining, fatally wounded "real" Aboriginal culture. Recent research challenges the "fatal impact" model of colonization with much more complex pictures of accommodation and resistance. In particular, detailed oral histories recorded by Shaw (1981; 1983; 1986) give the lie to the view that all Aboriginal attachments to country had been broken by the incursion of pastoralism (a view that may be seen as part of Stanner's Great Australian Silence). These records document the names and significance of many places in the Kununurra–Lake Argyle region. The widespread and "profound sadness" to which Shaw refers among many Aboriginal people is poignantly expressed by Bulla Bilinggiin (already quoted in the introduction).

> My grandfather in the same way took the *Djadu* [the sacred artefact] back right back to this country. He left it in a big cave over on the hump of a hill close to the river bank and it was drowned. It's finished now, that's the full strength of it. We have only the singing part, that's all. The rest is under water ...
>
> I wanted to get it out. I didn't know they were going to put this backwater right up to Argyle [the Argyle Dam and Lake]. I should have shifted that Thing myself but I was too late behind. The water was all over then. No good looking. Yes, it made me feel sorry for that. I had a feeling for that. I was roaming too much in that country, you know, going around that country all the time. I don't like to look at it [the water]. My private Law is under water now ...
>
> We went out on a boat and I showed a museum feller the place, you know, where it was drowned. That Thing, all that was just like what you call a map for the whole of the earth, see? That's the proper Law. That was a round thing, round like a turtle buried there. It was only Wood you know, one board, see, just like a turtle. If you got it and brought it into this country you could just bluff everybody, bluff anybody. They couldn't say, That's my land, it's my land, that my land,' they couldn't do it. The white man couldn't climb over it. You could tell him, 'This is my country. See, this my land. This is my property.' Oh, you can put it in the book now but it's all under water. (Shaw 1986, 171–72)

Shaw's work also emphasizes the long history of Aboriginal attempts formally to regain land that they had never ceded (e.g. Shaw

1981, introduction), with limited success. Whether as a smokescreen or as a genuinely held belief, the "productive" use of land was regularly invoked as a justification for denying Aboriginal rights.

> The last meeting of Wyndham–East Kimberley Shire Council decided that granting of Long Michael Plain and Coolibah Pocket to the Aboriginals would be detrimental to the future of the area concerned which has long-term possibilities of irrigation and should be retained as a connecting tourist route between the two lakes. It also decided that none of the land in the vicinity of Lake Argyle, including Golden Gate, should be released until the potential of the lake had been fully explored and Aboriginals had demonstrated their ability to fully use land already granted to them. (*Northern Times* 2 Nov. 1973, quoted in Shaw 1981, 26)

In case there is any doubt about the rights of contemporary Aboriginal people to participate in determining the futures of the Kimberley region, a detailed study by Crough and Christopherson (1993) shows them to form the long-term demographic base of the region and to be fundamental to much of the regional economy. For example, based on the 1991 census, approximately 45 percent of the resident Kimberley population are Aboriginal people, and 30 percent of the Wyndham-East Kimberley Shire (Crough and Christopherson 1993, 22–23). Aboriginal people are much more likely (83 percent) to have lived in the same statistical local area five years ago than non-Aboriginal people (35 percent) (23). Moreover, "If the value of production of the Argyle diamond mine is excluded from estimates of the regional economy, then spending attributable to Aboriginal people in the Kimberley region represented approximately 40 percent of the income of the Kimberley regional economy in 1991–92" (265).

Although many aspects of Aboriginal relations to land remain invisible unless explicitly articulated to outsiders, archaeological evidence offers a physical expression of Aboriginal settlement and occupation. The process and results of archaeological work in relation to the inundation of Lake Argyle are detailed by Dortch (1972; 1977). Subsequent work on the excavated materials showed that the Miriwun shelter dated to at least eighteen-thousand years before the present.

Archaeological evidence threatened or compromised by Ord Stage II includes rockshelter occupation sites and rock art complexes that attest to a long period of occupation and interaction with the landscape (Fullagar et al. 1996; Tacon et al. 1997). Importantly, there is also evidence of continuing association with the country in the post-European period, when Aboriginal pastoral workers were laid off during the wet season, visiting sites on foot and carrying out ceremonies (Head and Fullagar 1997).

In the draft public environmental review for Ord Stage II the management objective in relation to Aboriginal culture is expressed as "to ensure that changes to the biological and physical environment resulting from ORIA-M2 do not adversely affect cultural associations with the area." This document recognizes that potential impacts include "increased competition and reduced access to areas for hunting, fishing and ceremonies" and "increased conflict with other land users." Three proposed management strategies are flagged: "increased emphasis on communication with Aboriginal stakeholders and groups"; "encourage involvement of Aborigines in construction and development activities"; and "include cross-cultural awareness training for all new workers and residents" (Sinclair Knight Merz 1997, table B). This is not to deny that Aboriginal people have agency in this process, nor imply that there is unanimity in attitudes towards Ord Stage II. As Davies and Young (1996) have shown for other parts of the region, Aboriginal people and communities continue to employ a range of strategies in dealing with land management issues. Rather I am concerned to identify the views of land within which such participation and negotiation is constrained. There is little opportunity for Aboriginal people to express an alternate reading of the empty land through their detailed associations, named places and land-based responsibilities.

The Idealization of Agricultural Land Use

Agricultural production was mooted for the Kimberley as early as 1841, with the publication of George Grey's *Journals of Two Expeditions of Discovery in North Western Australia*. Grey wrote of the country around the mouths of the Prince Regent and Glenelg Rivers: "[t]he cultivated production for the growth of which the country and climate seem best adapted are cotton, sugar, indigo and rice" (quoted in Graham-Taylor 1978, 20). The British need for cotton—and desire to find a source outside America but within the Empire—kept this crop at the forefront of debates from Grey's time through to the 1920s.

Implicit in the agricultural vision of the monsoonal tropics is the enabling mechanism of harnessing water, specifically the large quantities which fall in a short period of the year. (The corollary is a perception of unharnessed water as "wasted.") Storing huge volumes of water in an environment climatically attuned to seasonal flushing has of course environmental consequences. A number of scientific concerns about the environmental and human health consequences of Stage I have been raised (e.g. Stanley 1975; Millington 1975; Charters 1975). Shaw (1983, 22) reports Aboriginal concerns about the health impacts of heavy fertilizer and insecticide applications to the original cotton crops. They also noticed fish losses in the Ord River below the drainage outlet.

Other environmental problems have related to overgrazing in the upper reaches of the Ord catchment prior to the dam being built, which fed high rates of sediment deposition into the dam. Management options included improved catchment management, dredging, and raising the spillway to increase the yield (Ord Catchment Public Forum, 6 Sept. 1991, Kununurra). Both the former and the latter have been carried out, and sustainable water yield is now promoted vigorously to potential developers: "Despite initial set-backs, the scheme has developed into an agricultural oasis in what was an extensive cattle grazing region. Success in the development of a viable agricultural system on the Ord could provide the basis for the establishment of many more irrigation areas on rivers throughout the north of Australia" (Agriculture Western Australia 1995, 5). Why an agricultural oasis is preferable to extensive cattle grazing—let alone hunting and gathering—is not explained, yet much is assumed; the most "productive" use of the land, in terms of calories extracted or dollars made per hectare, is presented as a given, as not requiring any justification.

Once again, it is too early to tell what the environmental outcomes of Stage II will be, despite a rhetoric that suggests that all potential problems are being taken care of. Indeed it is arguable whether we already understand the impact of the original dam on the long-term ecology of the region, twenty-five years being a short time in ecosystems. My point here is not to argue the environmental merits or demerits of the scheme, although the evidence available suggests that attention to these has been little more than cursory; rather it is to focus on the way that the environment has been constructed as awaiting the creative hand of agriculture to fulfill its true potential. In her analysis of the language associated with pre- and post-dam landscapes, Arthur (1997) shows how a landscape of "deficiency" and "excess" is transformed by the dam into one of "light" "energy and" "fertility."

Agriculture and Tourism

As the landscape of the alluvial plains becomes increasingly domesticated, there is likely to be a conflict with the demands of the other main arm of development in the region, tourism. Tourism throughout the Kimberley depends on images of isolation and adventure, marketing the region as "Australia's last frontier." Although in recent years depiction of that frontier has included images of latter day pioneers wresting rockmelons, sunflower seeds, and corn from the harsh and unforgiving landscape, there is likely to be a limit to this symbiosis between agriculture and "adventure" tourism.

This ambiguous relationship between agriculture and tourism is illustrated by further examples. Backpackers—many from overseas—are identified as an important sector of the tourist market because they stay in the area longer than other tourists and often seek casual work in horticulture: "There is therefore a strong synergistic link between this sector of the tourism market and the projected expansion of agriculture/horticulture provided for in ORIS Stage 2" (Naralup Associates 1996, 6). At the same time, the document identifies one of four reasons why East Kimberley tourist growth is likely to exceed the state average as "the growing relative importance of nature-based tourism and interest in indigenous culture."

The intertwining economic fate of agriculture and tourism is discussed in a 1993 economic evaluation of Stage II. The growing tourist demand is in the area of "rustic, unique experiences," yet the key to meeting that demand is the upgrading of Kununurra Airport to international status (Hassall and Associates P/L 1993b, 26). Justification for such an investment is also tied to the complementary service it would provide for "high-value, low-volume agricultural products that are suited to air freight" (26). Moreover, agricultural development will enhance confidence in investment for tourism by extending the presently restricted tourist season in two ways: increased airport access will improve accessibility at times when road access is inhibited by wet weather, and an enlarged agricultural industry will lead to increases in business and family visits that are more likely to be year-round (27). At the heart of these predictions then is the intensifying contradiction that although the tourist and agricultural industries need each other because they both need the Kununurra airport, the images of nature that underpin each are mirror images. It remains to be seen whether a fecund production and trade zone for internationally competitive agriculture can keep itself rugged, remote, and wild for tourists. This is not yet an actual land use conflict—Ord Stage II is not on land of particular interest to adventure tourism—but a conflict of images. Contradictory images can clearly be maintained in the face of considerable evidence to the contrary; the historical construction of an empty land and of fatally wounded Aboriginal cultures, for example, is pervasive even in this region with a large Aboriginal population. Contemporary Aboriginal people face the further parallel contradiction that tourism wants their culture, or at least images of it, but the land-based relationships that underpin social identity are being systematically undermined by the alienation of further land for agriculture.

Destiny and Development: Naturalizing the Inevitable

The three colonial conceptualizations have been consistently utilized throughout the twentieth century by people and organizations for whom the Ord River Irrigation Scheme and associated developments represent the natural order of human progress in northwestern Australia. Arthur (1997) discusses the way the creation of Lake Argyle is presented as an act of redemption, of completing the creation. However, the naturalization extends beyond images of land and people to the political and agro-industrial process itself, for which a key strategy to entrenching and maintaining development is to naturalize its inevitability. Thus present decision-making is situated as a continuation of strategic and visionary, as opposed to ad hoc and opportunistic, past decisions. If urgency can continually be invoked, alternative perspectives such as Aboriginal ones can be cast in the role of impediment.

> The processes of decision-making on the Ord River Scheme involved a seemingly endless sequence of small, incremental and uncoordinated adjustments on the part of both the Commonwealth and the Western Australian governments . . .
> Each individual decision relied on what had gone before and in turn influenced future decisions. Early, low cost decisions such as the decision in 1959 to construct the Diversion Dam on the Ord River, built up a momentum that made later, higher cost decisions such as the decision to go ahead with the Main Dam, imperative. (Graham-Taylor 1978, ii, 15–16)
>
> We have come a long way. We are not turning back. (Premier Court in the *West Australian*, 23 July 1974, cited in Graham-Taylor 1978, 399)

> The Ord Irrigation Project is the result of careful engineering, agricultural investigation and planning. (Agriculture Western Australia 1995, 4)

> Australia is the driest inhabited continent in the world. To not use the water that is available in the area would be a travesty. (Senator David Brownhill, Parliamentary Secretary to the Minister for Trade and to the Minister for Primary Industries and Energy, quoted in the Kimberley Echo, 17 July 1997)

In a political arena of competing myths, the big picture is likely to look better if it can also be presented as carefully thought out and strategically implemented. The Ord irrigation project may be an engineering marvel, but its depiction as an example of thorough and inclusive regional planning cannot be sustained, as Graham-Taylor's detailed study shows. (Indeed, as she emphasises, there is much we have yet to find out about Stage I because of the thirty-year embargo on certain commonwealth archives.)

Part of the momentum for Stage II has been created by the huge volume of capital investment that occurred in Stage I. As an economic evaluation of Stage I makes clear, the only way to see an economic return on that investment is to keep going: "It is our judgement that if the Ord Project is to ultimately provide a net positive return to the nation, the release and development of additional land for irrigated agricultural production must be facilitated" (Hassall and Associates P/L 1993a: 78). Hassall's cost-benefit analysis of the Ord project for the period 1958/59 to 1990/91 shows "a net loss to the nation of (1990/91) $492 million" (44); turning this into a net benefit by 2020/21 depends on further development not being prevented (36). Thus a number of documents make it clear that "the Governments of Western Australia and the Northern Teritory are committed to developing the Ord River Irrigation Scheme to its full potential."

Such a big picture creates its own momentum, including an aura of inevitability consistent with the view of agriculture as the most productive form of land use and thus an option to be pursued wherever possible. Ord Stage II may be a fait accompli, but it is one with a range of possible futures, along a spectrum between a white elephant and a productive, socially harmonious oasis. The actual social and ecological outcomes will depend partly on the extent to which the myths discussed here match real people's aspirations. On present evidence Aboriginal people's aspirations—focused primarily on regaining access to and control over the country—have little in common with the goal of being the sugarbowl of southeast Asia. Nor is it clear that the latter vision is either economically or ecologically sustainable.

"Selling Paradise and Adventure"

My critique of the myths on which the Ord River Irrigation Scheme has been founded offers no support for a replacement set of myths based on simplistic conceptualizations of "timeless" people living in a "pristine" environment, yet many images in common usage within the tourism industry come dangerously close to this vision of the Kimberley. Waitt (1997) explores how the Australian Tourist Commission has defined and packaged an Australian identity to position Australia within the international tourism market. This process requires Australia to be differentiated from competing products in markets including North America, Japan, Europe, and other parts of Asia. Waitt argues that the representations of landscape have changed very little from the nineteenth century, with the myths of "Arcadian paradise" and "adventurer's frontier" still dominating. This is partly to meet the escapist motivations of a clientele who overwhelmingly live in metropolitan centers: "[T]o meet the demands of adventurers the landscape of the interior (The Red Centre) is symbolised in the visual text [television advertisements] as a wild, rugged, vibrantly red "wilderness" . . . all of course devoid of people (a founding concept of colonial appropriation)" (Waitt 1997, 50). Moreover, representations of indigenous people in the advertisements are as part of the landscape, ahistorical and romantic. The visual images of Aborigines used are male, loin-clothed, and holding spears. By contrast, because the vast majority of Australians live in coastal cities, "[c]ityscapes are represented as the familiar; locations of sophisticated civilisations from which the fantasy of escape can begin" (50).

National images commodified for overseas consumption are potentially very different from Australians' images of themselves, let alone the lived experience of most Australian lives. Nevertheless, the depictions have similarities. Waitt discusses ways in which overseas perceptions of Australian landscape and peoples can have repercussions that eventually affect that local lived experience; for example, "Predominance of representations of Australia as a rural paradise and wilderness have already had significant negative impacts upon levels of foreign investment from Asia" (1994, 10). Moreover, these outside impressions are also becoming influential in domestic environmental debates (as discussed further in chapter nine).

Summerland

Apart from the hype and the legend, what is it that beckons half a million people to the Penguin Parade? It offers the excitement of the outdoors at night with the security of a cinema, the waiting for a ritual of nature (apparently resilient to the regular presence of an audience) to commence. Eager kids arrive hours before dusk and are cold and grumpy by the time it comes. Parents encourage, eyes straining to pick the first black patches in the ink and white floodlit surf zone. The penguins tease, a few loners surfing in, then scurrying back to wait for the mob. They gather in the curl of the waves, letting them crash emptily on the beach. Suddenly, they're here. Some kids are still cold and grumpy and unenchanted, and leave soon after the first few batches. Others wait, fascinated, until the floodlights are turned off and the colony is left to enjoy its family life in the dark, noisy peace. The show is over.

I have an interest to declare here, for my family's house is one of those earmarked for removal on the back of a truck. Mine are the children of a transitional generation. Not for them the chance to devegetate sand dunes with their pirate games. On a summer's day there are just too many of them; there would be no sand dunes left. They must follow the fenced track to the beach and back again. At the same time, they are the last generation to sleep with the penguins and to proudly take visitors under the back steps to see them. (But not to touch: Frighten a penguin into vomiting up their daily catch and you will have the blood of a starving chick on your hands. It is a moral dilemma for a curious seven-year-old.) Soon, the back steps will be gone, although they might leave the chimney footings for nesting boxes; for their children, and for their children's children, it will be the boardwalk, the interpretive center, and taxidermy. In one sense today's Australian children have access to much better environmental education than was the case twenty or thirty years ago. For many the holiday experience at Phillip Island now includes nature walks and junior ranger activities, in an environment characterized by the rehabilitation of past damage. However, primarily because of the problem of numbers, that experience is more distant from and less engaged with a nature than can be touched, held, eaten, chased, and rollen in.

Where the houses have been removed, the spaces have been recolonized with little wooden boxes, looking like angular igloos but with fold-up bits on the lid to allow the environmental manager to monitor things. The surrounds are landscaped—sand is mounded around and planted. It has the deadening commuter feeling of the outer suburbs—some of these patches are close to a kilometer from the beach. But what else can you do with a growing population?

I have no argument with any of this restoration. I am quite happy for public policy here to be racist towards plants and animals, to get rid of the northern invaders. I suppose what annoys me is the statement that "there are no recorded sites of historical significance" (PIPRCM 1989, 13). Follies, mistakes, ugliness, difference. Are such things historically insignificant? The Cat Bay jetty, teetering and beyond repair, but there. A fibro shack—if it was in Antarctica it would be a national treasure. And just as intrusive. There are ambiguities here that need to be articulated in order to decide how useful they are. Domestic and residential dimensions of contemporary human life are considered incompatible with this environment; the visitor is encouraged. The history of Aboriginal residence is celebrated and legally protected as part of this nature; the archaeology of Euro-Australian activity is evidence of cultural impact and therefore physically removed. However, the Aboriginal life to be permitted is explicitly prehistoric; there is silence on any contemporary Aboriginal attachment. Two hundred years ago Aboriginal people utilized a wide range of food resources; today's nature cannot be eaten. Nor is it to be touched; today's visitors are enjoined in several languages to "Take nothing but photos, leave nothing but footprints."

8

Aboriginality, Hunter-Gatherers, and Tradition

> While in a Western political-economic tradition, the idea of a sentient landscape is preposterous, the starting point for the commoditization of the northern landscape and for the Northern Territory land rights act is the spiritual relationship between Aborigines and the "living landscape" . . . By promoting difference as a commodity value—the startling difference between an objective and a spiritual view of the countryside—the actual difference in perspective is threatened to be subsumed into a common market system . . . And Aborigines must themselves maintain a particular form (the traditional man and woman) in order for them to remain commodities in the economy of difference.
>
> —Povinelli, *Labor's Lot: The Power, History and Culture of Aboriginal Action*

Philosopher Val Plumwood critiques that version of ecofeminist thought that replaces Virginia Woolf's "angel in the house" with the "angel in the ecosystem." Woolf's angel was "intensely sympathetic," "utterly unselfish," and above all, "pure" (Woolf [1931] 1993, 357). In terms of their relation to nature this myth is widely applied to Aboriginal people as well as to women, in the forms of the Noble Savage and the Earth Mother. Plumwood's analysis of the way that it operates against women is apposite also for Aboriginal people: "[u]nlike the more usual misogynist accounts which western culture provides of women, it recognises strengths in women's way of being, but it does so in an unsatisfactory and unrealistic way, and again fails to recognise the dynamic of power" (1993, 9). Moreover, as the Earth Mother is twinned with the Whore, so the alternative to the Angel in the Ecosystem is the Future Eater (Flannery 1994).

This is just one of a number of cross-cutting essentialisms relating to the Aboriginal-land relationship. To be sure, essentialism—with its connotation of fundamental natures (often but not necessarily based in biology)—is possibly too fixed a term for these themes. Of greater importance than terminology is an examination of the ways that such themes can be empowering and/or disempowering, and for whom. Aboriginal people have much to gain by emphasizing their powerful attachments to the land, but where does this leave urban Aborigines whose attachments have been broken? For example (as discussed in chapter one), recognition of certain Aboriginal rights in legislation carries the attendant risk of reifying particular expressions of Aboriginality as the authentic ones. The interplay of local, national, and international processes and images is also an important theme of this analysis. On the one hand Aboriginality has become increasingly commodified for international tourism, but on the other hand international human rights forums provide new avenues for Aboriginal political struggles when national ones do not deliver.

I begin by analyzing two themes that are susceptible to essentializing approaches. The first is "Aboriginality," something that is usually defined as a question of ethnicity, race, and/or culture; the arena in which these contested definitions play out most often today is the relationship between indigenous people and the state. The second is "hunter-gatherers," a term that still has wide academic currency but that can seem quaint in public discourse. As we have seen, the notions of hunters and gatherers have historically been defined in economic terms, as particular ways of making a living; contemporary academic discussions, however, focus more on the question of whether hunter-gatherers should be seen in social terms, in the way that they authorize for example particular types of land use. Little of this analysis has filtered beyond the academy, so that part of the dilemma is that mainstream Australia (perhaps subconsciously) conflates the notion of Aboriginality with images of stone-tipped spears, wooden digging sticks, and witchetty grubs. Thus a third essentialism, that of "tradition," threads through the other two. As Pred and Watts argue, "[t]he realm of 'tradition' or 'custom' provides much of the symbolic raw material around which local communities, interest groups, and classes rework and refashion the modernizations of capitalist transformation" (1992, 15). Moreover, these dilemmas must be understood in a nested political context, encompassing both intra-Aboriginal perceptions and identity and their interactions with the wider society.

Aboriginality

The category of Aboriginality or Aboriginal identity is constructed in a number of different ways, by different forces, for different reasons; thus, these identities can compete and coexist. To argue over which one is the most appropriate is to miss the practical point that a range of different actors are simultaneously creating images. For example, Weaver (1984) distinguishes between public and private ethnicity, while Langton (1994) distinguishes three contexts of construction of Aboriginality: Aboriginal people interacting with each other; stereotyping and mythologizing by white people without first-hand contact with Aboriginal people; and in dialogue between Aboriginal and non-Aboriginal subjects.

Cowlishaw argues that Australian anthropologists maintained a submerged definition of Aborigines as a race even after they had rejected biological race as an appropriate variable for categorization; even with the shift to social anthropology and its interest in the unsullied traditional cultures of northern and central Australia, "the concept of discrete *a priori* categories of human beings ... isometric with the concept of race" remained central (1987, 223). This focus implicitly denied both the authenticity of Aboriginal people in for example country towns and cities and also the historical experience of those understood as traditional. Some of the ensuing debate among anthropologists is discussed here, but it is important to note that a related debate was commencing among historians.

Attwood (1989) reviews the historical investigation of Aborigines since the 1960s in three stages: oppositional, revisionist, and Aboriginal. Oppositional history is exemplified by the work of Charles Rowley and the early Henry Reynolds, as critical of government policy and bringing to light the violence of the European invasion. The revisionist stage Attwood sees as trying "to understand contact from the point of view of Aborigines rather than Europeans, and to cast Aborigines as active agents rather than passive objects shaped and controlled by European colonisers" (1989, 136–137). There was a tendency, Attwood argues, for early workers to take a bipolar approach to "Aborigines" and "Europeans," although later examples show greater complexity in patterns of acculturation and accommodation. In Attwood's final stage, Aboriginal stories of their own past differed "in both form and content," emphasizing "loyalty to familial roots and kinship bonds, strong historical identification with place, continuing associations with the rhythms of the physical world, and the enduring pull of the religious realm" (140, 141).

> I think that the way the aboriginal peoples came to be Aborigines—as an ethnic group in itself and for itself—should be the subject of inquiry. This means focusing not on their "being" but on their "becoming" ... [W]e will not reach a proper understanding of the recent history of the aboriginal peoples here until we see Aborigines as a social and cultural formation, an historical—and hence changing—category arising from processes which can only be studied as these evolve over a considerable period of time. (149)

In 1992, Attwood contended "that power, knowledge and Aborigines are mutually constitutive—that they produce and maintain one another through discursive practices which can be known as Aboriginalism" (1992, ii). He distinguishes between "hard" and "soft" primitivism in colonial representations of the (ig)noble savage. Early romantic depictions—"soft"—are echoed by recent ones that express our desire for the "deep past European Australians ostensibly feel they have never had, and a spirituality they have apparently lost" (iv; see also Lattas 1992 and Murray 1992b). Frontier representations in contrast were mostly "hard," out of fear of the indeterminate nature of Aborigines. Following Cowlishaw's point about the burdens of inauthenticity, Attwood contends: "Since 1788 European representations of Aborigines have undoubtedly undergone considerable change but basic forms of Aboriginalist knowledge and power have not altered ... And such is the burden of a totalising concept of Culture that Aborigines 'writing back' against Aboriginalism tend to be caught within its paradigms" (Attwood 1992, xi).

The political implications of three discourses on Aboriginality—descent, persistence, and resistance—were examined by Hollinsworth (1992). He preferred resistance because it is "more dynamic, theoretically elucidatory and politically inclusive" (137). Response to Hollinsworth's preference for dynamism was heated from a number of sources. Mudrooroo Nyoongah criticizes the anti-essentialist position (its political stance against racism notwithstanding) by reminding us that

> Aboriginal thought does strongly incline towards the essentialist position: the template of the Dreaming ancestors being the guide to the present and future, that is conservation rather than revolution. This

conservative stance in Aboriginal thought is strengthened by references to "strong blood," "purest genes," or even the "Aboriginal souls" postulated by some Aborigines I have been conversing with. (1992, 156–57)

Lattas argued that "Hollinsworth's paper is an example of the way essentialism has become the new buzz-word for conflating and confusing all perceived wrongheadedness in the social sciences" (1992, 160).

Beckett asked, "Why then do such qualities as spirituality and closeness to the land remain at the heart of both Aboriginal and non-Aboriginal constructions of Aboriginality? Hollinsworth blames the anthropologists for fetishizing the 'tribal' Aboriginal," but (Beckett argues) it is more deeply rooted in Australian culture (1992, 166). These and other references illustrate that essentialisms can be both empowering and constraining (Lattas 1993; see also Langton 1993 on constructing the stereotype of the drunken Aborigine).

One context in which this power is played out has been the incorporation of Aboriginality into discussions of Australian national identity. For Hamilton, "It is as if the whole question of Australian identity is being reopened through an appropriation of the Aboriginal presence as a sanction for the settler presence in the country—indeed, for the presence of Australia as part of a world cultural scene" (1990, 23). Hamilton traces the historical roots of this process via two circuits of meaning. From pastoral times (pre–World War II) we have the good, real Aborigine, "clearly associated with 'the bush,' with nature, with mystic power and 'tribalism.' " The converse circuit is associated with "towns or cities, loss of cultural identity, lack of control and 'detribalisation' " (21). Hamilton argues that disengaging with the bush and creating pan-Aboriginality as essential leaves a path of authenticity open for urban Aborigines.

> These two circuits of meaning have retained a singular power up to the present day. However, more recent events have challenged and reordered their signifiers. Part of this challenge has arisen from Aborigines themselves . . . This new circuit of meaning attempts to overcome the distinction between "bush" and "city," and neutralise the image of Aborigines as natural and, therefore, non-cultural. Instead, it draws on images of power, of an intimate, mystic and indissoluble link with the land, and the perpetuity of Aboriginality as an essential identity irrespective of its location . . . This circuit of meaning has to a significant extent been constructed by Aborigines themselves. (21–22)

Hamilton locates the image's appropriation by the wider society in themes such as the environmental movement and the commodification of Aboriginal art. Moreover, it is not separate from societal consciousness of the high antiquity of Aboriginal occupation, including at the highest levels of government. Left unspoken so far in these discussions is the question of whether this makes Aboriginality something we can all aspire to.

For cultural geographers it is the multiplicity of such voices which is of increasing interest, together with analysis of how they interact to construct landscape and place. For example, the location "Redfern," an inner suburb of Sydney, or even more precisely "Eveleigh Street," is sufficient to evoke in the Australian consciousness a ghetto displaying "the full range of symptoms of social pathology" (Anderson 1993, 314). Anderson challenges its popular conception as a "naturally evolved slum" (331) by showing how its development as an Aboriginal housing project arose when Aboriginal activists "armed with a counter-hegemonic language of 'Aboriginality' " (316) and their white supporters were able to situate the project within a broader rhetoric of "land rights," which in the early 1970s fitted the agenda of the newly elected federal Labor government of Gough Whitlam. The various actors all had their own interests in the project, some competing and some overlapping.

Hunter-Gatherers

Although it crosscuts the more political construction of "Aboriginality," the notion of "hunter-gatherers" is important here because it is a category closely tied to land and to the way that land is appropriated and used. Although Aboriginality has both emic and etic uses, hunter-gatherer is a categorization applied from the outside; individual Aboriginal people often refer to each other as "a good hunter," but it is not a term with wide currency that they use to define their group identity.

Hunter-gatherers have long been distinguished from agriculturalists partly on the basis of attributes that they lack. They do not have cultigens, they do not clear vegetation, they are not sedentary; in summary, they do not have a discernible impact on their environment. Although anthropological and archaeological research now clearly shows the distinction to be wanting, for both empirical and theoretical reasons (as discussed in chapters two and three), it has been extremely persistent. Why has the dualism between hunter-gatherers and agriculturalists been so entrenched in Western thought for so long? Is it simply a residue of colonial anthropology or is there something more fundamental at issue? The debate is a continuing one; my purpose here is not to resolve it but to highlight several issues that have implications for the way that Aboriginal people and their relations to land are perceived today.

As we have seen, the placement of hunting societies at the base of the evolutionary ladder—clearly influenced by the colonial enterprise—stemmed also from their position in the geological strata of Europe. The persistence of the divide is in no small measure due to its apparently distinctive archaeological signature. Davidson argues that instead of the Mesolithic being a meaningful transition between fishing-gathering-hunting lifeways and agriculture, "it is an artefact of the methods of study of archaeologists—not a fundamental division in the progress of human evolution" (1989, 75). Today in the heartland of the Neolithic there is considerable debate about exactly what the Neolithic is (Thomas 1991; Gosden 1994) and the extent to which an economic revolution actually occurred. Is this then a dichotomy that might be archaeologically useful because visible, but otherwise has little to recommend it?

Recent scholarship has tended to focus on the social differences between hunter-gatherers and agriculturalists. Davidson suggested that rather than one being the evolutionary outcome of the other, they represent two different choices made by different groups; each were separate outcomes of the more generalized subsistence strategies at the end of the Pleistocene. The differences between the two—and the reasons for agriculture's widespread dominance—lie in the way that land and resources are appropriated; following Ingold (1980; 1986), these are characterized as collective appropriation for fisher-gatherer-hunters and individual appropriation for agriculturalists.

Chase (1989a) maintains that there is something distinctive about hunter-gatherer lifeways and that it lies in the ways in which resource use is socially authorized. (This is particularly interesting because his earlier work [Chase and Sutton 1981; Hynes and Chase 1982] is widely cited for its demonstration of the subsistence similarities between Cape York Aborigines and New Guinean horticulturalists.) Chase notes that

> even today, in Aboriginal societies where social integration is emically perceived as exhibiting unbroken continuity with the pre-European period and where it is exhibited through fine-grained interpretations of the landscape in terms of sites, territories, and spiritually authorized human action, agricultural practices are still not accepted, even though other European technologies and artefacts have been adopted. (1989a, 52)

He argues, following Giddens, that interactions with particular natural environments and with other groups reflexively "draw upon local traditional authority from the past and, at the same time, they create the interaction windows for the future" (45–46). Intensification of social and cultural filters results not in change towards agriculture but in a resistance to major interpenetration; with their "complex and deeply integrated religious beliefs and practices, societies such as those in Aboriginal Australia may have passed a critical threshold of receptivity to major alteration which would be required for acceptance of agricultural practices from neighbours or visitors" (51). Although Chase's arguments have not to my knowledge been addressed in the wider literature, there are clearly opposite views; for example, in a recent overview, "the link between production on the land, the transmission of knowledge, and the reproduction of social formations among hunter-gatherers may not universally distinguish hunter-gatherers from small-scale agricultural or pastoral societies. We have yet to define a rubicon with social consequence and substance that can systematically differentiate these societies" (Feit 1994, 438). Questioning of the categories themselves also raises the issue of whether Australian hunter-gatherers display traits generalizable to other groups.

While not explicitly addressing the differentiation debate, Povinelli offers important insights in her challenge to the theoretical divide between Aboriginal culture and economy. Povinelli's work with the Belyuen people of the Cox Peninsula, west of Darwin, takes further the idea of the conceptual transformation of the landscape in exploring how Belyuen women understand the transformative power of their labor. In the process Povinelli challenges the culturally specific ways in which hunter-gatherer productivity, work, and leisure have been measured by Western anthropology. For example, time not measurably economically "productive" on hunting trips is in fact productive in reinforcing social identity; "providing the conditions for country and people to 'find' the historical and mythic relationship that exists between them" (1993, 186), time spent "just sitting" contributes in turn to economic well-being. Povinelli thus argues against any easy disarticulation of cultural/ceremonial and economic/subsistence activity: "From an Aboriginal perspective all matter is the congealed labor of mythic action. While some mythic actions were concentrated in the Dreamtime past at certain, now sacred, sites, the land is more generally permeated by signs of present-day mythic intentionality and agency" (137).

In particular, Povinelli identifies four facets of the relationship between hunting action and cultural expression (see 1993, 139). First, the sentient landscape, with which all hunting trips interact, "most commonly encounters humans engaged in economic, not ritual, activity." Second, economic activity is understood as "the embodiment of human and mythic ancestral desire." Third, "hunting and gathering anchors local discourses of power and land tenure." Fourth, attention to the intersection of the cultural and the economic is important to understanding historical identity. The latter is seen in the way that laboring, landscape, and memory interact in a socially productive way:

> Belyuen Aborigines see social and cultural history in both the side products of their economic labor and the deliberate marks they make ... the lonely flapping of bright nylon strings left tied to poles once used to secure a mosquito net, the husked shells of various seasnails and crustacea left half-buried in the sands of a seasonal camp ... Even without the string or the shells, a place holds memory insofar as its use is remembered. Further, memories are seen as a product of work like other products of economic and mythic Dreaming action ... It is not enough to see land use as depositing social and historical debris to be gathered up and remembered, a kind of local archaeology of the self and social group. According to Belyuen Aborigines land use also creates and refashions the preexisting features of the countryside that are then put to use. (146)

Having explored some of the conceptual tensions in the notions of "Aboriginality" and "hunter-gatherer," I will use three example to show a range of contexts in which particular Aboriginal groups are living through some of these contradictions. As the case studies show, to see these situations as domination *or* resistance, or the people as victim *or* agent, would be too simplistic. Aboriginal people are dealing with externally imposed constraints, while reworking them to their own ends, in complex ways. It is these examples from the periphery, from locations of tension, that have the greatest potential to challenge and subvert perceptions built on the timeless primitive.

Hunter-gatherers, Sedentism, and the Cash Economy in the East Kimberley

As we have seen, the generational nomads came much later to the northwest than to the rest of the continent—only about a hundred years ago—so the echoes of their arrival still resound in the lives of living people. In contrast to the southeast, where the newcomers rapidly replaced the incumbents numerically, the northwest has been resistant for a century to white attempts to populate it and to open it up. The relatively recent timing of the incursions—and the bureaucratized nature of relationships between station management and their Aboriginal employees—has left a record of a different kind. Among the numerically significant Aboriginal population survive oral histories from the people whose parents and grandparents saw the first Europeans, the *kartiya* (whitefellas). Aboriginal people have had to contest a land ethic that rendered them and their relations to land invisible, all the while being constrained to participate within the new economy in order to survive. In this process, questions of Aboriginality, hunter-gatherers, and identity all intersect.

The particular story that I will examine here focuses on a space defined by kartiya boundaries, Legune Station, but is not fenced in by it. (The details of my narrative are drawn from Head 1994c). Legune Station was typical in that Aborigines were vital for the station labor force; at the same time, the highly seasonal climate provided the means for the curators of the country to fulfil their ceremonial responsibilities and to maintain their hunting and gathering skills. The wet season—bane of the kartiya because of its uncomfortable conditions and enforced idleness—was a time of release for Aboriginal people, who were all laid off until the next muster. Stories told by the first whites contain many of the images common to other parts of our story—the isolated frontier, the woman left alone with the children and the blacks, the bush blacks with frightening powers of observation and bush skills. By 1933 the Legune pastoral lease was still held by the English company famous for their manufacture of beef extract. At this time the residents included 11,423 cattle, 150 horses, 120 goats, and two mules.

> Regarding the general position, we find that the native and his lubra [Aboriginal woman] is being well treated by the lessees and in most cases the dependents are being fed and cared for.
> We find further that, whilst native labour is not generally over-efficient, it is a necessity to the pastoral industry at the present time (Pastoral Leases Investigation committee, quoted in Head 1994c, 174).

Detailed regulations governed the terms under which the pastoral lessee could employ Aborigines. The administration and monitoring of these has left a wealth of bureaucratic archival material, but we must read between the lines to imagine their impact on the daily lives both of the paternalists and of the recipients. Included in a 1952 census by a Patrol Officer Evans were Gypsy Mudtai and her children: Frank Dimget, born 1 July 1940; Friday Dedima, born 1 July 1941; Biddy Namera, born 1 July 1945; Kelly Djidjiginin, born 1 July 1947; and Harry Waupman, born 4 December 1950. Also recorded were Polly Wondunga and her children Bobby Porgundja (born 1 March 1949) and Sheila Nid-Burria (born 1 January 1951).

For a white historian it is jarring and untidy that people are here assigned arbitrary birthdays to correspond, for want of a better marker, with the new financial year. The lack of accuracy in something as fundamental as the date of birth seems to be an erosion of identity. This is compounded when the same person's name is recorded with a variety of spellings and impossibly contradictory birthdates. Records of claims made for maintenance of dependants show that Polly Wondanga, aged thirty, with her children Bobby and Sarah, was maintained throughout 1955. In the period 1 March to 30 June she was issued three yards of "cotten" material, one cardigan, and one blanket. Between July and December she received six yards of "cotten" material one "mosqueto" net, and four yards of "cotten" material for each of the children. In a 1972 census of Legune taken by Patrol Officer Cole, the residents include Polly Wundangu, estimated date of birth 1912.

I suspect that for Wandanga the fact that no one could work out exactly when she was born or how best to spell her name in English were the least of her worries. A far more profound erosion of her identity was the continued lack of acknowledgement of her rights to any of this country and the harrassment that was quite probably part of her daily life. The borders laid by Europeans over the East Kimberley continue to affect the lives of the people who live there. The first was the border between Western Australia and the Northern Territory. This particularly affects Aborigines, given the susceptibility of the Territory to federal control and influence; most dramatically, it means that in the Northern Territory Aborigines can claim land rights and in Western Australia they cannot. Such claims, however, are confined under the Land Rights Act to unalienated Crown Land or to pastoral leases held by Aborigines. Over sixty percent of the Northern Territory is held under pastoral leasehold, and it is the needs of groups displaced by this form of land alienation—who are ineligible to claim under the Land Rights Act—that have received much less attention in the public mind until recently. In its 1996 *Wik* decision, the High Court found that native title could survive the issuing of pastoral leases, but in the event of any inconsistency pastoral rights were to prevail. Through the late 1990s, there has been heated debate within Australia over the implications of this decision, with a bill before the federal parliament to further extinguish some of these rights in the name of "certainty" for mining and pastoral interests.

In 1986 an area of about seven square kilometers was excised from the Legune and Spirit Hills pastoral leases and returned to the forty-strong Marralam community as Crown Lease. Among the signatories were Polly Wandanga and Biddy Simon (fig. 22). The terms of the lease required the community to fence the area, install cattle grids on roads, maintain a firebreak along the boundary, and prevent accelerated soil erosion. A covenant precludes the keeping of cattle, pigs, or goats. Conversion to freehold after five years was to be dependent on continuous occupation (Head and Fullagar 1991). On the one hand, the area is clearly not large enough for forty people to live a hunting and gathering lifestyle, even presuming that was their goal and that a century of pastoralism had not irrevocably altered the available resources. On the other hand, the terms of the lease specifically prohibit land use options that are open to others, such as animal husbandry, although they are allowed to keep dairy cattle. (Apart from small herds on the irrigated pastures of the Ord River scheme, the nearest dairy cattle are probably three thousand kilometers away.) To white administrators, excisions were only ever meant as "living areas"; they have been criticized as "matchboxes" (Parsons 1986).

Such solutions as are being worked out are not particularly attractive to many Europeans. Both supporters and opponents of the "outstation" movement would like to cast it as a "going back" both in time and space—a return to a "traditional" lifestyle. The images jar with our vision of hunter-gatherers: the community gathered round the video, cheering on Rambo; Slim Dusty on the ghetto blaster; a production line of didgeridus for tourists to pay for a broken axle on the Hilux; Red Rooster chicken boxes in the bin after a trip to town.

In fact, bush meat and fish comprise a significant proportion of the diet (Head and Fullagar 1991), and when they have gone without, people talk about being "hungry for meat." Bush plant foods have been increasingly replaced by shop-bought carbohydrates such as bread, flour, and rice, for a complex suite of reasons. Nevertheless, traditional knowledge is maintained (fig. 23) and, for Marralam people, questions of subsistence and fulfilling expectations are secondary to the central goal of regaining access to and control over country, as custodian Biddy Simon tells:

Fig. 22. Biddy Simon *(left)* and Polly Wandanga *(right)* hunt for goanna in burnt *pandanus* woodland, Legune Station. Photograph by author.

We been like to come back and stay and we want country, you know? We like all this, we been missing very much you know, when we went to town and mission . . . I like to stay round this country or la station. Mission too many people, we only been there for might be ten years. In town and mission, Port Keats. I like to stay la this country. We been asking government to give us bit of land back, you know? And so we can teach our children how to run their own show when they come to be man and woman, you know? They'll understand, and so they can learn their children then . . .

This place we only been born la this station and all that, but our country back further up, you see. That's why we coming back to stay on this land, cause my mother been run this country and find Dad, over this side, when they been young, and have the family, you know. Eighty-one we been come here. Living for a while. Went back to town again when the wet come and we used to go back to town and stay there. And then when wet finish, back again. And still we been asking

Fig. 23. Biddy Simon digs for yams, Legune Station. Photograph by author.

them for grant money to give us, you know for build house and bit a block to stay on it. They been agreed all that straight away. I didn't find it hard from them, you know. And they been agreed for us straight away, cause we been have nothing.

We been talking to them why we coming back to the country. Give us bit a land back, to live on it. [See fig. 24.] We wanted house, water and things like that. We been asking them for money too.

We been just ask for enough for stay there, live, you know? Enough to sit down there. As long as manager don't want to stop us from camping places we know, you see.

We should be friendly and partner and all of that you know. We all la one land. Not only those getting away with this cattle business you know. And we getting nothing out of it. That not very good.

He only just holding for cattle, that's all and when he get all this money built up and he'll probably retire and give it away the station and go away, next bloke got to come and sit down, like that. (Head and Fullagar 1991, 42–43)

So how do people accommodate the grids laid over them? To what extent are they constrained by lines on other peoples' maps? The pattern of land use extends well beyond the boundaries of the excision, its

Fig. 24. Biddy Simon waters her garden, Marralam Outstation. Photograph by author.

viability therefore influenced by the formal and informal protections outside. These are in the form of "reservations" in pastoral leases, which permit the Aboriginal inhabitants of the leased land and those Aboriginal inhabitants of the Territory who in accordance with Aboriginal tradition are entitled to inhabit the leased land:

    a. to enter and be on the leased land;

    b. to take and use the natural waters and springs on the leased land;

    c. subject to any other law in force in the Northern Territory, to take or kill for food or for ceremonial purposes animals *ferae naturae* (of wild nature) on the leased land; and

    d. subject to any other law in force in the Northern Territory, to take for food or ceremonial purposes any vegetable matter growing naturally on the leased land (see Seaman 1984, 30; Boer 1989, 49–50.)

    Less clear is the extent to which fire, as an integral part of hunting strategies (particularly among women), is protected. A reading of official fire policies gives the impression that fire is a threat to the landscape and that everything is being done to minimize it. Indeed Aboriginal use of fire outside the prescribed early dry season burning-off period is technically illegal.

Despite the apparent increase in sedentism provided by houses, community mobility is high and resource use is spread across a number of different areas. Food and other goods go both to and from town. "Going back to the bush" is a simplistic reading of what is happening; "the best of both worlds" would be a better cliche.

All Aboriginal groups trying to regain access to or ownership of traditional lands have to conform to some extent to mainstream white perceptions of Aboriginality and Aboriginal land use. The common stereotype of "real" Aborigines as "the original conservationists," living in perfect "harmony with their environment" creates a backlash when people do not act in conformity with it. The stereotype contrasts the traditional past with the tainted present; Aboriginal accommodations to the colonizers are interpreted as the decay of a pristine culture rather than the creativity and flexibility of a dynamic one.

This is seen particularly in the marketability of various arts and crafts, where traditional and modern motifs and materials are combined (fig. 25). For example, a dillybag made by Biddy's mother sells to tourists in the arts and craft co-op in Kununurra. According to the label, the string is made from pandanus leaf rolled on the thigh. Before weaving, the string is boiled in water for a day with either the seeds or the roots of the bulmi plant; the seeds give a purple color, and the roots various shades of yellow. The dyed string is woven into a subtle striped pattern by weaving a simple knot, and a handle is attached. It must represent at least a week's work, and sells for $54.25. The same style of bag is also worked in acrylic yarns, in various color combinations including the black, red, and yellow of the Aboriginal flag, along with some much more garish examples depending on what wool was available. Although they are priced at $20–25, the tourists leave them sitting on the shelf for much longer.

At a more explicit, public level, there are different expectations to be met by Aborigines whose country happens to have been taken over by pastoralism or by national parks. Those trying to regain pastoral land meet an expectation that their land use will be "productive," while those in or in competition with parks are supposed to be "natural." A major bone of contention in parks is hunting and burning. Safety issues aside, burning is often frowned upon because tourists from thousands of kilometers away who have come to see wilderness do not like the look of blackened savannah. Although these expectations are usually implicit (and may not even be articulated by white managers to themselves) Aborigines are often acutely sensitive to the contradictions of the vision to which they are supposed to live up.

208   Reworking

Fig. 25. Jodie Hall paints on bark for sale, using a combination of materials including traditional ochres and PVC glue, Marralam Outstation. Photograph by author.

Welcome to a timeless land . . . It is CALM's privilege to preserve our national parks and reserves for visitors far into the future. We ask you to remember as you enjoy the Kimberley that this timeless part of Australia is fragile! (Western Australia Department of Conservation and Land Management [CALM] visitor information sheet, 1990)

They wanted me out and I wanted in because we got lot of dreamtime places to control. We should be recognised as traditional owners. That's our land, our country. (Chairman of Purnululu Aboriginal Corporation explaining his request for a living area within the Purnululu National Park, quoted in Coombs et al. 1989, 38)

We bin born and raised here. When we lose that country we'll be nothing. When we got a country back we'll be right. (Kija man, 1987, quoted in Coombs et al. 1989, 40)

A litterbag endorsed by the Bush Fires Board of Western Australia (1991) says, "Western Australia . . . too lovely to litter, too lovely to burn"; for many Aboriginal inhabitants of the East Kimberley, the country is too lovely not to burn. A road sign on the Victoria Highway in the Northern Territory near Keep River National Park proclaims, "We like our lizards frilled not grilled"; on outstations only a few kilometers away people love their lizards grilled.

Aboriginality and Land Rights

The interaction between internal and external perceptions as it is played out in land rights struggles is illustrated by the example of two different land rights committees operating in the South Australia country town of Port Augusta in 1981. Geographer Jane Jacobs (1988) argues that successful land rights claims depend not only on the internal cultural significance of the land but also the ability to articulate interest in the land in terms that fit government notions both of Aboriginality and of Aboriginal interests in land. These latter are constructed in a narrow field that depends heavily on the maintenance of "traditionality," expressed in such things as living on the land and speaking an Aboriginal language.

In the Port Augusta situation the two Aboriginal groups, the Adnyamathanha and the Kokatha, had had different experiences of the colonial process, which differentially affected their capacity to meet these externally imposed criteria. Jacobs uses three particular examples of the way that their interests in land were structured within this wider political arena. First, they used male elders to represent them publicly, "in part a response to the incorrect assumption among external agents that only Aboriginal men have a spiritual interest in the land" (1988, 255). Writing some time after the field research, Jacobs notes that this bias is being overcome, and it is now much more common for women's separate interests in land to be externally recognized.

Second, the reification of the concept of "sacred site" in the wider consciousness—and particular external definitions of what constitutes such sites—forced people to articulate their interests in land in these terms. Mundane occupation sites are less readily accommodated within external perceptions of the "sacred"; moreover, the idea of a site as a bounded entity acted against conceptualizations of land operating at a broader landscape level. Because the Adnyamathanha had a long-standing relationship with the government's official site recording authority, including participation in a site recording program, they "appear to have more sites and a more vital culture than the Kokatha"

(Jacobs 1988, 257). Many Aboriginal groups, including the Kokatha, have consciously resisted participating in site recording programs, due both to the sensitivity of the information recorded and to the fear of loss of control of knowledge about land. The prevalence of official registers provides the external agents with "control of the very information which is integral to the dialogue of land rights politics" (257). In this example, the Adnyamathanha were more successful than the Kokatha in competing for scarce political resources.

Jacobs's third example of the ways in which the political dialogues are structured is tribal territory and identity. Following colonization the Adnyamathanha lived mostly on a mission within their country. Because this settlement, Nepabunna, is within the topographically distinct Flinders Ranges, the association of people and place was further enhanced for external consumption. The Kokatha by contrast had to work much harder to publicly articulate their identity with a particular tract of land, partly because for them the colonization experience was characterised more by dispersal.

Although a number of details of this scenario have probably changed since the early 1980s—many government agencies for example have a broader conceptualization of "sites" than just dots on maps—the theme of having to conform to an externally imposed model of what constitutes Aboriginal authenticity is still valid in most parts of Australia. Rose (1996b) explores its operation in the Northern Territory Land Rights Act. She argues that Northern Territory Aboriginal people, with similarities of "history, modes of land tenure, systems of knowledge and proof," have been active agents in establishing the ritual and practice of the claims process over two decades. However, "the possibility is that in the post-Mabo era these land claims may become a canon of authenticity for proof of land tenure systems which could oppress and dispossess other Aboriginal people, not entirely because of the Act itself, but rather because of the cultural specificity of the claimants within its zone of applicability" (1996b, 52).

Aboriginality and Conservation

In the year following the battle over the Franklin River in Tasmania, conservation interest shifted to another battle front at the other end of the continent, the Daintree rainforest of northeast Queensland. In a study of the relationship between Kuku-Yalanji people and conservationists Anderson (1989) compared the understandings of the various actors. In particular he focused on Aboriginal support for a road being put through the forest, and conservationists' surprise at this stance. Anderson suggested

> that a model of interaction between Aborigines and Europeans which I have developed in other recent work has something to say about this seeming paradox of an Aboriginal man, born and bred in the bush, knowledgeable as few others are in this area about Bloomfield Aboriginal culture, welcoming with open arms a road development which would, at the very least, cut a swathe through and bring numerous Europeans into lowland rainforest areas used by the Kuku-Yalanji for camping, for hunting pigs and cassowaries and for gathering nuts, scrub hen eggs, and which, at worst, would disturb more than 30 burial sites and at least two important sacred sites. (1989, 219)

According to Anderson, Aboriginal behaviors are not "natural" or "given" but arise out of a particular political and economic context, whether in the past or in the present. Explanations for Kuku-Yalanji support for the road should be sought not in the notion that they were "untraditional" but in the fact of competition between two critical elements of their political economy: *jawunkarra* ("mobs") and *majamaja* ("bosses"). This political structure survived European arrival because individual Europeans with whom people had regular dealings (for example mission managers) were considered to be parallel in function to the majamaja. Only particular types of "intervention complexes" allowed groups to maintain themselves in this form. The Europeans had longterm residence; among the complex set of circumstances, "they had to have an adequate economic base; they had to need Aboriginal labour; they usually needed a language-learning capacity; and they required a strong physical and personal presence and a fictive kin relationship with locally prominent Kuku-Yalanji" (223).

Anderson argues that recent "hippie" immigrants to the area, seeking an alternative lifestyle, "represented an intervention complex which has affected Aborigines—by alienating land, preventing hunting and foraging access to other land, etc. Yet it is one that is lacking any enduring, particular social context" (1989, 224). This relationship, or lack of it, was thus seen not as neutral but as dangerous and hostile. These new settlers, for the Kuku-Yulanji, represented the entire conservation movement.

Whatever the attitudes of individual Aboriginal people, according to Anderson, their political economies did not have a concept of conservation because they did not need one: "Our culture is perhaps the only one that needs to invent and articulate such a concept, because ours is the only one which has had the capability to destroy the environment on the scale that we now have" (1989, 219). (This view is reflected also by Rose 1996c.) Thus, "as long as Aborigines are viewed as natural conservationists and not as political actors within complex systems involving both Aboriginal and European factors, this relationship will remain for the white conservationists one with ideological phantoms and not with real people" (Anderson 1989, 226).

The National Park

September 1991. Four Aboriginal men and a white archaeologist sit in the back of a landcruiser at the entrance to the national park. They are accompanying a Sacred Sites officer and a park administrator to a proposed camping area to make sure it is not placed too close to sacred sites. They wait in the midmorning heat outside the ranger's house as the two white bureaucrats gather the necessary paperwork. There is little conversation and flies gather inside the windscreen and under people's hats. The archaeologist shoos them in annoyance.

"Hey—careful. Careful now. You might kill them flies. You in national park now," chortles Paddy.

9

Beyond the Colonial Heritage in Environmental Debate

The education campaigns, membership drives and political campaigns of environmental organisations are an important barometer of colonial anxiety, inasmuch as they are the representations of the new generation of Australians seeking to establish a cultural security in landscapes full of colonial memories.

—Langton, "Art, Wilderness and *Terra Nullius*"

My proposal is that the tensions explored throughout this book—and encapsulated in Professor Marcia Langton's quote—may serve as starting points for a new kind of conversation about how Australians interact with each other and with the land. I have tried to build an argument that pays more careful attention than previous ones to the social dimensions of landscape construction. This is not to deny the increasing physical challenges to sustainable human occupation of the continent; rather it is precisely because of our demonstrable environmental problems that we need the best possible cultural understandings. Non-Aboriginal Australians need to understand both Aboriginal ecological relationships and our own as stemming from such social relationships. In neither cultural tradition does environmental impact flow automatically from race or from economic activity.

Australians have yet to develop the founding myths that will inspire us to work towards socially and environmentally sustainable occupation of our continent. As part of this process, there is a widespread yearning among non-Aboriginal Australians to draw on the strength and insights of Aboriginal attachments to the land—a yearning that goes hand in hand with bewilderment as to how precisely this could be done. We cannot as a society fish with a bamboo spear or subsist on the bush tucker so glossily portrayed in television series and on our coffee tables. With New Age exceptions, we are sceptical of spiritual relations that are portrayed as superstitious rather than grounded and pervasive. We know our society has been guilty of many appropriations. How do we listen and learn without continuing the process?

Are we to forego any lessons from Aboriginal ways of relating to land for fear of continuing the colonization process? To paraphrase Plumwood, can we really afford to lose such a powerful source of alternative vision and cultural challenge? No and no, but it is not quite what we might have expected; the Aboriginal voices heard in this book have not spoken of a land empty of humans. The clear and common perception is of a world brought into the human realm, socialized, domesticated by myths, narratives, songs, and art. The concept of land without designated human stewards is alien: "This land must belong to someone." Perhaps ironically, the backyard—the place held in such affection by many Australians—has more in common with Aboriginal constructions of the world than has the national park.

I start with a case study of an American scholarly debate that highlights the interaction between "scientific" and "postmodern" approaches in an Australian context. Following nine threads, I then explore the persistence of the colonial heritage in environmental debates and suggest ways that we can go beyond it. There are implications here for both practice and theory. My argument is that even green approaches to Australian environmental problems are hampered by a lack of awareness of the cultural context that has produced them. By identifying the ways in which our current solutions are still partly framed in colonialist terms, we can work towards better solutions. It is a measure of how deeply the dualistic framework of human relations to nature is embedded in our thinking that I fear that in critiquing concepts such as wilderness, I will be seen as an apologist for woodchipping, uranium mining, or cotton irrigation. The arguments that "because the Aborigines had an impact on the environment we can chop down this forest" or "because nature is a social construct we can do whatever we like to it" are untenable.

Indeed, as Gill argues, a critical approach to the "naturalisation" of landscape "can help in clarifying the bases of conflicts over resource management and conservation" (1994, 238). He was discussing the way that the rural community on Kangaroo Island, South Australia, had been marginalized by the National Parks and Wildlife Service emphasis on biophysical and visitor management. In this case the islanders had characterized their use of fire as similar to a "natural burn regime" in encouraging regeneration of vegetation. Park managers—aiming to prevent any further post-European modification of the environment—saw this as simplifying the vegetation over time. In this conflict there were thus two different views of what is "natural" for the Kangaroo Island environment. Gill argues that because "the social context of reserves has not been significantly addressed" (237) the land use conflict became more complex than it needed to be. Such is the appeal of the natural in these debates that even the mining industry, when its development ethos is challenged, seeks to position itself and its impacts as "natural" (McEachern 1995).

Because I have emphasised a range of ways of seeing the land, it is important here to clarify the ground on which I am arguing. I am in agreement with Gandy (1996) that although the world has a separate existence from us, our knowledge and understanding of it can only ever be partial and is mediated through social practice. In Australia as elsewhere the delineation of the extent of our "environmental problems" has come to us through positivist science; examples include holes in the ozone layer, measurements of soil degradation, estimates of the sustainability of logging operations, and mapping of lands affected by salinity. However, understanding the ways in which our knowledge is "mediated through social practice" is critical to working towards solutions. Moreover, these dynamics are thrown into relief by the other sorts of knowledge to which postmodern approaches have alerted us.

The threads of my argument, which are of course interwoven, are as follows.

1. Theorizing of environmental issues is not a waste of time, it is vital. Cross-cultural approaches must recognize not only the importance of talking but also the fact that the way that we talk and negotiate is an expression of power relations.

2. Dualistic approaches have severely limited our ability to deal with the central question of the human presence in Australia.

3. The environmental debate has become so deeply embedded in the rhetoric of persistence, continuity, and preservation of remnants that the vocabulary of change has been surrendered almost completely to the development lobby. As part of this process, Aboriginal people have become imprisoned by the same rhetoric; "tradition" is seen as something static and unchanging.

4. Imagery of arks and relics is differentially useful in different ecosystems. It may be appropriate in relation to old growth forests,

which can validly be depicted as continuing to survive against the climatic odds. For other types of forests, however, and for most arid zone ecosystems, we need a different sort of imagery.

5. Non-Aboriginal Australians need to historicize ourselves. Quick to see the impact of early Europeans on the Australian environment as an outcome of their own view of nature, we are somewhat slower to turn the critique upon ourselves. How does the notion of wilderness disempower Aboriginal people, for example? To what extent has the positioning of the Aborigines as "out there" contributed to a situation where the environment considered worth saving is also "out there," thus leading to a concentration on green rather than on brown issues—even though the latter affect the daily lives of most of the urban conservation lobby much more than do the former (James 1992)?

6. Supposedly universal environmental precepts such as biodiversity and conservation are themselves cultural constructs.

7. Some Aboriginal people and ecologists recognize the profundity of post-European landscape transformation in Australia. Acknowledging this "third nature" is likely to produce better environmental decisions than attempts to return to the past.

8. International conceptualizations of Australian environmental issues have an even stronger colonial heritage than do domestic ones. As international agreements have increasing influence in the political arena, this is of more than academic interest.

9. To remain useful and to resist becoming tomorrow's frozen essentialism, any new myths must recognize multiple layers of meaning, operate at a range of scales, and express their own ambiguities. We have one such myth already—*country*.

Postmodernism, Science, and Australian Feral Horses

The difficulty of threading a path through both science and cultural critique is shown in debates such as those between Symanski (1994) and Dear (1994) and between Demeritt (1994) and Cronon (1994) (see also Soper 1996). The discussion between Symanski and Dear—both Americans—about feral horses in Australia also illustrates other useful points—the interaction (or lack of it) between intellectual debates and on-the-ground issues, and overseas perspectives on "domestic" management problems—in the context of a vitriolic exchange on postmodernism. My main point, however—concerning science and cultural critique—is one considered peripheral by those authors; we can only ponder the role of place in influencing our respective positions.

Symanski summarizes changing estimates of the feral horse population in the Northern Territory during the 1970s and 1980s, arguing that the "problem" was redefined several times for various social and political reasons. He argues that there was no need to invoke postmodernism to explain these contested realities; rather, rigorous attention to the facts allows the correct interpretation to be chosen. In the process he appeals to the ecological reality of arid Australia as a basis for appropriate management decisions, including the necessity of culling horse populations. In his reply, Dear argues that Symanski's analysis could have been usefully informed by postmodernism, arguing that

> postmodernists are at the forefront of a reconceptualization of the relationship between people and the natural world. Among other things, this involves dismissal of the Man-Nature dualism and an ecology-based emphasis on the essential unity of the natural world . . . In practical terms, such viewpoints place greater emphasis on conservation and restoration rather than the exploitation of nature. (1994, 297)

For Dear, in this situation, conservation is equivalent to the rights of the horses not to be shot. However, as Symanski identifies in his subsequent response, an appeal to "essential" unity is an odd position for a postmodernist, particularly given recent deconstructions of old ecological realities (such as those discussed in chapter five). In particular, both these writers seem to have missed the point that there are other cultural constructions of Australia's feral animal "problem" than the ones that they discuss on the other side of the world.

Symanski dismisses "native disinterest" in the feral horse problem in a couple of sentences, arguing that Aboriginal people "have been slow to recognize land degradation associated with feral animals, in part because feral animals were, in their view, 'born to the country and therefore part of it' " (1994, 252). This is at least as important a "contested reality" as the actual numbers of horses, and it is one that needs to be problematized; if the intellectual reasons were not compelling enough, the increasing role of Aboriginal people in land management should be. Currently, Aboriginal managed land is around three times the size of Australia's government-managed conservation estate (15 percent versus 5 percent of land area) (map 13), and most Aboriginal

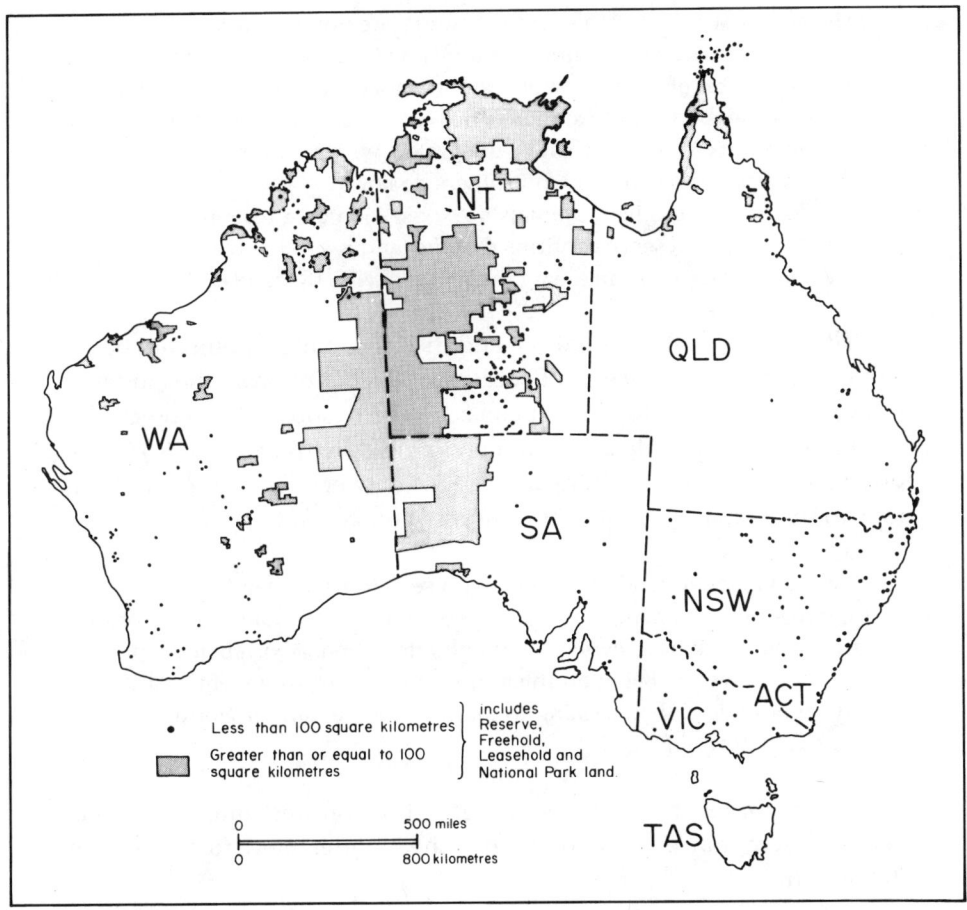

Map 13. Aboriginal land in Australia (simplifed after Horton 1994)

managed land is in the arid and semiarid zones. Any attempt to deal with feral animal "problems" that does not take account of Aboriginal perspectives is doomed to failure.

As Symanski recognizes, these animals are now seen by many Aboriginal people in central Australia as incorporated into the ecosystem. In some cases they are also now covered by Aboriginal law: "Wild pussy cat from here, some rabbit from here too. Pussy cat got Dreaming, some wild pussycat got Law" (quoted in Rose 1995, 122). In such cases—or in instances where feral animals have become important food resources—Aboriginal people will often oppose eradication programs.

> The effects of feral animals on the country are not seen as a cause for concern. It is seen as a natural phenomenon that animals eat the grass and raise a bit of dust. To separate the impact of feral animals from native species on these grounds is not seen as logical. People see the contemporary ecosystem as an integrated whole so they don't see some species as belonging while others do not.
>
> In many areas feral animals are looked on as a resource of the country. Their presence confirms that the land is productive and people derive pleasure from seeing them in the wild. (Rose 1995, 128)

This is not a simple situation, and discussion of it should not be divorced from an awareness that because of alienation from the land and its radical alteration since European settlement, subsistence choices for most Aboriginal people are extremely limited. Nevertheless, Rose emphasizes, there are significant differences between Aboriginal and European understandings of conservation management.

> Unlike European land managers, who seek to understand and manage their environment, Aboriginal people base their management on practices which have evolved through interaction. Aboriginal people see themselves as being an integral part of the environment and its dynamics rather than seeking to manipulate the natural world from outside. (1995: 90)

This carries over into perceptions of extinction and into Aboriginal peoples' acceptance of changes that they understand to be beyond their control.

> While most Aboriginal people were concerned about the fate of native animals there were few who accepted the finality of the concept of extinction. For most people those animals may be missing from their country now but they must still exist somewhere . . .
>
> The most common reason given for why animals had gone from the country was the fact that the old people who knew the Law had passed away. As a result the activities which are important for the health of the country had not been carried out, or were being done in a diminished capacity. (95, 97)

As recorded also by workers in other parts of Australia, the country is seen as being "sick" when traditional management practices are not carried out. This "looking after" includes both ceremonies and burning the bush.

It is interesting from an Australian perspective that this debate is seen overseas as an issue of animal rights, from Linda McCartney to the Queen of England to Michael Dear. Within Australia the dominant view both among scientists and among conservationists is that feral animals are problematic primarily because of their impact on land and soil degradation, as Symanski argues. Outside views of Australia as essentially empty are expressed by Linda McCartney: "Surely the Australian Government can find a bit of land in that vast country where the horses can live in peace" (quoted in Symanski 1994, 251). As one Australian scientist said in a debate with animal rights activists, "I speak for the soil." Dear's emphasis on conservation and restoration would undoubtedly invoke wide support (even from Symanski) but exactly what this should mean is by no means self-evident.

Theory, Talking, and Power in Environmental Debates

In the intense day-to-day context of environmental politics, many activists see theoretical debate as a waste of time—as fiddling while Rome burns. However, whether practitioners reflect on them or not, green political positions (like those of mining companies) arise out of particular cultural contexts that have political implications. Moreover, there are enlightening disagreements among political scholars over the influence of theory in the Australian environmental context. An example: Hay and Haward argue that wilderness-inspired movements have made a significant theoretical contribution in their presentation of an ecocentric position.

> [E]nvironment movements inspired *primarily* by the desire to preserve wilderness (rather than opposition to nuclear power) have been instrumental in providing the green movement with an ethical basis that, in its practical implications, is of an advanced radicalism. This involves notably the notion that moral standing is not an exclusively human quality, but that non-human nature is also morally "considerable" (a position denoted as bio- or ecocentrism). (1988, 433–34)

They contrast this position (common in Australasia and North America) with the European situation, where anti-nuclear issues and their focus on human well-being and survival dominate the green agenda. The irony is of course that wilderness is neither essential nor existential; the ecocentric can be profoundly Eurocentric.

Tellingly, Hay and Haward locate the future of green political theory in "countries (such as those of North America and Australasia) which have frontier traditions and embattled areas of remnant wilderness" (1988, 447). A similar claim is asserted by Eckersley, who (comparing particularly Europe and Tasmania) locates the relative emphasis on either anthropocentric or ecocentric thought in "the degree of human (or, more particularly, European) domestication of the landscape" (1990, 70). It is no accident that ecocentric or wilderness-focused attitudes persist in putatively postfrontier societies, because they can be located exactly within the frontier mentality. Moreover, our identification and resolution of these issues is still profoundly influenced by what we understand to be the relationship between hunter-gatherer peoples (the indigenous peoples of those postfrontier societies) and their environment; whether in ecological or in philosophical debates, the question of naturalness is always at least partly framed in terms of the presence or activities of aboriginal peoples (Taylor 1990; Callicott 1991; Rolston 1991).

On the question of the role of theory, Doyle and Kellow disagree with Hay and Howard:

> But these "high theorists" have had little to do with the everyday practice of the environment movement in Australia . . . In short, the development of environmental politics in this country has been profoundly anti-intellectual. Much environmental action is built around the notion of urgency, that the time available to "save the planet" is severely limited. (1995, 10–11)

Doyle and Kellow see this political focus as leading to such emphases as the "cuddly animal syndrome" and the concern with rainforest preservation at the expense of soil degradation (11).

Theorizing is clearly important in the reflections it provides on (for example) the choice of priorities for political engagement. It is vital for clarifying the cultural bases of different environmental positions; this is particularly important when many non-Aboriginal people want to draw inspiration from Aboriginal attachments to land. However, in valuing the process of talking and thinking, we must pay careful attention to the ways in which power structures the debates.

Aboriginal people speak often of whitefellas stumbling blindly round the country, bumping into things, because they do not stop to listen either to the land or to the people who speak for particular parts of it (Povinelli 1993; Rose 1996c). Appropriate processes of listening and of negotiation are time-consuming, labor-intensive, and inconsistent with decisionmaking predicated on an image of urgency, whether for a development application or out of a sense of ecological crisis. However, not to take the necessary time is to enact decisions that may themselves be unsustainable.

Helen Ross (1995) shows how the processes of natural resources negotiation need themselves to be intercultural. Appropriate timing is one of the points she covers, speaking of the "ripening" of issues; others include recognition of the differences in decision-making procedures in Aboriginal and in non-Aboriginal society. Thinking about how to think and talk about things is an important prerequisite to nitty-gritty debates over (for example) the appropriate use of fire, harvesting of animal foods, or mining on Aboriginal land.

The Deception of Dualism

As argued by Plumwood, there are dangers in uncritically reversing the categories in a dualistic model in which "contrasting concepts (for example, masculine and feminine gender identities) are formed by domination and subordination and constructed as oppositional and exclusive" (Plumwood 1993, 31). Plumwood emphasizes that rejecting dualism does not mean rejecting dichotomies or differences, indeed she argues for a nonhierarchical concept of difference to be constructed in place of the dismantled dualisms. At the same time, she is attuned to the postmodern dilemma of having discarded a discredited identity (say, "woman") but having no positive identity to reclaim as a basis for political action: "A better route to subversion . . . would treat woman's identity as an important if problematic tradition which requires critical reconstruction, a potential source of strength as well as a problem, and a ground of both continuity and difference with traditional ideals" (1993, 64).

The logical structure of dualism includes the characteristic of "radical exclusion," with its "denial or minimisation of continuity", this "helps to establish separate 'natures' which explain and justify widely differing privileges and fates" (49). Both sides need to appear homogeneous to conform to and confirm their "nature," and the process of stereotyping is important in this. James (1992) argues that "it is through repetition that a stereotype gains cultural currency and authenticity," because after constant and consistent presentation of a relation between terms, such a link accrues [the] status of a natural category" (Edmunds and James 1992, cited in James 1992, 208).

Wilderness provides perhaps the best example of land use constructed within such a framework. Authors such as Nash (1967), Tuan (1971), and Powell (1977) have shown that definitions of wilderness, although constantly changing, have always been dualistic and ambivalent. For example, Tuan argues that there was a shift from previous centuries, when the city was seen as sacred and the wilderness as profane, to the twentieth century, when the attributions have been reversed; the wilderness has been elevated to the sacred and the city is now profane. Despite these and other demonstrations of its social construction, wilderness remains an extraordinarily persistent ideal in the West; this is true not only in popular culture, where the "essence" of wilderness is often invoked, but also in the highest levels of international management agreements.

Plumwood (1993, 162) identifies the dilemmas arising from this dualism as on the one hand the denial of difference between the nonhuman and the human, and on the other retaining the gulf between the two. The false choices generated by this dualism (215) lead to arguments such as "everything's really natural" (therefore, presumably, we can do no wrong) or conversely that nothing is natural (emphasising the apartness of nature). As Plumwood identifies,

> The use of hyperseparated concepts of human and nature which rule out the ground of interaction and demand that true nature exclude all human influence makes the concept of wilderness extremely problematic in relation to indigenous peoples who both sustain and are sustained by their land and its ecosystems. The forest gardens and tended landscapes which are home for such peoples come to be viewed by the master consciousness as pure nature, in which humans, if they have a place at all, wander and live "as the beasts of the forest." (163)

The romanticist wilderness position faces two cultural dilemmas in trying to create or to restore pure nature. The first arises in facing the people who think of a particular landscape not as wilderness but as "country" (Sultan 1991), who may see "wilderness" as just the next wave of colonial dispossession. A further irony perceived by Aboriginal people is that it is their stewardship that has created and maintained the landscape that others now value. The second dilemma is that creating an ecosystem without people is a necessarily social enterprise because such an ecosystem would be new—not seen in Australia for at least sixty thousand years, and then under very different boundary conditions. Of course there are good reasons why at the end of the twentieth century we might want to create such areas, but we should not be under any illusion: the social investment in keeping people and their impacts out will be an expensive one and will command resources that are then not available for other areas. The impracticality of a completely hands-off management strategy is now widely recognized, given that designated wilderness areas can never be completely isolated. Moreover, intellectual honesty demands that we claim such landscapes as our own cultural construction rather than depicting them as a reestablishment of past conditions.

Throughout this book I have used a range of examples that destabilize stereotypes both of Aborigines and of the land. However, it is important to problematize not only the subject matter but also the way that debates are constructed. Part of the problem in decolonizing discussions of Aboriginal land use is that virtually all of the images considered helpful to conservation debates have been ones related to impacts.

Impacts-Based Models and the Rhetoric of Persistence and Continuity

Aborigines, like other indigenous peoples, have provided a metaphor of people who tread lightly on the earth. Thus, what many Euro-Australians mean when they support "traditional" land use in say, national parks is hunting with spears on foot. For Aboriginal people, however, as we have seen, traditional land use is that undertaken with the appropriate social authorizations, according to law; the technology involved is a secondary issue, and the actual impacts that are the outcome are variable. Although there are many examples in the literature of authorized usage corresponding to what Westerners would call a conservationist ethic, such as leaving enough for next time, there are also examples where the social imperative to "clean up the country" and to imprint a human signature upon it leads to (for example) the burning of fire-sensitive vegetation communities. The conflation of tradition with particular ecological impacts disempowers those Aboriginal people acting outside of the stereotype of "harmonious" usage; more than that, it is of limited assistance in helping us to deal with our own gumbooted ecological footprint, supporting much higher population levels and resource utilization of much greater intensity.

That indigenous land use challenges the conceptual basis for many conservation strategies is illustrated by the issues raised in accommodating it within the International Union for the Conservation of Nature (IUCN) system for categorizing protected areas. This system "has the advantages of international recognition providing a convenient approach for comparison of the various reserve systems across jurisdictions" (Thackway et al. 1996, 20). Five original categories vary along an axis of "degree of human intervention," with protected areas managed for science or wilderness protection at the "natural" end and protected areas managed for landscape/seascape conservation and recreation at the "artificial" end (20–21). (It is interesting to note the privileging of "science," both as a reason for the highest level of landscape protection and as an activity focused on natural rather than on artificial landscapes.) A sixth category, added later, includes protected areas managed for sustainable use of natural ecosystems; Thackway et al. note that "it does not fit neatly into the general pattern" (21), but lies about halfway along the conceptual continuum. It is this category that is the basis for negotiation of indigenous protected areas. However, as Thackway et al. discuss, there are a number of issues that arise in trying to deal with indigenous land use along a continuum between "natural" and "artificial" activities. One is the "thin end of the wedge" argument: permitting any flow of goods and services will lead to commercial exploitation, for example of forest areas. Another is the IUCN distinction between natural values and cultural values, with the former having priority. As discussed below, such a distinction ignores the extent to which key concepts such as biodiversity and conservation are themselves culturally shaped.

Aspirations to primitive, unpeopled environments have intensified over time, in response (many would argue) to the fullness of most of the world. One example of interest is the ways in which photographic representations of wilderness areas have changed over time in their depiction of human presences. Flanagan contrasts the first known photo of the Franklin River, taken in 1890, with the Peter Dombrovskis photo of the Rock Island bend that played a central role in the Franklin campaign in the early 1980s (Flanagan and Pybus 1990). The 1890 photo shows the photographer's dingy moored in the foreground; the Dombrovskis photo—published in national newspapers on the eve of the 1983 election with the caption "Could you vote for a party that would destroy this?"—betrays no sign of a human presence. Elsewhere, Flanagan shows that there was another, earlier way of conceptualizing things within the green movement. The move to flood Lake Pedder (in southwest Tasmania) under a much larger lake to generate hydroelectricity is widely seen as the defeat that galvanized the green movement in Tasmania; that defeat spawned the United Tasmania Group (UTG), the world's first green political party.

> The UTG's vision was at once determined and crusading yet capable and tolerant of numerous expressions. If, for example, we take the pictures of Lake Pedder used by the UTG to draw attention to their cause, what is striking is the variety of aesthetic responses to Pedder: bushwalking snap shots jostle with modernist and abstract and romantic images, sometimes within the same photograph. In contrast, by the late 1970s TWS [the Tasmanian Wilderness Society] was using only one style of imagery: the high Romantic. (Flanagan 1990, 204)

Compromise, Arks, and Relics

The persistence of the view that the most appropriate criterion for assessing human relations to nature is along a continuum of impacts (see also Lesslie 1995) makes it very difficult to reconceptualize the problem: "The dilemma is a very real one. Environmental goods are what economists term 'lumpy': they cannot readily be compromised. You cannot really have 'semi-wilderness,' but you can readily have a diminishing area of wilderness as compromise decisions erode its margins" (Kellow 1990, 204). In terms of the big picture, is a larger area with minimal impact more or less compromised than a diminishing area with humans absent?

This notion of compromise, usually used in discussion of the extent to which environmentalists should become incorporated into mainstream politics, has a theoretical dimension as well. Kellow (1990) shows how the pragmatic and the philosophical are linked by exploring the victory over the Franklin River in Tasmania; widely lauded as one of the great environmental achievements of the 1970s and 1980s, the Franklin River victory did not come without costs, including a more environmentally hostile state government. Moreover, Kellow argues, the purist view both of wilderness and of politics has concentrated large amounts of energy and resources in fighting for the "residuals" at the expense of the less sexy but more severe environmental problems. The so-called cuddly animal or mist-covered rainforest syndromes make it much harder to fight successfully on banal issues such as soil degradation.

The notion of remnants surviving on the Australian ark—influenced by the insights of environmental prehistory (as discussed in chapter five)—conditions the debate in several ways. Doyle and Kellow show the links between remnants and a sense of urgency, in the feeling that "it's not too late" to save the last pockets (although it presumably soon will be). They argue further that a focus on the ark also contributes to a bias towards particular environments: "To preserve environments because they are unique (among other things) is really a 'Noah's Ark' approach. It concentrates on gathering a smattering of threatened environments, and neglecting the problems of the larger environments with less 'sex appeal'. One such area that has suffered this fate is the rural environment which, paradoxically, includes those areas that suffer most degradation on an everyday basis" (Doyle and Kellow 1995, 12).

This argument takes us back to the great ecological diversity of the continent. Although the ark metaphor and the notion of relic are highly appropriate for some environments—for many rainforests, for example, which persist in a remnant state for a variety of historical reasons (map 14)—they limit our ability to conceptualize a range of other environmental issues. Not even all "forests" are equal; different taxa within dry rainforest patches have been differentially categorized as "refugia" and as "opportunistic." We do not seem to have yet developed useful imagery and myth for the savannahs of northern Australia, say, or for the chenopod shrublands of the southern part of the arid zone. Some components of rangelands ecosystems have been advantaged by the long-term trend to aridity, so to categorize and manage them as "remnants" may not be appropriate. This is not to deny the major environmental problems on the rangelands, but to seek a more accurate vocabulary for conceptualizing—and ultimately managing—those problems. Is it simply a matter of making our questions more systematic and contextual? What does it mean to describe Australia as biological "ark"? How vulnerable is it? How resilient is it? Which components of ecosystems are "relic"? Which are "opportunistic" and "flexible"?

"Biodiversity Is a Whitefella Word"

The ecocentric perspectives described above by Eckersley and by Hay and Haward as being more inclusive than green arguments that focus

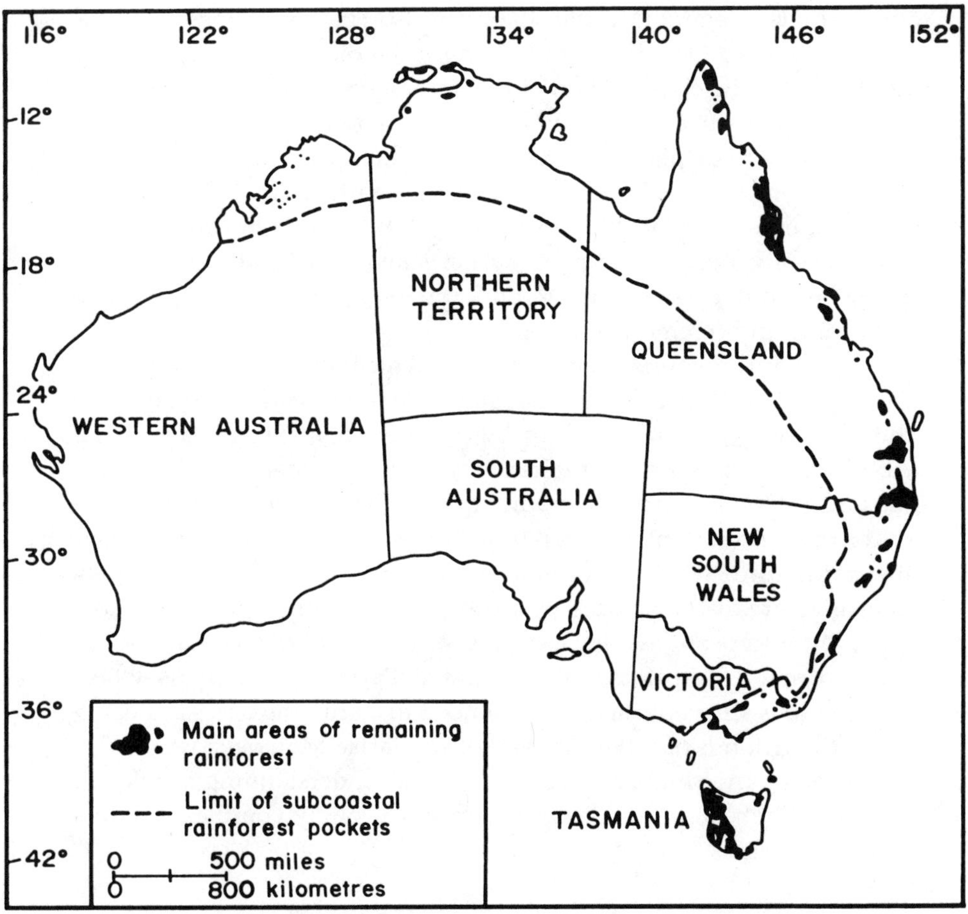

Map 14. Distribution of rainforest in Australia (simplified after Adam 1986)

on human utilitarian values may be so, but they also have strong Eurocentric dimensions of which we need to be aware. Listening to indigenous cultures means accepting challenges to the way that we perceive and classify the natural world. The discussion of feral animals and extinction (above) provides one example; Rhys Jones's and Betty Meehan's work in Arnhem Land provide others. In her study of Gidjingali classification of mollusca, Meehan collected molluscs belonging to 106 formal Linnaean species. Gidjingali people named ninety-seven of these, and placed them into fifty-four taxa; edible shellfish have very specific classifications, while many noneconomic species are lumped into a single category (Meehan 1982; see also Hiatt and Jones 1988). As Jones observes, "One of the underlying principles . . . was thus strictly utilitarian . . . the classification of the human predator" (1991, 30).

Is biodiversity as measured in numbers and types of species a universal measure of planetary survival? Not only is species a mutable category, but the available evidence suggests that Aboriginal assessments of ecosystem health and viability take a more holistic view. In her overview Rose's examples (1996c) show that healthy country is that where human stewards are undertaking appropriate actions such as burning and ceremonial activity.

There are of course many ways in which Western scientific and Aboriginal understandings of sustainable ecosystems overlap, and there are many examples now in Australia of scientists, managers, and Aboriginal owners working together. In emphasizing examples where the understandings are offset rather than identical, I am not being critical of these important projects. It is, however, important to recognize that most cases where Aboriginal people are acknowledged as joint managers are also instances where their ownership rights are recognized by European law, for example in the well-known examples of Kakadu and Uluru-Kata Tjuta National Parks. In situations where ownership is still contested, we still need to clarify the bases of negotiation, the grounds of difference and of similarity. Moreover, we need to ask whether any single model of ecological understanding provides a strong enough basis for dealing with increasingly complex environmental problems.

Third Nature

A good example of such a problem is the issue of restoration: following European colonization, are we confronted with such a transformed ecology that attempts at environmental restoration are not only intellectually misguided but in practice completely lacking in feasibility? This issue is widely discussed—in different ways—both by Aboriginal people and by ecologists, but less often by environmentalists, miners, or foresters. For extractive industries of all types, restoration of the environment has become an important part of the rhetoric associated with political permissions for their activities. Of course, the practice is something else again; as many people argue, replanting trees is not the same as restoring a forest.

The desire for places lacking human signatures is clearly strong. Given the difficulty of finding areas that meet even a "compromised" set of wilderness criteria after two hundred years of European impacts, there is likely to be an increased focus on the concepts of "renovating" and "restoring" natural areas. I do not want to argue against the practice of restoration per se, but if it includes obliterating the historical record there are hidden dangers (cf. Griffiths's 1991 discussion of cattlemen's huts in the Victoria high country). If, for example, our descendants a century or two hence were to believe that we had bequeathed them an untouched environment, they could perhaps live in happy innocence. However, if we bequeath them a historical record of how their environment came to be, we greatly increase their ability to deal with their own ecological problems (which we can only presume will be even more considerable than ours). As part of this process it is important to keep working towards an understanding of the human role in the creation of the various environments of Australia, a role that is still very patchily understood.

The theme of introduced plants and animals now being part of Australian ecosystems is expressed by many Aboriginal people. In addition to the examples documented in central Australia in Rose 1995 (some of which have already been discussed), Povinelli records the amusement and frustration of Belyuen women who are continually being asked by researchers to show them "traditional" foods: "All of these bush foods are Aboriginal, mangoes and everything, animals too, cows; let the researchers photograph anything now" (1993, 128). There is a parallel view among ecologists aware of the profundity of post-European landscape change, particularly in arid areas: "There are no 'natural' arid systems. Man will always have the responsibility because man, both black and white, has altered the land by his activities" (Graetz 1988, 138). As a society, however, we remain reluctant to grapple with the conceptual demands and responsibilities of the new ecosystems, couching many environmental debates in terms of returning things to a previous state. Even the scientific community is only just beginning to ask how postcolonial ecological research might operate in terms of sampling and analysis.

Debates over kangaroo culling—such as those that filled an entire issue of *Australian Zoologist*—show that aspirations to restore present-day ecosystems to an undamaged precolonial state draw on two further dualisms: the dichotomy perceived between agricultural and nonagricultural economies, and a further dichotomy between introduced and native biota. Sue Arnold, representative of Australians for Animals, asks:

> Will our descendants laugh or will they cry when they hear the story of people who, in spite of being surrounded by an abundance of fruit, vegetables, meat and fish, decided to kill their wildlife. Will they laugh or cry over their primitive antecedants, who in their wisdom believed that if they "farmed" kangaroos this would be beneficial to the human and animal populations. (1994, 143)

Peter Rawlinson, for the Australian Conservation Foundation, argues the basis on which, say, kangaroos and sheep could be treated differently.

> Wildlife species are those plants and animals living in an uncultivated or undomesticated state, that is they exist outside agriculture. Native Australian species are those that existed on the continent before the introduction of agriculture in 1788 which includes indigenous species such as the macropods that evolved here. These usages are entirely consistent with the definitions of native wildlife in the Commonwealth's Australian National Parks and Wildlife Act 1975 and the Wildlife Protection (Regulation of Exports and Imports) Act 1982. (1988, 130)

Nevertheless, those indigenous species now operate in ecosystems influenced, and in many cases degraded by agriculture. How might our understanding of this "third nature" and its management be improved if themes now embedded in the postcolonial practice of the humanities—interpenetration, accommodation, resistance—could be harnessed and reworked for the natural sciences?

International Perceptions: Layers of Other

As the management of protected areas becomes increasingly incorporated into international as well as into domestic management strategies (Wensley 1996), cross-jurisdictional understanding of environmental and of indigenous issues is likely to become more important. With the exception of the tourism theme, the literature has yet to pay appropriate attention to how these cultural understandings differentially affect policy development.

Linda McCartney's comments on feral horses (referred to earlier in this chapter) exemplify the view that Australia might be one place that the rest of the world can consider as "other," as "empty," and as the locus of pilgrimage and of salvation. (This parallels the suggestion of the role that the desert plays in the urban Australian psyche.) The most vocal campaigns overseas have been mounted in support of Australian fauna rather than flora or physical landscapes. Gordon Grigg, one of the first zoologists to propose commercial kangaroo harvesting as a solution to land degradation by sheep, accused Greenpeace of campaigning against this in Europe and America by arguing that the kangaroo was on the verge of extinction. Most Australians, he suggested, "seem to have accepted that there really are plenty of kangaroos and that the populations are not threatened by harvesting" (1988, 125). This is not to suggest that there was widespread support within Australia for kangaroo harvesting; in fact there was considerable opposition, stemming partly from the kangaroo's dual status as rural pest and as national symbol, most evocatively on the tail of Qantas jets. The introduction of kangaroo meat to restaurant menus in Australia has met with mixed reactions. However, domestic understandings are one issue; international ones deserve more systematic research in the future. In particular the articulation of long-distance arguments almost solely in the currency of animal rights needs to be better understood. This works in the opposite direction as well: Australians are extremely attuned to the situations of Japanese whales and of Canadian seals, less so to the subsistence and cultural needs of indigenous people in those two countries.

Country: A Peopled Land

In searching for new sustaining and sustainable myths, I suggest that the term *country* is a good starting point. Its multiple meanings flag the many ambiguities that attend the human presence in Australia, and it also provides the ground for a meeting of Aboriginal and non-Aboriginal aspirations. The usage of *country* in Aboriginal English is explored by Deborah Bird Rose, who defines country as "a nourishing terrain," noting that it "is not only a common noun but also a proper noun. People talk about country in the same way that they would talk about a person" (1996c, 7). Country can refer not just to the land but also to the sea and the sky. For most white Australians country signifies an affection for the rural (at the same time as it possesses more generalized meanings). Paradoxically, then, attention to Aboriginal ways of seeing country turns us back to sources of strength within our own tradition. Lowenthal has argued that while Australians are cynical about celebration of the past at a national or state level, "the best-loved Australian past is genuinely local. It is the nearby, intimate, family background that matters most, to old and new Australians alike" (1990, 49). (This point is also made strongly by Griffiths 1996.)

The third understanding of *country* of relevance here is the nation state, and the responsibility of this particular nation state for an entire continent encompassing great bio- and geodiversity. The local attachments and responsibilities thus interact with national and international ones. Consciousness of this interplay of scales is an important tool in assessing competing claims in environmental debates. In terms of the continent as a whole, a more rigorous examination and comparison of the scale of impacts, both in space and in time, helps us to demonstrate that not all impacts are equal, nor all changes equally desirable.

Although each of these meanings is interesting and relevant, it is perhaps the interplay between them that is most important; this very ambiguity prevents any one view becoming authoritarian and ideological. As Eagleton, discussing Barthes's view of language, argues: "The 'healthy' sign ... is one which draws attention to its own arbitrariness—which does not try to palm itself off as 'natural' but which, in the very moment of conveying a meaning, communicates something of its own relative, artificial status as well" (1983, 135).

10

Conclusion

Australians are having trouble with the past. We are not sure whether it is over or not.

I write this on 17 December 1997, the day after we cremated Ted Matthews, the last surviving Australian of the sixteen thousand or so who landed at Anzac Cove, Gallipoli, on 25 April 1915. The Turkish defenders provided solid resistance, but a beachhead for the Allied landing was secured and maintained for the following eight months. This brave and costly campaign is widely remembered as a baptism of blood for the young Australian nation. The governor-general, Sir William Deane, told the state funeral that Mr. Matthews's death marked "a final break in a living thread that united us Australians with the complete Anzac epic." Prime Minister John Howard linked the spirit born at Gallipoli to another great theme in the mythology of national identity, the struggle against a harsh and fickle land: it "may seem to slumber but arises to draw new breath when needed, amid ash-filled skies, flooded ground or the rubble of a disaster." Both men called for Ted Matthews's memory—and his injunction that we never forget the evils of war—to be honored by all Australians. Far from being a fading legend, Gallipoli and its annual commemoration Anzac Day, seem to have remained vigorous because rather than in spite of the passing of the original soldiers. Many young Australians are interested in exploring the legend for their own generation, and Anzac Cove and the Gallipoli Peninsula have become an important place of pilgrimage for backpackers.

Yesterday was also the day when the federal government gave its official response to the Stolen Generations report (discussed in chapter three above). The Federal Minister for Aboriginal Affairs, Senator John Herron, announced a financial package to facilitate family reunions; however, the government declined to apologize for the removal of

Aboriginal children from their families or to pay direct cash compensation for persons affected. Although this was a past that was still happening at least forty years after Gallipoli, it is one that we are now to consider over: "You might as well go and ask the British for an apology for coming to Australia with the convicts," said Senator Herron.

Some pasts are to be considered over and done with, and suggested symbolic gestures are brushed aside as irrelevant; other pasts are actively maintained through the reproduction of symbols. Memories of distant times are to be fostered; grief at happenings in our own lifetime is not to stop us from getting on with things.

I have explored in this book some of the multiple ways in which the past is intertwined with the present. The biophysical landscape provides particular types of inheritance, which people have reworked into their own presents over many millenia. In our turn, we rethread the stories and the land into the mosaic of a fuller, busier world.

There is a rhythm, an echo, in all of the areas we have visited. The tracks of the pioneers were made quite literally by someone else. From the English fens to the parkland of southeastern Australia to the campo of Paraguay, newcomers are surprised to find open spaces in new lands and are shocked when the owners get upset about sheep stamping out Yam-daisies. If terra nullius is a myth that must be discarded in discussions of the ownership of the continent, then it must be similarly discarded when we create and preserve landscapes. The concept of "land belonging to no one" could persist for so long only because it went with "land use unacknowledged by the colonizer," "landscape perception unrecognized by the colonizer," and "human imprint on the land unnoticed by the colonizer." What does it mean for us that for someone else the land was already known, named, bounded, occupied, home? These are not questions that can be answered quickly. Owning a past that even in the late 1990s is still being radically revised is one of those issues that must be allowed to "ripen." This cannot be cold storage ripening, however, where fruits are warehoused and left to themselves; rather, they must be fed and watered with thinking, talking, and questioning.

Dealing with the colonial legacy is only one of the challenges. Australian landscapes of the twenty-first century will be influenced also by social constructions of nature that are neither Aboriginal nor European in ancestry. I have referred to the increasingly global scale of environmental debate. We have not to my knowledge even begun to ask about the ways of seeing the Australian natural world that the new immigrants are bringing from countries such as Vietnam, Thailand, Turkey, or South Africa, to name a few. These are the perspectives—many of which have been hewn into their present form in environments much more similar to Australia than is northwest Europe—that will increasingly influence the shape of the land both in urban and in rural areas.

Glossary
Works Cited
Index

Glossary

Archaeology: the study of the human past through analysis of material remains.
Billy: metal can or pot for boiling water or cooking over a campfire.
Cycad: tropical or subtropical gymnosperm plant of the order Cycadales.
Drover: person whose occupation is the driving of sheep or cattle, especially to and from market.
ENSO: El Niño Southern Oscillation phenomenon. A cross-Pacific pattern of oceanic and atmospheric circulation, which oscillates on an approximately decadal timescale. During El Niño years usual upwelling of cold water off the Peruvian coast does not occur, the southeast trades are weaker, and ocean temperature is lower. Consequently there is a rainfall deficit over northern Australia.
Glacial: a cold phase during an ice age. A glacial maximum is the period of largest ice sheet extension.
Gondwana: ancestral southern hemisphere supercontinent, comprising Antarctica, Australia, and parts of South America, Africa, and India.
Holocene: an epoch of the Quaternary comprising the time since the Pleistocene, i.e. approximately the last ten thousand years.
Interglacial: the time period between two glacial stages, during which there is an amelioration of climate. The Holocene is an interglacial period.
ka: thousands of years.
Luminescence dating: methods that calculate the time since minerals were last exposed to heat or light. Includes thermoluminescence (TL) and optically stimulated luminescence (OSL).
Megafauna: a suite of large fauna, including mammals, birds, and reptiles that became extinct in the late Quaternary.
Moiety: a form of social organization in which people and natural phenomena are divided into two categories.
Native title: land rights that preexisted the extension of British sovereignty over Australia, recognized by Australian common law in the 1992 High Court *Mabo* case.

Paleoecology: study of the relationship between fossil organisms and their environments.

Pleistocene: the first epoch of the Quaternary, approximately two million years ago to ten thousand years ago.

Quaternary: the younger of the two periods of the Cainozoic, approximately the last two million years.

Radiocarbon dating: method of determining the time since the death of an organic material by measuring the proportion of the C-14 isotope within its carbon content.

Radiometric dating: methods based on measuring the rates of decay of radioactive elements within samples.

Sacred site: particular places in or features of the landscape that are closely associated with Aboriginal totemic history. The term is not Aboriginal but is now frequently used in legislative contexts. Popular usage often obscures the variety of sites and their attendant meanings.

Squatter: in eastern Australia a squatter was a pastoralist occupying crown land outside the limits of settlement. By the mid-nineteenth century such occupation had been regularized and validated with lease tenures, and the word became synonymous with pastoralism.

Succession: the sequential development of changes within a plant community.

Terra nullius: the concept of vacant, uninhabited land, belonging to no one.

Works Cited

Adam, P. 1986. *Australian rainforests.* Oxford: Clarendon Press.
Agriculture Western Australia. 1995. *Ord River Irrigation Area.* Bulletin no. 4311. Kununurra, Western Australia: Agriculture Western Australia.
Allen, J. 1983. "Aborigines and archaeologists in Tasmania, 1983." *Australian Archaeology* 16, 7–10.
———. 1993. "Notions of the Pleistocene in Greater Australia." In *A community of culture,* edited by M. Spriggs, D. Yen et al., 139–151. Canberra: Australian National Univ.
Altman, J. C. 1981. "Hunting buffalo in north-central Arnhem Land: A case of rapid adaptation among Aborigines." *Oceania* 52, 274–85.
———. 1987. *Hunter-gatherers today.* Canberra: Aboriginal Studies.
Anderson, C. 1989. "Aborigines and conservationism: The Daintree-Bloomfield road." *Australian Journal of Social Issues* 24, 214–27.
Anderson, K. J. 1993. "Place narratives and the origins of inner Sydney's Aboriginal settlement, 1972–73." *Journal of Historical Geography* 19, 314–35.
Anderson, K. J. and F. Gale, eds. 1992. *Inventing places: Studies in cultural geography.* Melbourne: Longman Cheshire.
Aplin, G., S. G. Foster, et al., eds. 1987. *Australians: A historical dictionary.* Sydney: Fairfax, Syme, and Weldon Associates.
Arnold, S. 1994. "The morality of harvesting kangaroos." *Australian Zoologist* 24, 143–46.
Arthur, J. 1997. "An unobtrusive goanna." In *Tracking knowledge in north Australian landscapes,* edited by D. Rose and A. Clarke, 37–49. Darwin: North Australia Research Unit.
Atkinson, A., and M. Aveling, eds. 1987. *Australians 1838.* Sydney: Fairfax, Syme, and Weldon.
Attorney-General of Australia. 1994. "Commentary on the Native Title Act 1993." In *Make a better offer: The politics of Mabo,* edited by M. Goot and T. Rowse, 264–82. Sydney: Pluto.
Attorney-General's Department. 1997. "Legal implications of the High Court decision in the Wik Peoples—v—Queensland: Current advice." Canberra:

Attorney-General's Department. Found at www.dpmc.gov.au/native/wik.html.

Attwood, B. 1989. *The making of the Aborigines*. Sydney: Allen and Unwin.

———. 1992. "Introduction." In *Power, knowledge, and Aborigines*, edited by B. Attwood and J. Arnold, i–xvi. Melbourne: LaTrobe Univ. Press.

———. 1996. "Making history: Imagining Aborigines and Australia." In *Prehistory to politics: John Mulvaney, the humanities, and the public intellectual*, edited by T. Bonyhady and T. Griffiths, 98–116. Melbourne: Melbourne Univ. Press.

Australian Geological Survey Organisation (AGSO). 1996. *CLIMANZ IV: Quaternary climates of Australia and New Zealand. Abstracts*. Canberra: Australian National Univ.

Baker, R. M. 1989. "Land is life: Continuity through change for the Yanyuwa from the Northern Territory of Australia." Ph.D. diss., Univ. of Adelaide.

Barbour, M. G. 1995. "Ecological fragmentation in the fifties." In *Uncommon ground: Toward reinventing nature*, edited by W. Cronon, 233–55. New York: Norton.

Bartlett, R. 1993. "Mabo: Another triumph for the common law." In *Essays on the Mabo Decision*, 58–66. Sydney: Law Book Company.

Bate, W. 1962. *A history of Brighton*. Melbourne: Melbourne Univ. Press.

Bayly, L. A. 1973. "Westernport recreation capacity case study. Melbourne: Westernport Regional Planning Authority.

Beaton, J. M. 1983. "Does intensification account for changes in the Australian Holocene archaeological record?" *Archaeology in Oceania* 18, 94–97

Beckett, J. 1992. "Comment on Hollinsworth." *Oceania* 63, 165–67.

Bender, B. 1993. "Stonehenge—contested landscapes (medieval to present-day)." In *Landscape: Politics and perspectives*, edited by B. Bender, 245–80. Oxford: Berg.

———, ed. 1993. *Landscape: Politics and perspectives*. Oxford: Berg.

Birckhead, J., T. De Lacy, et al., eds. 1992. *Aboriginal involvement in parks and protected areas*. Canberra: Aboriginal Studies.

Bird-David, N. H. 1988. "Hunters and gatherers and other people—a reexamination." In *Hunters and gatherers 1: History, evolution, and social change*, edited by T. Ingold, D. Riches, and J. Woodburn, 17–30. Oxford: Berg.

Birks, H. H., H. J. B. Birks, et al., eds. 1988. *The cultural landscape—past, present, and future*. Cambridge: Cambridge Univ. Press.

Bishop, P., ed. 1988. *Lessons for human survival: Nature's record from the Quaternary*. Symposium proceedings no. 1. Sydney: Geological Society of Australia.

Blainey, G. 1975. *The triumph of the nomads: A history of ancient Australia*. Melbourne: Sun.

Boer, B. 1989. "The legal framework affecting Aboriginal people in the East Kimberley." *East Kimberley Working Paper (Australian National Univ., Canberra)* 30.

Bond, G. C., and A. Gilliam. 1994. "Introduction." In *Social construction of the past: Representation as power,* edited by G. C. Bond and A. Gilliam 1–22. London: Routledge.

Bonyhady, T., and Griffiths, T., eds. 1996. *Prehistory to politics: John Mulvaney, the humanities, and the public intellectual.* Melbourne: Melbourne Univ. Press.

Bowden, M. J. 1992. "The invention of American tradition." *Journal of Historical Geography* 18, 3–26.

Bowdler, S. 1981. "Hunters in the highlands: Aboriginal adaptations in the eastern Australian uplands." *Archaeology in Oceania* 16, 99–111.

———. 1993. "Views of the past in Australian prehistory." In *A community of culture: The people and prehistory of the Pacific,* edited by M. Spriggs et al., 123–38. Canberra: Australian National Univ.

Bowler, J. 1982. "Aridity in the late Tertiary and Quaternary of Australia." In *Evolution of the flora and fauna of arid Australia,* edited by W. R. Barker and P. J. M. Greenslade, 35–46. Adelaide: Peacock.

———. 1996. "Isotope stage 3: Lake levels." In *CLIMANZ IV: Quaternary climates of Australia and New Zealand. Abstracts.* Canberra: Australian National Univ.

Bowler, J., R. Jones, H. Allen, and A. Thorne. 1970. "Pleistocene human remains from Australia: A living site and human cremation from Lake Mungo, Western New South Wales." *World Archaeology* 2, 39–60.

Bowler, J., A. Thorne, and H. Polach. 1972. "Pleistocene man in Australia: Age and significance of the Mungo skeleton." *Nature* 240, 48–50.

Bowman, D. M. J. S. in press. "The impact of Aboriginal landscape burning on the Australian biota." *New Phytologist.*

Bowman, D. M. J. S. and W. J. Panton. 1993. "Decline of *Callitris intratropica* R. T. Baker and H. G. Smith in the Northern Territory: Implications of pre- and post-European colonization fire regimes." *Journal of Biogeography* 20, 373–81.

Bradley, R. 1993. *Altering the earth.* Edinburgh: Society of Antiquaries of Scotland.

Bradshaw, J. 1986. "Australia—the French Discovery of 1983." In *The Australian scapegoat: Towards an antipodean aesthetic,* edited by P. Fuller, 59–69. Perth: Univ. of Western Australia Press.

Bride, T. F. [1898] 1969. *Letters from Victorian pioneers.* Melbourne: Currey O'Neil.

Brown, B. 1983. *Wilderness News* 43.

Burch, E. S., and L. J. Ellanna, eds. 1994. *Key issues in hunter-gatherer research.* Oxford: Berg.

Butzer, K. W. 1992. "The Americas before and after 1492: An introduction to current geographical research." *Annals of the Association of American Geographers* 82, 345–68.

Byrne, D. 1995. "Buddhist *stupa* and Thai social practice." *World Archaeology* 27, 266–81.

Callicott, J. B. 1991. "The wilderness idea revisited: The sustainable development alternative." In *The ethics of the environment*, edited by A. Brennan, 235–43. Aldershot, England: Dartmouth.

Carter, P. 1987. *The road to Botany Bay: An essay in spatial history.* London: Faber and Faber.

Charters, A. D. 1975. "Ecology of trematodes and the Ord River Dam." In *Manmade lakes and human health*, edited by N. F. Stanley and M. P. Alpers, 137–48. London: Academic.

Chase, A. 1989a. "Domestication and domiculture in northern Australia: A social perspective." In *Foraging and farming: The evolution of plant exploitation*, edited by D. R. Harris and G. C. Hillman, 42–78. London: Unwin Hyman.

———. 1989b. "Perceptions of the past among north Queensland Aboriginal people: The intrusion of Europeans and consequent social change." In *Who needs the past? Indigenous values and archaeology*, edited by R. Layton, 169–79. London: Unwin Hyman.

Chase, A., and P. Sutton. 1981. "Hunter-gatherers in a rich environment: Aboriginal coastal exploitation in Cape York Peninsula." In *Ecological biogeography of Australia*, edited by A. Keast, 1818–52. The Hague: Junk.

Clark, R. L. 1983. "Pollen and charcoal evidence for the effects of Aboriginal burning on the vegetation of Australia." *Archaeology in Oceania* 18, 32–37.

Clarke, A., and R. Torrence, eds. in press. *Negotiating difference: Reinterpretations of intercultural encounters in Oceania.* London: Routledge.

Clement, C. 1991. "Australia's North-West: A study of exploration, land policy, and land acquisition, 1644–1884." Unpublished PhD thesis. Perth: Murdoch Univ.

Collier, J. 1911. *The pastoral age in Australia.* London: Whitcombe and Tombs.

Commonwealth of Australia. 1984. *Aboriginal social indicators 1984.* Canberra: Australian Government Publishing Service.

———. 1994. *Australia's biodiversity: An overview of selected significant components.* Biodiversity series paper no. 2. Canberra: Biodiversity Unit, Department of the Environment, Sport and Territories.

———. 1997. *Bringing them home: Report of the national inquiry into the separation of Aboriginal and Torres Strait Islander children from their families.* Sydney: Human Rights and Equal Opportunity Commission.

Conway, J. K. 1989. *The road from Coorain.* London: Mandarin.

Coombs, H. C., H. McCann, et al., eds. 1989. *Land of promises.* Canberra: Centre for Resource and Environmental Studies and Aboriginal Studies Press.

Cosgrove, R. 1989. "Thirty thousand years of human colonization in Tasmania: New Pleistocene dates." *Science* 243, 1703–5.

———. 1995. *The illusion of riches: Scale, resolution and explanation in Tasmanian Pleistocene human behaviour.* International series no. 608. Oxford: British Archaeological Reports.

Cosgrove, R., J. Allen, et al. 1990. "Palaeoecology and Pleistocene human occupation in south central Tasmania." *Antiquity* 64, 59–78.

Cowlishaw, G. 1987. "Colour, Culture and the Aboriginalists." *Man* (n.s.) 22, 221–37.
Crawfurd, J. 1863. "On the connexion between ethnology and physical geography." *Transactions of the Ethnological Society of London*, n.s. 2, 4–23.
Cronon, W. 1994. "Cutting loose or running aground?" *Journal of Historical Geography* 20, 38–43.
———. 1996a. "The Trouble with wilderness." In *Uncommon ground: Toward reinventing nature*, edited by W. Cronon. New York: Norton.
———, ed. 1996b. *Uncommon ground: Toward reinventing nature*. New York: Norton.
Crough, G., and C. Christopherson. 1993. *Aboriginal people in the economy of the Kimberley region*. Darwin: North Australia Research Unit.
Crowley, G. M., and A. P. Kershaw. 1994. "Late Quaternary environmental change and human impact around Lake Bolac, western Victoria, Australia." *Journal of Quaternary Science* 9, 367–77.
Cutter, J. 1987. *Guesthouses on Phillip Island: A history*. N. p.
D'Costa, D. 1996a. "Full glacial and late glacial palaeoenvironments at Tower Hill, Western Victoria." In *CLIMANZ IV: Quaternary climates of Australia and New Zealand. Abstracts.* Canberra: Australian National Univ.
———. 1996b. "Interglacial palaeoenvironmental reconstructions at Egg Lagoon, King Island, Bass Strait." In *CLIMANZ IV: Quaternary climates of Australia and New Zealand. Abstracts.* Canberra: Australian National Univ.
Davidson, B. R. 1972. *The northern myth: Limits to agricultural and pastoral development in tropical Australia*. Mebourne: Melbourne Univ. Press.
Davidson, I. 1989. "Is intensification a condition of the fisher-hunter-gatherer way of life?" *Archaeology in Oceania* 24, 75–78.
Davies, J., and E. Young. 1996. "Taking centre stage: Aboriginal strategies for redressing marginalisation." In *Resources, nations and indigenous peoples: Case studies from Australasia, Melanesia and south-east Asia*, edited by R. Howitt, J. Connell, et al., 152–71. Melbourne: Oxford Univ. Press.
Davis, M. B. 1994. "Ecology and palaeoecology begin to merge." *Trends in Ecology and Evolution* 9, 357–58.
Dear, M. 1994. "Who's afraid of postmodernism? Reflections on Symanski and Cosgrove." *Annals of the Association of American Geographers* 84, 295–300.
Delcourt, P. A. and H. R. Delcourt. 1987. *Long-term forest dynamics of the temperate zone: A case study of late-Quaternary forests in eastern North America*. New York: Springer-Verlag.
Demeritt, D. 1994. "Ecology, objectivity and critique in writings on nature and human societies." *Journal of Historical Geography* 20, 22–37.
Denevan, W. M. 1992. "The pristine myth: The landscape of the Americas in 1492." *Annals of the Association of American Geographers* 82, 369–85.
Desmond, A., and J. Moore. 1991. *Darwin*. London: Penguin.
Dodson, J. R., ed. 1992. *The naive lands: Prehistory and environmental change in Australia and the south-west Pacific*. Melbourne: Longman Cheshire.

Dodson, J. R., R. Fullagar, et al. 1992. "Dynamics of environment and people in the forested crescents of temperate Australia." In *The naive lands: Prehistory and environmental change in Australia and the south-west Pacific*, edited by J. R. Dodson, 115–59. Melbourne: Longman Cheshire.

Dodson, J. R., R. Fullagar, et al. 1993. "Humans and megafauna at Cuddie Springs, NSW." *Archaeology in Oceania*. 28, 93–99.

Dortch, C. 1972. "Archaeological work in the Ord reservoir area, East Kimberley." *A.I.A.S. Newsletter* 3, 13–18.

———. 1977. "Early and late stone industrial phases in Western Australia." In *Stone tools as cultural markers*, edited by R. V. S. Wright, 104–32. Canberra: Australian Institute of Aboriginal Studies.

Doyle, T., and A. Kellow. 1995. *Environmental politics and policy making in Australia*. Melbourne: Macmillan.

Duncan, J., and N. Duncan. 1988. "Rereading the landscape." *Environment and Planning D: Society and Space* 6, 117–26.

Eagleton, T. 1983. *Literary theory: An introduction*. Oxford: Basil Blackwell.

Eckersley, R. 1990. "The ecocentric perspective." In *The rest of the world is watching*, edited by C. Pybus and R. Flanagan, 68–78. Sydney: Pan Macmillan.

Edgeworth David, T. W. 1923. "Geological evidence of the antiquity of man in the Commonwealth: With special reference to the Tasmanian Aborigines." *Papers and Proceedings of the Royal Society of Tasmania*, 109–50.

Edmunds, M., and R. James. 1992. *Black and white and read all over*. Canberra: Australian Institute of Aboriginal and Torres Strait Islander Studies.

Etheridge, R. 1890. "Has Man a Geological History in Australia?" *Proceedings of the Linnean Society of New South Wales* 15, 259–66.

Evernden, N. 1992. *The social creation of nature*. Baltimore: Johns Hopkins Univ. Press.

Faegri, K. 1988. "A model for describing the cultural landscape." In *The cultural landscape—past, present, and future*, edited by H. H. Birks et al., 1–6. Cambridge: Cambridge Univ. Press.

Feit, H. A. 1994. "The enduring pursuit: Land, time and social relationships in anthropological models of hunter-gatherers and in subarctic hunters' images." In *Key issues in hunter-gatherer research*, edited by E. S. Burch and L. J. Ellanna, 421–40. Oxford: Berg.

Flanagan, R. 1990. "Return the people's Pedder!" In *The rest of the world is watching*, edited by C. Pybus and R. Flanagan, 194–210. Sydney: Pan Macmillan.

Flanagan, R., and C. Pybus. 1990. "Green images." In *The rest of the world is watching*, edited by C. Pybus and R. Flanagan, 157–69. Sydney: Pan Macmillan.

Flannery, T. F. 1994. *The future eaters: An ecological history of the Australasian lands and people*. Sydney: Reed.

Flood, J. 1980. *The moth hunters*. Canberra: Australian Institute of Aboriginal Studies.

———. 1983. *Archaeology of the dreamtime*. Collins: Sydney.
Forster, S. G. 1981. "Aboriginal rights and official morality." *The Push from the Bush: A Bulletin of Social History* 11, 68–98.
Frankel, D. 1984. "Who owns the past?" *Australian Society* 3, no. 9: 14–15.
———. 1993. "Pleistocene chronological structures and explanations: A challenge." In *Sahul in review: Pleistocene archaeology in Australia, New Guinea, and Island Melanesia*, edited by M. Smith, M. Spriggs, and B. Fankhauser, 24–36. Canberra: Department of Prehistory, Australian National Univ.
———. 1995. "The Australian transition: Real and perceived boundaries." *Antiquity* 69, 649–55.
Fullagar, R., and J. Field. 1997. "Pleistocene seed-grinding implements from the Australian arid zone." *Antiquity* 71, 300–307.
Fullagar, R., D. M. Price, et al. 1996. "Early human occupation of northern Australia: Archaeology and thermoluminescence dating of Jinmium rockshelter, Northern Territory." *Antiquity* 70, 751–73.
Furby, J. 1995. "Megafauna under the microscope: Archaeology and palaeoenvironment at Cuddie Springs." Unpublished Ph.D thesis, Univ. of New South Wales, Sydney.
Gagan, M. K., L. K. Ayliffe, et al. 1996. "Near-weekly records of ENSO-monsoon dynamics at 5ka BP from Great Barrier Reef corals." In *CLIMANZ IV: Quaternary climates of Australia and New Zealand. Abstracts* Canberra: Australian National Univ.
Gandy, M. 1996. "Crumbling land: The postmodernity debate and the analysis of environmental problems." *Progress in Human Geography* 20, 23–40.
Gaughwin, D. 1983. "Coastal economies and the Western Port Catchment." M. A. Thesis, La Trobe Univ.
Gelder, K., and J. M. Jacobs. 1995. "Uncanny Australia," *Ecumene* 2, 171–83.
Gibson, R. 1992. *South of the west: Postcolonialism and the narrative construction of Australia*. Bloomington: Indiana Univ. Press.
Gill, E. D. 1955a. "Aboriginal midden sites in western Victoria dated by radiocarbon analysis." *Mankind* 5, 51–54.
———. 1955b. "Radiocarbon dates for Australian archaeological and geological samples." *Australian Journal of Science* 18, 49–52.
Gill, N. 1994. "The cultural politics of resource management: The case of bushfires in a conservation reserve." *Australian Geographical Studies* 32, 224–40.
Glacken, C. J. 1967. *Traces on the Rhodian shore: Nature and culture in Western thought from ancient times to the end of the eighteenth century*. Berkeley: Univ. of California Press.
Gliddon, J. W. 1958. *Phillip Island in picture and story*. Melbourne: Wilke.
Goot, M., and T. Rowse, eds. 1994. *Make a better offer: The politics of Mabo*. Sydney: Pluto.
Gosden, C. 1989. "Prehistoric social landscapes of the Arawe Islands, West New Britain Province, Papua New Guinea." *Archaeology in Oceania* 24, 45–58.

———. 1994. *Social being and time*. Oxford: Blackwell.
Gott, B. 1982. "Ecology of root use by the Aborigines of southern Australia." *Archaeology in Oceania* 17, 59–67.
———. 1983. "Murnong—*Microseris scapigera:* A study of a staple food of Victorian Aborigines." *Australian Aboriginal Studies*, 1983/2, 2–17.
Gould, S. J. 1987. *Time's arrow, time's cycle*. Cambridge, Mass.: Harvard Univ. Press.
Graetz, R. D. 1988. "Kangaroos, sheep and the rangelands: The ecological issues." *Australian Zoologist* 24, 137–38.
Graham-Taylor, S. 1978. "A history of the Ord River scheme: A study in incrementalism." Unpublished Ph.D. thesis. Perth: Murdoch Univ.
Gregory, J. 1904. "The antiquity of man in Victoria." *Proceedings of the Royal Society of Victoria* 17, 120–44.
Gregson, N. 1992. "Beyond boundaries: The shifting sands of social geography." *Progress in Human Geography* 16, 387–92.
Griffiths, T. 1991. "History and natural history: Conservation movements in conflict?" In *The humanities, and the Australian environment*, edited by D. J. Mulvaney, 87–111. Canberra: Australian Academy of the Humanities.
———. 1996. *Hunters and collectors: The antiquarian imagination in Australia*. Cambridge: Cambridge Univ. Press.
Grigg, G. 1988. "Kangaroo harvesting and the conservation of the sheep rangelands." *Australian Zoologist* 24, 124–28.
Grinker, R. R. 1992. "History and hierarchy in hunter-gatherer studies." *American Ethnologist* 19, 160–65.
Grove, R. H. 1995. *Green imperialism: Colonial expansion, tropical island Edens, and the origins of environmentalism, 1600–1860*. Cambridge: Cambridge Univ. Press.
Haddon, A. C. 1924. *The races of man and their distribution*. Halifax: Milner.
Hale, H., and N. Tindale. 1930. "Notes on some human remains in the Lower Murray Valley, South Australia." *Records of the South Australian Museum* 4, 145–218.
Hall, M. 1994. "Lifting the veil of popular history: Archaeology and politics in urban Cape Town." In *Social construction of the past: Representation as power*, edited by G. C. Bond and A. Gilliam, 167–84. London: Routledge.
Hallam, S. J. 1975. *Fire and hearth*. Canberra: Australian Institute of Aboriginal Studies.
Hamilton, A. 1990. "Fear and Desire: Aborigines, Asians, and the national imaginary." *Australian Cultural History* 9, 14–35.
Haraway, D. 1989. *Primate visions: Gender, race, and nature in the world of modern science*. New York: Routledge.
Harvey, D. 1989. *The condition of postmodernity*. Oxford: Blackwell.
Hassall and Associates P/L. 1993a. "The Ord River irrigation project past, present and future: An economic evaluation. Stage 1," Prepared for Kimberley Water Resources Development Office, Perth.

Hassall and Associates P/L. 1993b. "The Ord River irrigation project past, present and future: An economic evaluation. Stage 2." Prepared for Kimberley Water Resources Development Office, Perth.

Hay, P. R., and M. G. Haward. 1988. "Comparative green politics: Beyond the European context?" *Political Studies* 36, 433–48.

Haynes, C. D. 1985. "The pattern and ecology of munwag: Traditional Aboriginal fire regimes in north-central Arnhemland." *Proceedings of the Ecological Society of Australia* 13, 203–14.

———. 1991. "Use and impact of fire." In *Monsoonal Australia: Landscape, ecology, and man in the northern lowlands,* edited by C. D. Haynes, M. G. Ridpath, and M. A. J. Williams, 66–71. Rotterdam: Balkema.

Head, G. 1970. *William and Sarah Head, our pioneer ancestors: Family history 1838–1970.* Melbourne: Humphrey and Formula.

Head, L. 1990. "Conservation and Aboriginal land rights: When green is not black." *Australian Natural History* 23, 448–54.

———. 1992. "Australian Aborigines and a changing environment—views of the past and implications for the future." In *Aboriginal involvement in parks and protected areas,* edited by J. Birckhead, T. De Lacy, and L. Smith, 47–56. Canberra: Aboriginal Studies.

———. 1994a. "Both ends of the candle? Discerning human impact on the vegetation." *Australian Archaeology* 39, 82–86.

———. 1994b. "Landscapes socialised by fire: Post-contact changes in Aboriginal fire use in northern Australia, and implications for prehistory." *Archaeology in Oceania* 29, 172–81.

———. 1994c. "Aborigines and pastoralism in northwestern Australia: Historical and contemporary perspectives on multiple use of the rangelands." *Rangeland Journal* 16, 167–83.

———. 1995. "Meganesian barbecue: Reply to Seddon." *Meanjin* 54, 702–9.

———. 1996. "Rethinking the prehistory of hunter-gatherers, fire, and vegetation change in northern Australia." *The Holocene* 6, 481–87.

Head, L., and R. Fullagar. 1991. " 'We all la one land': pastoral excisions and Aboriginal resource use." *Australian Aboriginal Studies.* 1991/1: 39–52.

———. 1997 "Hunter-gatherer archaeology and pastoral contact: Perspectives from the northwest Northern Territory, Australia." *World Archaeology* 28, 418–28.

Head, L., C. Gosden, et al. 1994. "Social landscapes." *Archaeology in Oceania* 29 (3).

Headland, T. N. 1997. "Revisionism in ecological anthropology." *Current Anthropology* 38, 631–46.

Headland, T. N., and L. Reid. 1989. "Hunter-gatherers and their neighbors from prehistory to the present." *Current Anthropology* 30, 43–66.

Herbertson, A. J., and F. D. Herbertson. 1914. *Man and his work: An introduction to human geography.* London: Adam and Charles Black.

Hesse, P. 1996. "The late Quaternary Tasman Sea dust record of Australian region climate." In *CLIMANZ IV: Quaternary climates of Australia and New Zealand Abstracts*. Canberra: Australian National Univ.

Heusser, L. E., and G. van der Geer. 1994. "Direct correlation of terrestrial and marine paleoclimatic records from four glacial-interglacial cycles—DSDP site 594 southwest Pacific." *Quaternary Science Reviews* 13, 273–82.

Heyward, M. 1995. "Alan Moorehead." *Voices* 5, 79–89.

Hiatt, L. R., and R. Jones. 1988. "Aboriginal conceptions of the workings of nature." In *Australian science in the making*, edited by R. W. Home, 1–22. Cambridge: Cambridge Univ. Press.

Hills, E. R. 1991. "The imaginary life: Landscape and culture in Australia." *Journal of Australian Studies* 29, 12–27.

Hirsch, E., and M. O'Hanlon, eds. 1995. *The anthropology of landscape: Perspectives on place and space*. Oxford: Clarendon.

Hobsbawm, E. 1983. "Introduction: Inventing traditions." In *The Invention of Tradition*, edited by E. Hobsbawm and T. Ranger, 1–14. Cambridge: Cambridge Univ. Press.

Hobsbawm, E., and T. Ranger, eds. 1983. *The Invention of Tradition*. Cambridge: Cambridge Univ. Press.

Hocking, B. 1993. "Aboriginal law does now run in Australia." In *Essays on the Mabo decision*, 67–85. Sydney: Law Book Company.

Hollinsworth, D. 1992. "Discourses on Aboriginality and the politics of identity in urban Australia." *Oceania* 63, 137–55.

Hoorn, J. 1993. "Exposing the lie of terra nullius: Joseph Lycett's Awakabal album." *Art and Australia* 30/31, 77–83.

Horton, D. R. 1979. "The great megafaunal extinction debate: 1879–1979." *The Artefact* 4, 11–25.

———. 1982. "The burning question: Aborigines, fire, and Australian ecosystems." *Mankind* 13, 237–51.

———. 1986. "Seasons of repose: Environment and culture in the late Pleistocene of Australia." In *The Pleistocene perspective, vol. 2*. London: Allen and Unwin.

———. 1991. *Recovering the tracks: The story of Australian archaeology*. Canberra: Aboriginal Studies.

Horton, D. R., ed. 1994. *The encyclopaedia of Aboriginal Australia: Aboriginal and Torres Strait Islander history, society and culture*. Canberra: Aboriginal Studies Press.

Howitt, A. 1898. "On the origin of the Aborigines of Tasmania and Australia." *Australasian Association for the Advancement of Science* 7, 723–58.

Howitt, R., and S. Jackson. in press. "Some things *do* change: Indigenous rights, geographers, and geography in Australia." *Australian Geographer*.

Hynes, R. A., and A. Chase. 1982. "Plants, sites, and domiculture: Aboriginal influence upon plant communities in Cape York Peninsula." *Archaeology in Oceania* 17, 38–50.

Ingold, T. 1980. *Hunters, pastoralists, and ranchers.* Cambridge: Cambridge Univ. Press.
———. 1986. *The appropriation of nature.* Manchester: Manchester Univ. Press.
Iwasaki-Goodman, M., and M. M. R. Freeman. 1994. "Social and cultural significance of whaling in contemporry Japan: A case study of small-type coastal whaling." In *Key issues in hunter-gatherer research,* edited by E. S. Burch and L. J. Ellanna, 377–400. Oxford: Berg.
Jacobs, J. M. 1988. "Politics and the cultural landscape: The case of Aboriginal land rights." *Australian Geographical Studies* 26, 249–63.
———. 1996. *Postcolonialism and the city.* London: Routledge.
James, R. 1992. "The political iconography of Aboriginality." *Oceania* 63, 207–21.
Jones, F. L. 1970. *The structure and growth of Australia's Aboriginal population.* Canberra: Australian National Univ. Press.
Jones, R. 1968. "The geographical background to the arrival of man in Australia and Tasmania." *Archaeology and Physical Anthropology in Oceania* 3, 186–215.
———. 1969. "Fire-stick farming." *Australian Natural History* 16, 224–28.
———. 1973. "Emerging picture of Pleistocene Australians." *Nature* 246, 278–81.
———. 1975. "The Neolithic, Palaeolithic, and the hunting gardeners: Man and land in the antipodes." In *Quaternary studies: Selected papers from IX Inqua Congress, Christchurch N.Z. 1973,* edited by R. P. Suggate and M. M. Cresswell, 21–34. Christchurch: Royal Society of New Zealand.
———. 1980. "Cleaning the country: The Gidjingali and their Arnhemland environment." *BHP Journal,* 10–15.
———. 1985. "Ordering the landscape." In *Seeing the first Australians,* edited by I. Donaldson and T. Donaldson, 181–209. Sydney: George Allen and Unwin.
———. 1990. "Hunters of the Dreaming: Some ideational, economic, and ecological parameters of the Australian Aboriginal production system." In *Pacific production systems: Approaches to economic prehistory,* edited by D. E. Yen and J. M. J. Mummery 25–53. Occasional Papers in Prehistory 18. Canberra: Department of Prehistory, Australian National Univ.
———. 1991. "Landscapes of the mind: Aboriginal perceptions of the natural world." In *The humanities and the Australian environment,* edited by D. J. Mulvaney, 21–48. Canberra: Australian Academy of the Humanities.
———. 1992. "Philosophical time travellers." *Antiquity* 66, 744–57.
———. 1993. "A continental reconnaissance: Some observations concerning the discovery of the Pleistocene archaeology of Australia." In *A community of culture: The people and prehistory of the Pacific* edited by M. Spriggs, et al., 97–122. Canberra: Australian National Univ.
Keating, P. 1993. "Prime minister's address to the nation." In *Make a better offer: The politics of Mabo.* edited by M. Goot and T. Rowse, 235–38. Sydney: Pluto.
Kellow, A. 1990. "Spoiling for a fight or fighting over the spoils? Resource and environmental politics and policies in Australia towards 2000." In *Australia towards 2000,* edited by B. Hocking, 198–214. London: Macmillan.

Kershaw, A. P. 1975. "Late Quaternary vegetation and climate in northeastern Australia." In *Quaternary studies: Royal Society of New Zealand bulletin 13,* edited by R. P. Suggate and M. M. Cresswell, 181–87. Wellington: The Royal Society of New Zealand.

———. 1976. "A Late Pleistocene and Holocene pollen diagram from Lynchs Crater, north-eastern Queensland, Australia." *New Phytologist* 77, 469–98.

———. 1985. "An extended late Quaternary vegetation record from north-eastern Queensland and its implications for the seasonal tropics of Australia." *Proceedings of the Ecological Society of Australia* 13, 179–89.

———. 1986. "Climatic change and Aboriginal burning in north-east Australia during the last two glacial/interglacial cycles." *Nature* 322, 47–49.

Kershaw, A. P., G. M. McKenzie, et al. 1993. "A Quaternary vegetation history of northeastern Queensland from pollen analysis of ODP site 820." *Proceedings of the Ocean Drilling Program, Scientific Results* 133, 107–14.

Kiernan, K., R. Jones, et al. 1983. "New evidence from Fraser Cave for glacial age man in south-west Tasmania." *Nature* 301, 28–32.

Kuklick, H. 1993. *The savage within: The social history of British anthropology, 1885–1945.* Cambridge: Cambridge Univ. Press.

Kuper, A. 1988. *The invention of primitive society: Transformations of an illusion.* London: Routledge.

Landes, D. S. 1983. *Revolution in time: Clocks and the making of the modern world.* Cambridge, Mass.: Harvard Univ. Press.

Langford, R. 1983. "Our heritage—your playground." *Australian Archaeology* 16, 1–6.

Langton, M. 1993. "Rum, seduction and death: 'Aboriginality' and alcohol." *Oceania* 63, no. 3: 195–206.

———. 1994. "Aboriginal art and film: The politics of representation." *Race and Class* 35, 89–106.

———. 1995/96. "The European construction of wilderness." *Wilderness News* 143, 16–17.

———. 1996. "Art, wilderness and *terra nullius*." In *Ecopolitics IX Conference papers and resolutions,* edited by R. Sultan et al., 11–24. Darwin: Northern Land Council.

Lansbury, C. 1970. *Arcady in Australia: The evocation of Australia in nineteenth-century English literature.* Melbourne: Melbourne Univ. Press.

Lattas, A. 1992. "Wiping the blood off Aboriginality: The politics of Aboriginal embodiment in contemporary intellectual debate." *Oceania* 63, 160–64.

———. 1993. "Essentialism, memory, and resistance: Aboriginality and the politics of authenticity." *Oceania* 63, 240–267.

Lawson, H. 1984. *A camp-fire yarn: Complete works 1885–1900.* Sydney: Lansdowne.

Layton, R. 1989. "Introduction: Who needs the past?" In *Who needs the past? Indigenous values and archaeology,* edited by R. Layton, 1–20. London: Unwin Hyman.

Lee, R. B. 1992. "Art, science, or politics? The crisis in hunter-gatherer studies." *American Anthropologist* 94, no. 1: 31–54.
Lesslie, R., and M. Maslen. 1995. *National wilderness inventory Australia: Handbook of procedures, content, and usage.* Canberra: Australian Heritage Commission.
Lines, W. J. 1992. *Taming the great south land: A history of the conquest of nature in Australia.* Sydney: Allen and Unwin.
Livingstone, D. 1991. "The moral discourse of climate: Historical considerations on race, place, and virtue." *Journal of Historical Geography* 17, 413–34.
———. 1992. *The geographical tradition: Episodes in the history of a contested enterprise.* Oxford: Blackwell.
Longmore, M. E. 1996a. "The mid-Holocene 'Dry': Calibration of palaeowater depth as a surrogate for effective precipitation using sedimentary LOI in the perched lake sediments of Fraser Island." In *CLIMANZ IV: Quaternary climates of Australia and New Zealand. Abstracts.* Canberra: Australian National Univ.
———. 1996b. "Palaeoclimatic evidence from perched lake sedimentary records on Fraser Island, Southeast Queensland." In *CLIMANZ IV: Quaternary climates of Australia and New Zealand. Abstracts.* Canberra: Australian National University.
Lourandos, H. 1983. "Intensification: a late Pleistocene–Holocene archaeological sequence from southwestern Victoria." *Archaeology in Oceania* 18, 81–94.
Lourandos, H., and A. Ross. 1994. "The great 'Intensification Debate': Its history and place in Australian archaeology." *Australian Archaeology* 39, 54–62.
Lowenthal, D. 1978. "Australian images: The unique present, the mythical past." In *Readings in Australian arts*, edited by P. Quartermaine, 84–94. Exeter, England: Univ. of Exeter.
———. 1990. "Uses of the past in Australia." In *Australia Towards 2000*, edited by B. Hocking, 46–54. London: Macmillan.
Lowie, R. H. 1920. *Primitive society.* New York: Boni and Liveright.
Lubbock, J. 1878. *Pre-historic times, as illustrated by ancient remains, and the manners and customs of modern savages.* London: Frederic Norgate.
———. [1870] 1978. *The origin of civilisation and the primitive condition of man.* Chicago: Univ. of Chicago Press.
Lucas, D., and J. Russell-Smith. 1993. "Traditional resources of the South Alligator floodplain: Utilisation and management. Volume 1." Consultancy report to the Australian Nature Conservation Agency, Canberra.
Magowan, F. 1994. " 'The land is our *Marr* (essence), it stays forever': The *yothu-yindi* relationship in Australian Aboriginal traditional and popular musics." In *Ethnicity, identity, and music*, edited by M. Stokes, 135–56. Oxford: Berg.
Marsh, G. P. [1864] 1965. *Man and nature.* Cambridge, Mass.: The Belknap Press of Harvard Univ. Press.

Mazel, A. D. 1992. "Changing fortunes: 150 years of San hunter-gatherer history in the Natal Drakensberg, South Africa." *Antiquity* 66, 758–67.

McBryde, I. 1985. "Thomas Dick's photographic visison." In *Seeing the first Australians*, edited by I. Donaldson and T. Donaldson, 137–63. Sydney: Allen and Unwin.

———. 1992. "The past as symbol of identity." *Antiquity* 66, 261–66.

McCarthy, F. 1948. "The Lapstone Creek excavation: Two culture periods revealed in eastern New South Wales." *Records of the Australian Museum* 22, 1–34.

McEachern, D. 1995. "Mining meaning from the rhetoric of nature—Australian mining companies and their attitudes to the environment at home and abroad." *Policy, Organisation, and Society* 10, 48–67.

McGlone, M. S., A. P. Kershaw, et al. 1992. "El Niño/southern oscillation and climatic variability in Australasian and South American palaeoenvironmental records." In *El Niño: Historical and paleoclimatic aspects of the southern oscillation*, edited by V. Markgraf and H. Diaz, 435–62. Cambridge: Cambridge Univ. Press.

McGrath, A. 1991. "Travel to a distant past: The mythology of the outback." *Australian Cultural History* 10, 113–24.

Mearns, L. 1994. "To continue the dreaming: Aboriginal women's traditional responsibilities in a transformed world." In *Key issues in hunter-gatherer research*, edited by E. S. Burch and L. J. Ellanna, 263–88. Oxford: Berg.

Meehan, B. 1982. *Shell bed to shell midden.* Canberra: Aboriginal Studies.

———. 1991. "Wetland hunters: some reflections." In *Monsoon Australia: Landscape, ecology, and man in the northern lowlands*, edited by C. D. Haynes, M. G. Ridpath, and M. A. J. Williams, 197–206. Rotterdam: Balkema.

Meinig, D. W. 1962. *On the margins of the good earth.* Adelaide, South Australia: Rigby.

Mercer, D. 1993. "Victoria's National Parks (Wilderness) Act 1992: Background and issues." *Australian Geographer* 24, 25–32.

Merrilees, D. 1968. "Man the destroyer: Late Quaternary changes in the Australian marsupial fauna." *Journal of the Royal Society of Western Australia* 51, 1–24.

Millington, A. J. 1975. "Agricultural implications of the Ord River Dam." In *Man-made lakes and human health*, edited by N. F. Stanley and M. P. Alpers, 113–36. London: Academic.

Moorehead, A. 1963. *Cooper's Creek.* London: Hamish Hamilton.

Morgan, L. H. [1877] 1907. *Ancient society, or Researches in the lines of human progress from savagery through barbarism to civilization.* New York: Henry Holt.

Morphy, H. 1993. "Colonialism, history, and the construction of place: The politics of landscape in northern Australia." In *Landscape: Politics and perspectives*, edited by B. Bender, 205–44. Oxford: Berg.

———. 1995. "Landscape and the reproduction of the ancestral past." In *The anthropology of landscape: Perspectives on place and space,* edited by E. Hirsch and M. O'Hanlon, 184–209. Oxford: Clarendon.
Moser, S. 1995a. "The 'Aboriginalization' of Australian archaeology." In *Theory in archaeology: A world perspective,* edited by P. Ucko, 150–77. London: Routledge.
———. 1995b. "Archaeology and its disciplinary culture: The professionalisation of Australian prehistoric archaeology." Ph.D. diss., Univ. of Sydney.
Moult, A., and L. Meier. 1983. *Australia the beautiful, wilderness.* Sydney: Weldon.
Mulvaney, D. J. 1961. "The stone age of Australia." *Proceedings of the Prehistoric Society* 27, 56–107.
———. 1971. *Discovering man's place in Nature.* Sydney: Sydney Univ. Press.
———. 1975. *The prehistory of Australia.* Revised ed. Ringwood, Victoria: Penguin.
———. [1958] 1990. "The Australian Aborigines 1606–1929: Opinion and fieldwork." In *Through white eyes,* edited by S. Janson and S. Macintyre, 1–44. Sydney: Allen and Unwin.
Mulvaney, D. J., and E. B. Joyce. 1965. "Archaeological and geomorphological investigations on Mt. Moffatt Station, Queensland, Australia." *Proceedings of the Prehistoric Society* 31, 147–212.
Murray, T. 1992a. "Tasmania and the constitution of 'the dawn of humanity.' " *Antiquity* 66, 730–43.
———. 1992b. "Aboriginal (pre)history and Australian archaeology: The discourse of Australian prehistoric archaeology." In *Power, knowledge, and Aborigines,* edited by B. Attwood and J. Arnold, 1–19. Melbourne: La Trobe Univ. Press.
———. 1996. "Aborigines, archaeology and Australian heritage." *Meanjin* 55, 725–35.
Murray, T., and J. Allen. 1995. "The forced repatriation of cultural properties to Tasmania." *Antiquity* 69, 871–73.
Nanson, G. C., D. M. Price, et al. 1996. "TL evidence of palaeoclimate and flow regime changes in Australia, pre Stage 7 to the present." In *CLIMANZ IV: Quaternary climates of Australia and New Zealand. Abstracts.* Canberra: Australian National Univ.
Naralup Associates. 1996. "Ord irrigation project: Population planning study." [Perth].
Nash, R. 1967. *Wilderness and the American mind.* New Haven: Yale Univ. Press.
National Trust of Australia, Victoria. 1974. "Preservation of the Mornington Peninsula and Westernport." Unpublished report. Melbourne: National Trust of Australia, Victoria.
Nettheim, G. 1994. "The uncertain dimensions of native title." In *Make a better offer: The politics of Mabo,* edited by M. Goot and T. Rowse, 55–65. Sydney: Pluto.

Northern Territory Tourist Commission. 1993. *Come share our culture: A guide to Northern Territory Aboriginal tours, arts, and crafts.* Darwin: Northern Territory Tourist Commission.

Nyoongah M. 1992. "Self-determining our Aboriginality: A response to 'Discourses on Aboriginality and the politics of identity in urban Australia.' " *Oceania* 63, 156–57.

Owen, R. 1879. "Extinct animals of the colonies of Great Britain." *Proceedings of the Royal Colonial Institute* 10, 267–97.

Pardoe, C. 1992. "Arches of radii, corridors of power: Reflections on current archaeological practice." In *Power, knowledge, and Aborigines,* edited by B. Attwood and J. Arnold, 132–41. Melbourne: La Trobe Univ. Press.

———. 1993. "The Pleistocene is still with us: Analytical constraints and possibilities for the study of ancient human remains in archaeology." In *Sahul in Review,* edited by M. A. Smith, M. Spriggs, and B. Fankhauser, 81–94. Canberra: Department of Prehistory, Australian National Univ.

———. 1994. "Bioscapes: The evolutionary landscape of Australia." *Archaeology in Oceania* 29, 182–90.

Parsons, M. 1986. "The 'matchbox' solution only inflames the problem: Obtaining living areas on pastoral leases." In *Science and technology for Aboriginal development,* edited by B. Foran and B. Walker, Sec. 2–12. Melbourne: Commonwealth Scientific and Industrial Research Organisation.

Pearson, N. 1994. "From remnant title to social justice." In *Make a better offer: The politics of Mabo,* edited by M. Goot and T. Rowse, 179–84. Sydney: Pluto.

Pearson, S. 1996. "The last 3500 years in seven sites in central Australia: An interesting place and an interesting time." In *CLIMANZ IV: Quaternary climates of Australia and New Zealand. Abstracts.* Canberra: Australian National Univ.

Perdue, T. 1995. "Women, men, and American Indian policy: The Cherokee response to 'civilization.' " In *Negotiators of change: Historical perspectives on Native American women,* edited by N. Shoemaker, 90–114. New York: Routledge.

Peschel, O. 1876. *The races of man and their geographical distribution.* London: Henry King.

Peterson, N. 1985. "The popular image". In *Seeing the first Australians,* edited by I. Donaldson and T. Donaldson, 164–80. Sydney: Allen and Unwin.

Phillip Island Penguin Reserve Committee of Management (PIPRCM). 1989. *Phillip Island Penguin Reserve management plan.* Melbourne: Department of Conservation, Forests, and Lands.

Plumwood, V. 1993. *Feminism and the mastery of nature.* London: Routledge.

Povinelli, E. A. 1993. *Labor's lot: The power, history, and culture of Aboriginal action.* Chicago: Univ. of Chicago Press.

Powell, J. M. 1977. *Mirrors of the New World: Images and image-makers in the settlement process.* Folkestone, England: Dawson and Son.

———. 1980. "Taylor, Stefansson, and the arid centre: An historic encounter of 'environmentalism' and 'possibilism.' " *Journal of the Royal Australian Historical Society* 66, 163–83.

———. 1993. *Griffith Taylor and "Australia Unlimited": The John Murtagh Macrossan Lecture for 1992.* Brisbane: Queensland Univ. Press.

———. 1994. "Strangers and lovers: Disputing the legacy of environmental history." In *Identifying Australia in postmodern times,* edited by L. Dobrez, 87–104. Canberra: Bibliotech.

Prakash Reddy, G. 1994. "Hunter-gatherers and the politics of environment and development in India." In *Key issues in hunter-gatherer research,* edited by E. S. Burch and L. J. Ellanna, 357–76. Oxford: Berg.

Pratt, K. L. 1994. " 'They never ask the people': Native views about the Nunivak Wilderness." In *Key issues in hunter-gatherer research* edited by E. Burch and L. Ellanna, 333–56. Oxford: Berg.

Pred, A., and M. J. Watts. 1992. *Reworking modernity: Capitalisms and symbolic discontent.* New Brunswick, N. J.: Rutgers Univ. Press.

Presland, G. 1983. *An archaeological survey of the Melbourne metropolitan area.* Melbourne: Victoria Archaeological Survey.

Price, C. 1987. "Immigration and ethnic origin." In *Australians: Historical statistics,* edited by W. Vamplew, 2–22. Sydney: Fairfax, Syme, and Weldon.

Price, T. D., and J. A. Brown, eds. 1985. *Prehistoric hunter-gatherers: The emergence of cultural complexity.* New York: Academic.

Prichard, J. C. 1826. *Researches into the physical history of mankind.* London: John and Arthur Arch.

———. 1851. *Researches into the physical history of mankind.* 4th Ed. London: Houlston and Stoneman.

———. 1855. *The natural history of man; Comprising inquiries into the modifying influence of physical and moral agencies on the different tribes of the human family.* London: H. Balliere.

Pulleine, R. 1928. "The Tasmanians and their stone-culture." *Australasian Association for the Advancement of Science* 19, 294–314.

Rackham, O. 1995. *The History of the countryside.* London: Weidenfeld and Nicholson.

Radcliffe-Brown, A. R. 1930. "Applied Anthropology." *Australian and New Zealand Association for the Advancement of Science* 20: 267–80.

———. [1929] 1958. "Historical and functional interpretations of culture in relation to the practical application of anthropology to the control of native peoples." In *Method in social anthropology: Selected essays by A. R. Radcliffe-Brown,* edited by M. N. Srinivas, 39–41. Chicago: Univ. of Chicago Press.

———. [1923] 1958. "The methods of ethnology and social anthropology." In *Method in social anthropology: Selected essays by A. R. Radcliffe-Brown,* edited by M. N. Srinivas, 3–38. Chicago: Univ. of Chicago Press.

Ramos, A. 1994. "From Eden to limbo: The construction of indigenism in Brazil." In *Social construction of the past: Representation as power,* edited by G. C. Bond and A. Gilliam, 74–88. London: Routledge.
Ratzel, F. 1896. *The history of mankind.* London: Macmillan.
Rawlinson, P. 1988. "Kangaroo conservation and kangaroo harvesting: Intrinsic value versus instrumental value of wildlife." *Australian Zoologist* 24, 129–38.
Renfrew, C. 1973. *Before civilization: The radiocarbon revolution and prehistoric Europe.* London: Jonathan Cape.
Reynolds, H. 1987a. "Aborigines." In *Australians 1888,* edited by G. Davison, J. W. McCarty, and A. McLeary, 117–32. Sydney: Fairfax, Syme, and Weldon.
———. 1987b. *The law of the land.* Ringwood, Victoria: Penguin.
Riddett, L. A. 1990. *Kine, kin, and country: The Victoria River district of the Northern Territory 1911–1966.* Darwin: North Australia Research Unit.
Ritchie, J., ed. 1990. *Australian dictionary of biography. Volume 12: 1891–1939* Melbourne: Melbourne Univ. Press.
Ritter, D. 1994. "The 'rejection of terra nullius' in *Mabo:* A critical analysis. Unpublished honours thesis. Perth: Univ. of Western Australia.
Roberts, C. 1995. *Australia's Kimberley.* Broome, Western Australia: Kimberley Images.
Roberts, N. 1989. *The Holocene: An environmental history.* Oxford: Basil Blackwell.
Roberts, R. G., R. Jones, and M. A. Smith. 1990 "Thermoluminescence dating of a 50,000 year old human occupation site in northern Australia." *Nature* 345, 153–56.
Robertson, K. 1973. *Myrtleford: Gateway to the Alps.* Adelaide: Rigby.
Robertson, M., K. Vang, et al. 1992. *Wilderness in Australia: Issues and options.* Canberra: Australian Heritage Commission.
Rolston, J. 1991. "The wilderness idea reaffirmed." In *The ethics of the environment,* edited by A. Brennan, 370–77. Aldershot, England: Dartmouth.
Rose, B. 1995. *Land management issues: Attitudes and perceptions amongst Aboriginal people of central Australia.* Alice Springs: Central Land Council.
Rose, D. B. 1996a. "Rupture and the ethics of care in colonized space." In *Prehistory to politics: John Mulvaney, the humanities, and the public intellectual,* edited by T. Bonyhady and T. Griffiths, 190–215. Melbourne: Melbourne Univ. Press.
———. 1996b. "Histories and rituals: Land claims in the Territory." In *In the age of Mabo: History, Aborigines, and Australia,* edited by B. Attwood, 35–53. Sydney: Allen and Unwin.
———. 1996c. *Nourishing terrains: Australian Aboriginal views of landscape and wilderness.* Canberra: Australian Heritage Commission.
Ross, H. 1995. "Aboriginal Australians' cultural norms for negotiating natural resources." *Cultural Survival Quarterly* 19, 33–38.

Ross, H., E. Young, et al. 1994. "Mabo: An inspiration for Australian land management," *Australian Journal of Environmental Management* 1, 24–41.
Roth, H. L. 1887. "On the origin of agriculture." *Journal of the Royal Anthropology Institute* 16, 102–36.
Rousseau, J. J. [1755] 1973. "A discourse on the origin of inequality." In *The Social Contract and Discourses.* London: Dent.
Rowse, T. 1994. "How we got a Native Title Act." In *Make a better offer: The politics of Mabo,* edited by M. Goot and T. Rowse, 111–32. Sydney: Pluto.
Russell-Smith, J. 1991. "Classification, species richness, and environmental relations of monsoon rain forest in northern Australia." *Journal of Vegetation Science* 2, 259–78.
Russell-Smith, J., and C. Dunlop. 1987. "The status of monsoon vine forests in the Northern Territory: A perspective." In *The rainforest legacy,* edited by G. Werren and A. P. Kershaw, 227–88. Canberra: Australian Heritage Commission.
Sanderson, M. 1988. *Griffith Taylor: Antarctic scientist and pioneer geographer.* Ottawa: Carleton Univ. Press.
Sauer, C. O. 1952. *Agricultural origins and dispersals.* New York: American Geographical Society.
Sauer, C. O. 1956. "The agency of man on the earth." In *Man's role in changing the face of the earth,* edited by W. L. Thomas, 49–69. Chicago: Univ. of Chicago Press.
Sauer, C. O. [1944] 1965a. "A geographic sketch of early man in America." In *Land and life,* edited by J. Leighly, 197–245. Berkeley: Univ. of California Press.
Sauer, C. O. [1958] 1965b. "Man in the ecology of tropical America." In *Land and life,* edited by J. Leighly, 182–93. Berkeley: Univ. of California Press.
Schaffer, K. 1988. *Women and the bush: Forces of desire in the Australian cultural tradition.* Cambridge: Cambridge Univ. Press.
Schrire, C. 1984. "Interactions of past and present in Arnhem Land, Australia." In *Past and present in hunter gatherer studies,* edited by C. Schrire, 67–93. New York: Academic.
Seaman, P. 1984. *The Aboriginal land inquiry.* Perth: Ministry of Aboriginal Affairs, Western Australia.
Seddon, G. 1975. "Phillip Island: Capability, conflict, and compromise." Melbourne: Report to the Westernport Regional Planning Authority, Centre for Environmental Studies, Univ. of Melbourne.
Shaw, B. 1981. *My country of the pelican dreaming.* Canberra: Australian Institute of Aboriginal Studies.
———. 1983. *Banggaiyerri: The story of Jack Sullivan.* Canberra: Australian Institute of Aboriginal Studies.
———. 1986. *Countrymen: The life histories of four Aboriginal men.* Canberra: Australian Institute of Aboriginal Studies.

Shoemaker, N., ed. 1995. *Negotiators of change: Historical perspectives on Native American women.* New York: Routledge.
Short, J. R. 1991. *Imagined country: Environment, culture, and society.* London: Routledge.
Sick, W. 1969. "Geographical substance." In *Biogeography and ecology in South America,* edited by E. J. Fittkau et al., 449–74. The Hague: Junk.
Simmons, I. G. 1989. *Changing the face of the earth: Culture, environment, history.* Oxford: Basil Blackwell.
Sinclair Knight Merz 1997. "Draft Executive Summary Ord River irrigation project stage 2 development. M2 Development Area Public Environmental review." Prepared for Western Australian Department of Resources Development Perth.
Singh, G., and E. A. Geissler. 1985. "Late Cainozoic history of vegetation, fire, lake levels, and climate, at Lake George, New South Wales, Australia." *Philosophical transactions of the Royal Society of London, Series B* 311, 379–477.
Singh, G., A. P. Kershaw, et al. 1981. "Quaternary vegetation and fire history in Australia." In *Fire and the Australian biota,* edited by A. M. Gill, R. H. Groves, and I. R. Noble, 23–54. Canberra: Australian Academy of Science.
Smith, B. 1984. *European vision and the South Pacific.* Sydney: Harper and Row.
Smith, L. 1994. "Heritage management as postprocessual archaeology?" *Antiquity* 68, 300–309.
Smith, M. A. 1987. "Pleistocene occupation in arid Central Australia." *Nature* 328, 710–11.
Smith, M. A., M. Spriggs, et al., eds. 1993. *Sahul in review: Pleistocene archaeology in Australia, New Guinea, and Island Melanesia.* Canberra: Department of Prehistory, Research School of Pacific Studies, Australian National Univ.
Smith, S. J. 1990. "Social geography: Patriarchy, racism, nationalism." *Progress in Human Geography* 14, 261–71.
Sollas, W. J. 1915. *Ancient hunters and their modern representatives.* London: Macmillan.
Solway, J., and R. Lee. 1990. "Foragers, genuine or spurious: Situating the Kalahari San in history." *Current Anthropology* 31, 109–46.
Soper, K. 1996. "Nature/'nature.'" In *FutureNatural: Nature, science, culture,* edited by G. Robertson, M. Mash, L. Tickner et al., 22–34. London: Routledge.
Souter, G. 1968. *A peculiar people: The Australians in Paraguay.* Sydney: Angus and Robertson.
Sparks, C. D. 1995. "The land incarnate: Navajo women and the dialogue of colonialism, 1821–1870." In *Negotiators of change: Historical perspectives on Native American women,* edited by N. Shoemaker, 135–56. New York: Routledge.
Speth, W. W. 1977. "Carl Ortwin Sauer on destructive exploitation." *Biological Conservation* 11, 145–60.

Spiegel, A. D. 1994. "Struggling with tradition in South Africa: The multivocality of images of the past." In *Social construction of the past: Representation as power*, edited by G. C. Bond and A. Gilliam, 185–202. London: Routledge.

Stanley, N. F. 1995. "The Ord River Dam of tropical Australia." In *Man-made lakes and human health*, edited by N. F. Stanley and M. P. Alpers, 103–12. London: Academic.

Stanner, W. E. H. 1965. "Religion, totemism, and symbolism." In *Aboriginal man in Australia*, edited by R. M. Berndt and C. H. Berndt. Sydney: Angus and Robertson.

———. 1969. *After the dreaming: The Boyer Lectures 1968*. Sydney: Australian Broadcasting Commission.

Stewart, O. C. 1956. "Fire as the first great force employed by man." In *Man's role in changing the face of the earth*, edited by W. L. Thomas, 115–33. Chicago: Univ. of Chicago Press.

Stocking, G. W. 1987. *Victorian anthropology*. New York: Macmillan.

Strzelecki, P. E. D. 1845. *Physical description of New South Wales and Van Diemen's Land*. London: Longman, Brown, Green, and Longmans.

Sultan, R. 1991. "A voice in the wilderness? Aboriginal perspectives on conservation." *Habitat* 19, no. 3: 1.

Symanski, R. 1994. "Contested realities: Feral horses in outback Australia." *Annals of the Association of American Geographers* 84, 251–69.

Tacon, P. S. C. 1991. "The power of stone: Symbolic aspects of stone use and tool development in western Arnhem Land, Australia." *Antiquity* 65, 192–207.

———. 1994. "Socialising landscapes: The long-term implications of signs, symbols, and marks on the land." *Archaeology in Oceania* 29, 117–29.

Tacon, P. S. C., R. Fullagar, S. Ouzman, and K. Mulvaney. 1997. "Cupule engravings from Jinmium-Granilpi (northern Australia) and beyond: Exploration of a widespread and enigmatic class of rock markings." *Antiquity* 71, 942–65.

Taylor, S. G. 1990. "Naturalness: The concept and its application to Australian ecosystems." *Proceedings of the Ecological Society of Australia* 16, 411–18.

Taylor, T. G. 1919a. "Climatic cycles and evolution." *Geographical Review* 8, 289–328.

———. 1919b. "The settlement of tropical Australia." *Geographical Review* 8, 84–115.

———. 1921. "The evolution and distribution of race, culture, and language." *Geographical Review* 11, 54–119.

———. 1938. "Correlations and culture: A study in technique." *Annual meeting of the British Association for the Advancement of Science*, 103–38 Cambridge: British Association for the Advancement of Science.

———. 1940. *Australia: A study of warm environments and their effect on British settlement*. London: Methuen.

———. 1946a. *Environment, race, and migration: Fundamentals of human distribution: With special sections on racial classification and settlement in Canada and Australia.* Toronto: Univ. of Toronto Press.

———. 1946b. *Our evolving civilization: An introduction to geopacifics.* London: Geoffrey Cumberlege.

Taylor, T. G., and F. Jardine. 1924. "Kamilaroi and white: A study of racial mixture in New South Wales." *Journal of the Royal Society of New South Wales* 58, 268–95.

Tehan, M. 1994. "Practising land rights: The Pitjantjatjara in the Northern Territory, South Australia, and Western Australia." In *Make a better offer: The politics of Mabo*, edited by M. Goot and T. Rowse, 34–54. Sydney: Pluto.

Thackway, R., S. Szabo, et al. 1996. "Indigenous protected areas: A new concept in biodiversity conservation." In *Biodiversity: Broadening the debate* 4, 18–34. Canberra: Australian Nature Conservation Agency.

Thomas, J. 1991. *Rethinking the Neolithic.* Cambridge: Cambridge Univ. Press.

Thomas, N. 1994 *Colonialism's culture: Anthropology, travel, and government.* Cambridge: Polity.

Tindale, N. B. 1959. "Ecology of primitive aboriginal man in Australia." In *Biogeography and ecology in Australia*, edited by A. Keast, R. L. Crocker, and C. S. Christian, 36–68. The Hague: Junk.

Tindale, N. B. 1974. *Aboriginal Tribes of Australia.* Berkeley: Univ. of California Press.

Town and Country Planning Board, Victoria 1971. "Phillip Island: A report." Melbourne: Victorian Government Printer.

Trigger, D. S. 1997. "Mining, landscape and the culture of development ideology in Australia." *Ecumene* 4, 161–80.

Tuan, Y.-f. 1971. "Man and Nature." *Association of American Geographers, Resource Paper* 10.

Tylor, E. B. 1891. *Primitive culture: Researches into the development of mythology, philosophy, religion, language, art, and custom.* London: John Murray.

Ucko, P. 1994. "Foreword." In *Social construction of the Past: Representation as power*, edited by G. C. Bond and A. Gilliam, xiii–xv. London: Routledge.

Western Australia. 1996. *Ord River irrigation project: A review of its expansion potential.* Governments of Western Australia and Northern Territory.

Western Australia and Northern Territory. 1997. "Terms of reference for expressions of interest in the development of Ord River irrigation area—stage 2." Perth: Department of Resources Development.

Waitt, G. 1994. "The Republic of Korea's foreign direct investments in Australia." *Australian Geographical Studies* 32, 191–213.

———. 1997. "Selling paradise and adventure: Representations of landscape in the tourist advertising of Australia." *Australian Geographical Studies* 35, 47–60.

Ward, R. 1967. 1952. *Man makes history.* Sydney: Shakespeare Head.

Warner, W. L., A. R. Radcliffe-Brown, et al. 1928. "Some aspects of the Aboriginal problem in Australia." *The Australian Geographer* 1, 67–69.
Weaver, S. M. 1984. "Struggles of the nation-state to define Aboriginal ethnicity: Canada and Australia." In *Minorities and mother country imagery,* edited by G. L. Gold, 182–210. St Johns: Institute of Social and Economic Research, Memorial Univ. of Newfoundland.
Wensley, P. 1996. "International law and policy developments." In *Environmental outlook no. 2: Law and policy,* edited by B. Boer, R. Fowler, and N. Gunningham, 1–17. Sydney: Federation.
Wenzel, G. W. 1994. "Recent change in Inuit summer residence patterning at Clyde River, East Baffin Island." In *Key issues in hunter-gatherer research,* edited by E. S. Burch and L. J. Ellanna, 289–308. Oxford: Berg.
Wessel, T. R. 1976. "Agriculture, Indians, and American History." *Agricultural History* 50, 9–20.
White, J. P. 1994. "Honk if you've seen Sahul." *Review of Archaeology* 15, 6–10.
———. 1996. "Australia: An archaeological region." Paper presented to Australian Archaeological Association Conference, Normanville, South Australia.
White, J. P., and J. F. O'Connell. 1982. *The prehistory of Australia, New Guinea, and Sahul.* Sydney: Academic.
White, M. E. 1986. *The greening of Gondwana.* Sydney: Reed.
White, R. 1981. *Inventing Australia: Images and identity 1688–1980.* Sydney: George Allen and Unwin.
Wilderness Society. 1983. *The Franklin Blockade.* Hobart: The Wilderness Society.
Willems-Braun, B. 1997. "Buried epistemologies: The politics of nature in (post) colonial British Columbia. *Annals of the Association of American Geographers* 87, 3–31.
Williams, N. M. 1982. "A boundary is to cross: Observations on Yolngu boundaries and permission." In *Resource managers: North American and Australian hunter-gatherers,* edited by N. M. Williams and E. S. Hunn, 131–54. Canberra: Australian Institute of Aboriginal Studies.
———. 1986. *The Yolngu and their land: A system of land tenure and the fight for its recognition.* Canberra: Australian Institute of Aboriginal Studies.
Williams, N. M., and E. S. Hunn, eds. 1982. *Resource managers: North American and Australian hunter-gatherers.* Canberra: Australian Institute of Aboriginal Studies.
Williams, N. M., and D. Mununggurr. 1989. "Understanding Yolngu signs of the past." In *Who needs the past? Indigenous values and archaeology,* edited by R. Layton, 70–83. London: Unwin Hyman.
Wilmsen, R., and J. Denbow. 1990. "Paradigmatic history of San-speaking peoples and current attempts at revision." *Current Anthropology* 31, 489–524.
Woolf, V. [1931] 1993. "Professions for women." In *A room of one's own and three guineas,* 356–61. London: Penguin.

Young, E. 1992. "Hunter-gatherer concepts of land and its ownership in remote Australia and North America." In *Inventing places: Studies in cultural geography*, edited by K. Anderson and F. Gale, 255–72. Melbourne: Longman Cheshire.

Yunupingu, M. 1994. "Yothu Yindi: Finding balance." *Race and Class* 35, 113–22.

Index

Italic page number denotes illustration.

Aboriginal arts and crafts, 155, 207, *208*
Aborigines, population estimates, 58–59, 67
Advertising, 99–101
Africa, 19, 37, 53, 112
Agricultural land use, 184
Agriculture, 44, 113; and Aborigines, 57–58; and American Indians, 64; and civilization, 62; and gender, 20, 64; and hunter-gatherers, 41, 52, 155; and irrigation, 3, 174; and New Guinea, 29; and perception of uninhabited land, 179–80; and property, 64–65; and tourism, 186–87. *See also* Hunter-gatherers; Ord River Irrigation Scheme/Area
Alaska, 20–21
America, 71. *See also* North America
American Indians, 64
Andaman Island, 50
Angel in the ecosystem, 192
Angel in the house, 192
Antarctica, 112
Anzac Cove, 235
Apartheid, 25
Araucaria, 97
Argyle diamond mine, 177, 182, 183
Aridity, 52, 112–16, 128. *See also* Desert
Arnhem Land, 89, 97, 101, 229; rainforest on, 113; Yolngu of northeast, 139, 140 *141*

Arrernte, 101
Arts and crafts, 155, 207, *208*
Atherton Tablelands, 46
Australian Archaeological Association, 133
Australian Constitution, 68
Australian Geographer, 72
Australian Labor Party, 137
Australian Tourist Commission, 15, 189
Australopithecus, 102
Authorship, 11
Awakabal, 118, *119*

Babies in the Bush, 160
Banks, J., 35
Bass Strait, 92
Belyuen, 199–200, 231
Bilinggiin, Bulla, 3, 182
Biodiversity, 22, 217, 228
Bioscape, 17
Blackburn decision, 146–48
Blue Mountains, 94
Bogong moths, 82
Brazil, 24
Brighton, U.K., *56*
Brighton, Vic., 56, *57*
Brown, Bob, 130–31, 136–37
Buddhism, 28
Buffalo River Valley, 82, *83, 84*
Bulletin, The, 68, 158

Bungle Bungles, 175
Bunya Mountains, 121
Burning. *See* Fire
Bushfires, 136
Bush Fires Board, W.A., 208
Bushmen, 75

California, 136
Callitris, 128
Cambridge Gulf, W.A., *115*
Campo, 158–60
Canary Islands, 37
Cape Town, 27
Casuarina, 123–24
Cave Bear, 39
Charcoal analysis, 16, 123–24
Chenchu, 22
Cherokee, 64
Clan, 147
Clementsian succession, 116, 126–27
Conservation movement/ conservationists, 6, 9, 21, 130–32, 133–36; in western countries, 23. *See also* Daintree; Franklin River
Constitution of Australia, 68
Continental scale, 30
Cook, Captain J., 34–35
Coopers Creek, 79, 115
Country, 11, 217, 233–34
Cuddie Springs, 98, 124
Cultural heritage, 9, 25, 27, 108, 178–79. *See also* International heritage agreements
Cycads, 103

Daintree, 210–12
Darwin, Annie, 60
Darwin, Charles, 38, 55, 121
Darwin, Charles and Emma, 60
Darwinism, 35, 37
Davidson, B. R., 181
Deane, Sir William, 235
Desert, 78–80, 112, 233. *See also* Aridity
Devon Downs, S. A., 93
Dick, Thomas, 72, *73*

Dioscorea. *See* Yams
Djilamatang, 82
Domain, 145
Domiculture, 145
Domus, 145
Downe, Kent, 60
Dreaming/Dreamtime: and Canberra, 139; dimensions of, 99, 102; feral animals incorporated into, 219; and Stanner, 71; as unchanging, 25
Duduroa, 82
Durack, Kim, 175
Dust storm, Melbourne, 135

Earth Mother, 172
Edgeworth, David, 45
Egg Lagoon, 116
Elcho Island, N.T., 102
ENSO, 117
Environmental determinism, 45, 48
Environmental impact assessment, 178
Environmental restoration, 165, 170–71, 231
Etchingham, Sussex, 55, *56*
Eucalyptus, 97, 123–24, 127
Europe, 39, 62, 80, 91
Excisions from pastoral leases. *See* Pastoral leases
Eyre, E. J., 40

Fire: Aboriginal use of, 104, 117–23, 144, 207, 220; Ash Wednesday, 136; biota adapted to, 29; and evolutionary status, 36–37; on Kangaroo Island, 215–16; and landscape transformation, 16, 225; in national parks, 207; and succession, 127–28
Fire-stick farming, 104, 122
Franklin River, Tas., 133, *134*, 226–27
Fraser Island, 116–17
Fraser (Kutikina) Cave, 133–34
Fraser, Malcolm, 136
Fruit trees, 125

Gallipoli, 235–36
Garden metaphor, 63
Gardiner, John, 56
Gardiners Creek, 56, *57*, *58*
Gender and hunter-gatherers, 20, 64–65
Geographical Society of New South Wales, 72, 74
Gidjingali, 229–30
Gill, Edmund, 93
Gillies, Janet, 84
Gipps, Sir George, 66
Glacken, Clarence, 6–8
Gleasonian vegetation change, 116, 126–27
Gondwana, 112
Gordon River, 133
Goudhurst, Kent, 55, *56*
Great Australian Arid Period, 122
Great Barrier Reef, 117
Great Smoky Mountains, Tennessee, 121
Greenpeace, 233
Grey, George, 40, 184
Gurmanamana, Frank, 139

Hall, J., *208*
Hawke, Bob, 149
Head, Edward, 59
Head, Sarah (nee Ellis), 55, 56, 58, 60, 157
Head, Walter, 157, 160–62
Head, William, 55, 56, 59, 60, 157
Head, William Jr., 58–59
Hidden Lake, 116
High Court of Australia, 41, 66–67, 146, 202. *See also* Mabo; Native Title Act
High pressure belt, 112
Holocene, 16, 103–4, 113, 117
Homo sapiens, 96
Horton, D. R., 121–22
Howard, John, 335
Howitt, 40
Hume and Hovell, 82
Hume, Hamilton, 82, 111
Hunter-gatherers: and agriculture, 41, 124, 155, 197; and gender, 20, 64–65; impact on landscape of, 61, 125, 197; and intensification, 103–4; landscape understanding of, 17–18; and ownership, 20, 147; and primitivism, 23–26; and property law, 36; revisionist debate over, 77. *See also* Agriculture; Tradition

India, 20–21, 37, 112
Intensification narrative in prehistory, 103–5, 107
International heritage agreements, 22, 29. *See also* Cultural heritage
International Union for Conservation of Nature, 226
Inuit, 23
Island metaphor, 63

Jackson, W., 122
Jaimathang, 82
Jinmium, 97, 101
Jones, Rhys, 122, 139, 229

Kakadu National Park, 130, 230
Kangaroo culling, 231–32
Kangaroo harvesting, 22
Kangaroo hunting, 38
Kangaroo Island, S.A., 215
Keating, Paul, 101, 149
Keep River, N.T., 175
Keilor Terrace, 93
Kenniff Cave, 94–95
Kent, *56*
Kershaw, Peter, 96–97
Kimberley Research Station, 175
King Island, 116
Kuku-Yalanji, 210–12
Kunwinjku, 101
Kutikina (Fraser) Cave, 133–34

Lake Argyle, 3, *4*, 133–34, 175, 183
Lake Eyre, 115
Lake George, 97, 111, 117, 123–24
Lake Mungo, 95, 97, 116

Land Rights, 62, 99, 149. *See also* Native Title Act
Land Rights Act (N.T.) (1976), 26, 148, 151, 202, 210
Lane, William, 157
Langton, Marcia, 214
Lapstone Creek, N.S.W., 93
Lawson, Henry, 160–62
Legune Station, N.T., 201–3
Little penguin *(Eudyptula minor)*, 170, 172–74
Lockean view of property, 62
Lowenthal, 80–81, 91
Lubbock, 38–39, 40, 50
Lycett, Joseph, 118, *119*
Lynchs Crater, Qld, 96, 111, 117, 123–24

Mabo, 67, 146, 149–51. *See also* High Court of Australia; Native Title Act
Macaulay, Hector and Jessie, 82
Madeira, 37
Malakunanja, 98
Malinowski, 77
Mammoth, 39
Man the Hunter conference, 65
Marralam, 203, *206, 208*
Marsh, George Perkins, 8–9, 15
Marshall decision, 66, 150
Matrilineal interests in land, 142
Matthews, Ted, 235
Mauritius, 37
McCartney, Linda, 221, 232
McGuffie, William, 83–84
McMahon, William, 3
Mediterranean, 7
Meehan, B., 229
Megafauna, 43, 50, 104, 118–22
Meinig, D., 73–74
Melbourne, dust storm, 135
Merrilees, D., 122–23
Mesolithic, 198
Microseris scapigera (Yam-daisy), 57–59, 85, 125, 236
Milirrpum v. Nabalco and the Commonwealth, 146
Minjambut, 82
Miriwoong, 3
Miriwun rockshelter, 183
Mitchell, Thomas, 40, 57
Monte, 158–60
Moore, Janet, 109
Moore, William, 83–84, 109
Moorehead, Alan, 78, 79
Moral climatology, 49
Morgan, Hugh, 150, 151
Morphy, H., 140–45
Mt. Buffalo, 82
Mt. Hotham, 82
Mulvaney, John, 90
Murnong. *See* Yam-daisy
Murray River, 82
Murrumbidgee River, 82
Myrtleford, *84*

Names as property, 140
Natal Drakensberg, 24
National Geographic, 99
National Parks, 79, 207–9, 213, 225
National Trust, 171
Native Title Act (1993) 101, 150, 178. *See also* High Court of Australia; Mabo; Wik
Natsiq (ringed seal), 23
Navajo, 20
Neolithic, 198
New Age Travellers, 28
New Australia, 157, *159*
New Guinea, 29, 113, 149, 198
New Zealand, 149
Ngarigo, 82
Ngunawal, 82
Ningbingi, W.A., *120*
Noble Savage, 76, 192
Nog Nog Wah (Nug Nug), 83–84
Nolan, Sydney, 78
North America, 8, 62, 126–27
Nothofagus, 170
Nug Nug (Nog Nog Wah), *84*, 125–6
Nunivak, 116

Oakleigh, 60
Optically stimulated luminescence (OSL) dating, 97
Ord River, 3, *176, 177*; Irrigation Scheme/Area, 165, 174–89.
Ovens River Valley, 82, *83*
Owen, Richard, 121

Palaeoecology, 110–12
Paraguay, 158–60, *159*
Pastoral leases, 202–7
Patrilineal interests in land, 142
Penguin Parade, 165–74, 190–91
Peschel, 38, 42–43
Phillip Island, 165–74, *168, 169*, 190–91, 20
Phyllocladus, 116
Pleistocene, 28, 50, 94–95, 104
Pocohontas, 20
Point Macleay Mission, S.A., *70*
Pollen analysis, 16, 123–24
Port Augusta, 209–10
Port Phillip, 56, *57*
Portulaca oleracea, 41
Possibilism, 48
Postcards, 71
Postmodernism, 9–10, 27, 217–18
Pristine landscapes, 17, 25, 28, 110
Property, 36, 62, 63, 64
Public Lands Council of Victoria, 131

Quaternary, 28, 112

Radcliffe Brown, 74–76
Radiocarbon dating, 93, 103
Radiometric dating, 77, 98, 102, 107
Rainforest, 113, *115*
Raoni, Chief, 24
Ratzel, 36, 38, 76
Revisionist approaches in ecology, 126–28
Reynolds, H., 41, 150, 194

Riviera, French, 136
Robinson, G. A., 57
Roth, 64
Rousseau, 40, 63

Sacred site, 25–26, 179, 209
San, 24
Sauer, Carl O., 16, 119
Second nature, 6–7
Sheep, 58
Simon, Biddy, 23, 24, 202–5, *204*
Singh, Gurdip, 97, 123
Smith, Adam, 36
Social landscape, 17–18
Sollas, 38–39, 43, 107
South Africa, 24–25, 27, 75, 99
South America, 112
Southern Ocean, 30, 112
Spirit Hills station, 203
St. Helena, 37
Stanner, W. E. H., 70, 76–77, 147
Sting, 24
Stolen children/generations, 69, 235–6
Stone tools, 107
Strzelecki, 44
Stupa, 28
Sussex, *56*

Tandberg, Ron, 4, *5*
Tasman sea, 171
Tasmania: archaeological differentiation of, 30; dunes active in, 111; and Franklin campaign, 133–37, 226–27; and international agreements, 22; prehistory of, 92, 104–5; Walter Woods in, 162
Tasmanian Aboriginal Centre, 135
Tasmanian Aboriginal Land Council, 105
Tasmanians: evolutionary status of, 39, 46, 48, 52; extinction of, 75; Sauer's view of, 119
Tasmanian Wilderness Society, 134
Taylor, Griffith, 37, 74, 107

Terra nullius: in Blackburn decision, 146; and conservationists, 21; as discourse of power, 67, 150–51; and landscapes, 6, 236; parallels with India, 22
Thailand, 28
Thatcher, Margaret, 28
Thermoluminescence (TL) dating, 97
Thomas, William (Asst. Protector), 59
Time, Western and Yolngu views of, 151–55
Timeless land, 61
Tindale, N., 119–221
Tombs, The, 94
Tourism, 3, 15, 25, 101, 186–87
Toyota, 99–100, *100*
Tradition, 146, 148, 154–55, 193, 231
Tylor, 36, 37, 40

Uluru-Kata Tjuta National Park, 230
Unchanging people in an unchanging land, 89, 93, 104
United Tasmania Group, 227
U.S. Supreme Court, 66

Vegetation communities, 127
Victoria, 58, 68, 71, 82; prehistory of, 92–93

Walgalu, 82
Wandanga (Wondunga, Wundangu), Polly, 202–5, *204*

Wedge, J. H., *59*
Wessel, 64
Whaling, 23
White Australia policy, 46, 54
Whitlam, Gough, 197
Wik, 151, 202
Wilderness: changing definitions of, 224; and frontier societies, 221–23; as inspiration for literature, 80; and Nunivak, 20–21; official rhetoric of, 42; and people, 130–32, 179, 227; re-creation/restoration of, 3, 171
Wilderness Society, The, 133–34
Williams, N., 140–46
Winterigah, 82
Woods, Walter, 162
Woolly-haired rhinoceros, 39
World Archaeological Congress, 26
World Heritage, 29
Wurundjeri, 59–60

Yam-daisy *(Microseris scapigera)*, 57–59, 85, 125, 236
Yams *(Dioscorea* spp.), 41, 64
Yarra River, 56, *57*
Yolngu, 139–56, *141, 143*
Yothu Yindi, 155–56

Zamia, 64